ALL ABOUT HISTORY ANNUAL

This All About History Annual is a collection of the very best content from the magazine's last 12 months, and contains some of the most interesting people and stories from throughout history. You'll find tales that are known and loved, like the legend of Robin Hood, alongside some lesser-known but equally incredible stories, including the Night Witches of the Second World War. We have delved right back into Ancient times to get to know Cleopatra and the Aztecs, and explored the most amazing discoveries that helped form the modern world. We have included a broad selection of subjects here, from the ubiquitous to the unknown, to educate and excite as you expand your knowledge of the world's past. We hope that the subjects inside will help you to discover historical eras, icons and moments that you had never imagined, while learning about the stories you thought you knew in a new light.

ALL ABOUT HISTORY ANNUAL

Imagine Publishing Ltd
Richmond House
33 Richmond Hill
Bournemouth
Dorset BH2 6EZ
☎ +44 (0) 1202 586200
Website: www.imagine-publishing.co.uk
Twitter: @Books_Imagine
Facebook: www.facebook.com/ImagineBookazines

Publishing Director
Aaron Asadi

Head of Design
Ross Andrews

Production Editor
Alex Hoskins

Senior Art Editor
Greg Whitaker

Designer
Katie Mapes

Photographer
James Sheppard

Printed by
William Gibbons, 26 Planetary Road, Willenhall, West Midlands, WV13 3XT

Distributed in the UK, Eire & the Rest of the World by
Marketforce, Blue Fin Building, 110 Southwark Street, London, SE1 0SU
Tel 0203 148 3300 www.marketforce.co.uk

Distributed in Australia by
Network Services (a division of Bauer Media Group), Level 21 Civic Tower, 66-68 Goulburn Street, Sydney, New South Wales 2000, Australia Tel +61 2 8667 5288

ISBN 978 1910 155 882

Part of the ALL ABOUT HISTORY bookazine series

IMAGINE PUBLISHING

CONTENTS

VICTORY & DEFEAT

EXPLORATION & DISCOVERY

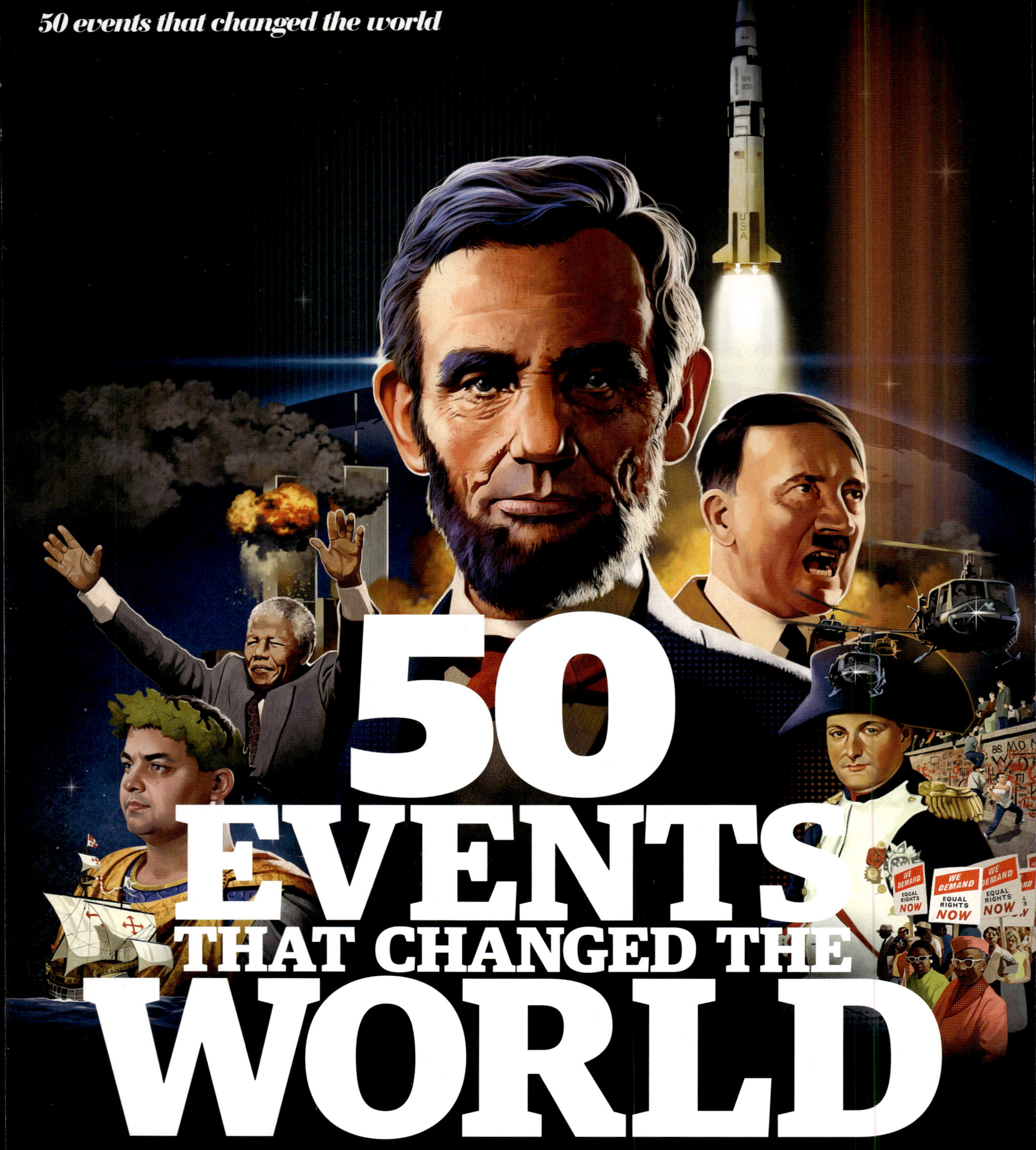

50 EVENTS THAT CHANGED THE WORLD

Ancient Greece to 9/11 – history's gamechangers revealed

20 JULY 1969

ONE GIANT LEAP FOR MANKIND

The first Moon landing

There was no way the United States was going to lose the Space Race. Although Soviet Russia seemed one step ahead at every turn, with Sputnik-1, Yuri Gagarin and Luna-2 – the first artificial satellite, the first man in space, and the first rocket to reach the Moon respectively – JFK told the American people on 25 May 1961 that the nation should "commit itself to achieving the goal, before this decade is out, of landing a man on the Moon, and returning him safely to the Earth."

Using Saturn rockets and veterans of Projects Mercury and Gemini, the process of developing a safe rocket that could make the journey and a safe return began. However, in 1967 the test launch of Apollo 1 ended catastrophically on the launch pad when an electrical fire in the cabin caused the death of all three from asphyxiation before help could get to them. But each successive Apollo mission flight brought them closer to their goal of the Moon, testing everything from navigation systems, docking procedures and lunar suits.

Finally, on 16 July 1969 – within John F Kennedy's anticipated time frame – the Apollo 11 mission launched on board a Saturn V rocket, containing astronauts Neil Armstrong, Buzz Aldrin and Michael Collins. It entered lunar orbit on 19 July, as Collins remained in the craft and Armstrong and Aldrin descended in the Lunar module Eagle. After fears that they had overshot their landing target, they set down on the Sea of Tranquillity. Aldrin took communion while Armstrong prepared to activate the shuttle's camera and step outside.

He descended the nine rungs to the Moon's surface and broadcast to a captivated world the words that would echo throughout history. "That's one small step for [a] man… one giant leap for mankind." Indeed, while it would be the American flag that was planted on the Moon, and President Nixon who would make a phone call to the astronauts, it was a demonstration of how far the entire human race had come.

Origins

- Russia and America obtain German technology **1945**
- Chuck Yeager breaks sound barrier **14 October 1947**
- The Space Race begins **1957**

Legacy

- Endless conspiracy theories
- Co-operative international space exploration
- Missions to explore Mars

A project initiated by Pericles in 447 BCE the Parthenon is often seen as an enduring symbol of Athenian democracy

508 BCE

DAWN OF DEMOCRACY

The first democratic, people-led government in Ancient Greece...

The Athenians certainly couldn't imagine life without democracy. Athens was one of the most prosperous of some 1,500 city-states (poleis) in 6th-century-BCE Greece, initially governed by an elite ruling minority. Internal unrest and costly conflict with its neighbours, however, gradually brought the city to its knees. Taking inspiration from rival Sparta, with its unusual egalitarian ethos, democracy was seen as an experiment that could unify society.

Shaped by Solon, Cleisthenes and Pericles - among others - and evolving over two centuries, every Athenian citizen was expected to get involved, though a randomly drawn, rotating council took care of day-to-day government. Forward thinking as it was, democracy was a totally different beast then - with women, foreigners and many others not represented. Nevertheless it laid the foundations for what is now a cornerstone of the modern world.

Origins

- Solon's reforms mean all Athenian citizens must participate in the Ecclesia (Assembly) **594 BCE**
- Cleisthenes introduces a policy of equal rights **508 BCE**

Legacy

- The French Revolution sees the ruling monarchy overthrown **1787-1799**
- Lincoln's 'government of the people, by the people, for the people' speech **1863**

11 SEPTEMBER 2001

THE DAY AMERICA WAS ATTACKED

The terrorist attacks of 9/11

"The sights were mind-boggling. I thought for a second a movie was being made."

Firefighter Mickey Kross was inside the World Trade Center's North Tower when it collapsed, yet even for those of us witnessing that indelible news footage on the other side of the world, his words resonate.

Just 46 minutes after American Airlines Flight 11 took off in Boston, five terrorists had taken over and flown the plane into the iconic building that would later tumble down around Kross. It was one of four hijackings that day, all of which hit their targets, except for one: United Flight 93's passengers reclaimed the plane and ensured it crashed out of harm's way in a Pennsylvanian field.

Everyone has an opinion about what caused 9/11, but more clear-cut are the effects. In the immediate sense, it resulted in the deaths of 2,996 people - the most ever in a single foreign attack on American soil. In the longer term, it forced the hand of American foreign policy. The War on Terror had begun.

Origins

- Soviet Union invades Afghanistan **December 1979**
- Al-Qaeda (The Base) emerges, calling on Muslims to join the 'holy war' **1988**
- First World Trade Center bomb kills six people **26 February 1993**

Legacy

- Launch of the War on Terror
- War in Iraq and Afghanistan
- Osama bin Laden is killed by US Navy SEALs **2 May 2011**

Gavrilo Princip is captured after killing Franz Ferdinand, which led to the start of the Eastern European conflict

MURDER AT SARAJEVO

28 JUNE 1914

Archduke Franz Ferdinand and his wife fell to the gunshots fired by 19 year-old Serbian nationalist Gavrilo Princip, as they drove through the city. Princip was one of a group of six Bosnian Serb assassins. Austria's retaliation was backed by Germany, and Europe exploded into conflict.

THE FIRST VACCINE

14 MAY 1796

The first vaccine for smallpox came courtesy of a microbiologist. Testing the rumour that milkmaids were immune from it because they had already contracted the similar illness cowpox, Edward Jenner took pus from Sarah Nelmes' cowpox blisters and successfully inoculated an eight year-old boy.

HIROSHIMA AND NAGASAKI: FEAR AND DREAD UNLEASHED

6 AUGUST 1945

When the US dropped an atomic bomb on Hiroshima, up to 80,000, of the population of 350,000, were killed immediately. The effects would be felt for decades as illness caused by the radiation brought the death toll to 140,000. The second attack on Nagasaki three days later ended the war at a terrible cost.

Little Boy and Fat Man caused damage that's felt today

FALL OF THE BERLIN WALL

1991

Built by East Germany in 1961 to keep the 'fascist' elements of the West out, the heavily guarded Berlin Wall became a significant symbol of the oppression of the Iron Curtain, by preventing people in the East from defecting and emigrating. With the decline of communist Russia, the wall could no longer be defended and was torn down by the people amid much celebration.

The first production line 1908

The assembly line was probably the greatest gift Henry Ford gave to the manufacturing industry. This production process brought the car to the engineers, rather than the other way around. It halved the time it took to create his Model T Ford and dramatically cut costs.

The five-day working week 1926

In May 1926, Detroit, Henry Ford instigated a second American revolution. He reduced the working week of Ford Motor Company's workers from six to five days and their working day from nine to eight hours. Productivity at Ford soared as a result of the new, two-day weekend, a practice so successful it was adopted worldwide and is standard today.

NAPOLEON SURRENDERS

1815

After being forced to abdicate by the French parliament, Napoleon Bonaparte requested protection from the British, who allowed him on board the British ship Bellerophon, commanded by Captain Thomas Byam Martin, where he was held in custody for some three weeks before exile to the island of St Helena in the South Atlantic.

THE LAST ROMAN EMPEROR

476 CE

By the late fifth century, the Roman Empire was rapidly losing its millennia-long grip on Europe and the Western World. The Vandals (an East German tribe) had already sacked and pillaged Rome once and, seeing Rome's weakness, others were rallying against their ruler. Germanic general Odoacer finally entered the capital and forced the last emperor of Rome, Romulus Augustus, into exile.

THE FIRST DEFENCE OF DEMOCRACY

SEPTEMBER 490 BCE

The Persian Empire wanted to punish Greece for supporting the Ionians. When the outnumbered Athenians attacked first at Marathon, the Persians struck for the weak middle of their line. The strongest troops were on the Athenian flanks, which decimated the invaders. The forces of democratic Greece had not only stood up to the forces of Persia, they crushed them.

BOSTON TEA PARTY

16 DECEMBER 1773

The American colonists' patience with the British parliament was at an end. Why should they obey a body they had no hand in electing? When The Sons of Liberty in Boston threw three ship loads of tea into the harbour, the shocked British were set on a path for war.

SLAVERY IS ABOLISHED

31 JANUARY 1865

Three years after the Emancipation Proclamation, and with the Civil War still raging, Abraham Lincoln took a bold step and pushed for the 13th Amendment to be approved by Congress. Even without the Southern representatives the vote barely made it through, but its success marked the start of a long fight for equality.

ROME ADOPTS CHRISTIANITY

28 OCTOBER 312 CE

Ancient Rome was a dangerous time to be a Christian, until the Emperor Constantine looked up before the Battle of Milvian Bridge and saw a flaming cross bearing the words "In this sign shalt thou conquer." Converted by his vision and his victory, Constantine's new faith began the Christianisation of the Roman Empire.

WOMEN GET THE VOTE

1918

Suffrage groups across the Western world began to make their voice heard in the mid-to-late 19th century, but by the beginning of the 20th century, women were still not counted among the number of those eligible to vote. It took over 50 years, World War I, and the tenacity of leading suffragette societies to get women the vote for the first time on both sides of the Atlantic.

6 JUNE 1944

THE BIGGEST INVASION

D-Day and the first step towards ending the Second World War

On 6 June 1944, the Allied Troops under the direction of General Dwight D Eisenhower and Bernard Montgomery took the first step towards breaking Hitler's stranglehold on Europe with a massive assault on the French coast – the largest amphibious attack in history.

In the preceding months the Allies had mounted a decoy operation, Operation Fortitude, in an attempt to convince the Axis forces that they would attempt to cross at Pas de Calais, where the English Channel is narrowest. Meanwhile, Operation Overlord had been poised since 1 May but favourable weather conditions were vital to the plan's success. After being postponed several times, Operation Overlord finally went into effect and the Allied forces set foot on Normandy beaches at 6:30am.

The troops taking part in the amphibious assault comprised 72,215 British and Canadian soldiers, and 57,500 Americans. They were divided to attack five targets, designated Utah (US), Omaha (US), Gold (UK), Juno (Canada), and Sword (UK), over 80 kilometres (50 miles) of coastline. With its cliff-top bunkers, which had not suffered much damage from the preceding aerial bombardment, Omaha was the most heavily defended, and the attacking US forces took heavy casualties before taking the beach. However, the decoy had worked. The German military was not alerted that an invasion was occurring until 4am. The attack did not just come from the sea, however. After midnight on 6 June, American, British and Canadian paratroopers were dropped into Normandy to facilitate the attack at Utah beach, which would give the Allies access to Cherbourg harbour. Due to the adverse weather conditions, many of the paratroopers missed their targets, but vital locations like Pegasus Bridge and the town of Sainte-Mère-Église would be captured.

At 6.00pm, Prime Minister Winston Churchill announced the invasion in the House of Commons. By midnight, each of the five beaches had been taken and the liberation of Europe from Nazi Germany was well underway.

Origins

- Five years of conflict **1939-1944**
- Germany's failed invasion of Russia **1941**
- America enters the war **1941**

Legacy

- Peace in Europe
- Atomic bombs and Japanese defeat
- Formation of the United Nations

A landing craft just vacated by invasion troops points towards a fortified beach on the Normandy Coast, June 6, 1944

START OF THE CRUSADES

1096

Launched by the Catholic church by Pope Urban II in 1095, the first crusade to retake the holy lands of Israel was originally to help the Byzantines repel the warring Turks, but soon evolved into a holy war to take back Jerusalem. The successful campaign was the first of many 'holy' crusades that transformed the Middle East.

COLUMBUS FINDS A NEW WORLD

12 OCTOBER 1492

Despite attempting to find an alternate route to the lucrative Indies, Columbus's journey across the Atlantic brought him to the Bahamas and on to Cuba. Although he wasn't the first European to set foot on the Americas, word spread about his discovery of a new continent across the ocean.

THE COMPASS IS INVENTED

1117

The first magnetic compasses, thought to have appeared in China during the Qin Dynasty, were not used for exploration, but rather for geomantic divination and feng shui. The magnetic compass continued to develop in China until its first recorded use for navigation in 1117, and was used by European sailors soon after, revolutionising navigation and opening the oceans to exploration.

THE PERSIAN EMPIRE FALLS

334-330 BCE

In roughly three years, Alexander the Great brought about the fall of the 200 year-old Persian Empire. Challenging Darius III's superior numbers in 334 BCE, Alexander won successive victories until his opponent fled from the battlefield at Gaugamela in 331 BCE. Persia's surrender ended one of the most formidable empires.

OIL IN SAUDI ARABIA

1938

The hunt for oil in Saudi Arabia began in 1922 but it wasn't until 1938 that eager American Max Steineke finally discovered a reserve of black gold, just weeks after having to plead with his employers for more time. The discovery changed the world's energy practices and its relationship with the Arab world.

"Workers of the world, unite!" 1848

Karl Marx and Friedrich Engels' Communist Manifesto is one of the most influential (and most quoted) political manuscripts. Its ethos of power to the working class has been the mandate of many coups since it was first published by German political refugees in London.

THE END OF THE AZTECS

1521

Having landed in the Yucatan Peninsula in Mexico in 1519, the Spanish discovered a wealthy native people known as the Aztecs, expanding their control beyond Mexico. That ground to a halt with an invasion led by Hernando Cortes. The Aztec population was devastated by new diseases like smallpox and were overthrown by the better armed invaders.

1989

INVENTING THE WORLD WIDE WEB

It's hard to imagine life without the Internet today, but it wouldn't exist if not for one man's vision

It's not as if technology that combined hypertext and the internet for globally sharing information wasn't around in 1989, but British physicist Tim Berners-Lee wanted to take it to another level. When Berners-Lee first proposed the World Wide Web for workers at CERN to co-ordinate their research, his supervisor Mike Sendall wrote: 'Vague but exciting'.

Collaborating with computer scientist Robert Cailliau the prototype software for the basic web system was demonstrated in 1990 on a NeXT computer, and it rapidly spread to other research labs and universities around the globe. With the development of versions for more ubiquitous Mac and PC environments, the World Wide Web was ready to make the leap from academia to mainstream. On 30 April 1993, CERN posted the source code for anyone to use, totally free of charge. Just two decades on, there are around 630 million websites and counting. You can see how far the web has come by taking a look at the first web page: http://info.cern.ch/hypertext/WWW/TheProject.html.

Origins
- Ted Nelson invents hypertext **1960**
- ARPANET goes live **29 October 1969**
- Ray Tomlinson sends the first email **9 October 1971**

Legacy
- The dawn of social networking
- Era of citizen journalism
- 'Gangnam Style' first to hit 1 billion YouTube views

WWW: vague but exciting

THE FIRST GOLD COINS ARE MINTED

546 BCE

Although gold had already been used as a currency for centuries before, and the first electrum (gold and silver alloy) coins were struck back in the seventh century BCE, the first proper gold coins were minted by King Croesus of the Lydians (modern-day Turkey). This rich nation used its pure gold currency as a statement of wealth and power.

JFK IS ASSASSINATED

22 NOVEMBER 1963

While being driven through Dealey Plaza in Dallas with his wife Jackie, John F Kennedy was shot and killed. His death sent shockwaves through the American people and fanned the flames of growing mistrust and fear of their government. There are those who still claim it wasn't Lee Harvey Oswald who pulled the trigger.

LENIN SEIZES POWER

25/26 OCTOBER 1917

On 25 October, Bolshevik forces laid siege to the Winter Palace in Petrograd, finally gaining entrance in the early morning and placing the members of the unpopular provisional government under arrest. The Russian people rallied behind the party of Lenin and Trotsky, who promised an exit from the First World War, food and equality.

WATT PERFECTS THE STEAM ENGINE

1796

The steam engine, invented by James Watt, did so much more than drive steam trains across the country. It kick-started the Industrial Revolution so that factories could be built anywhere, not just near rivers, and steam-driven machines could do the job of dozens of workers in a fraction of the time.

THE TENNIS COURT OATH

20 JUNE 1789

Political tensions were high when the National Assembly of nobles, clergy and common people gathered at the Palace of Versailles, Paris, on 20 June. They found that King Louis XVI had excluded them and convened in the tennis court where they swore to create a new French constitution – thus sowing the seeds of the French Revolution to come.

DARWIN TAKES AN OCEAN VOYAGE
1831-1836

Charles Darwin's discoveries on his voyage to South America on HMS Beagle would forever change our understanding of the world around us. Forming the idea that one species could change into another, he began work on his theory of natural selection and published *On The Origin Of The Species* on 24 November 1859.

Apartheid ends in South Africa 1994

Apartheid (the state of being apart) was legislated in 1948 in South Africa, with four racial groups classified and forced into segregation. After trade embargoes in the Eighties and growing civil unrest, its gradual breakdown culminated in Nelson Mandela's victorious abolition of the internationally hated regime.

LENIN DIES
21 JANUARY 1924

Lenin was bedridden and mute following three strokes by the time of his death. While Trotsky seemed to be the natural successor, he was efficiently sidelined and subsequently expelled by Stalin, paving the way for one of history's most appalling dictators.

WRITING IS INVENTED
3200 BCE

Writing sprung out of a need to keep records in court when memory proved insufficient. It was invented in Central and South America in the seventh century BCE and Mesopotamia (modern Iraq) in 3200 BCE. True writing is distinct from early bronze age symbols and the use of digits to keep records.

THE TURING MACHINE IS INVENTED 1936

It must be a strange thing, to invent something years before anyone could even conceive of needing it. Yet this is exactly what Alan Turing did when he invented the computer. Moreover, his invention was an intangible mathematical theory for a computer, rather than a working machine, which wasn't used until Turing's tenure at Bletchley Park.

ROSA PARKS REFUSES TO STAND 1955

When Rosa Parks was arrested for refusing to give up her seat in the 'coloured' section of the bus for a white passenger in Montgomery, Alabama, she became the rallying point for a nation that would no longer accept the injustice of racial segregation. "The only tired I was," she said, "was tired of giving in."

TELEVISION IS DEMONSTRATED
1924

Although the television wasn't the creation of a single inventor, John Logie Baird contributed two major improvements to its display and was the first to transmit an image – a flickering greyscale photograph reproduced just a few feet away from the source. He went on to demonstrate live moving images in 1926 and the TV was born.

9000 BCE

AGRICULTURE ARRIVES

The human race takes the first step away from hunter-gatherer culture and begins to settle down

The exact site, the exact reason, and the exact date of the invention of agriculture has yet to be pinpointed. Various theories have been put forth as to why, when and how men and women began to tend to and rear their own crops and livestock, with many variations on similar themes. However, it is generally agreed that the innovation occurred shortly after 9000 BCE, and that the site of the invention of agriculture was in what is now the known as the Fertile Crescent, in the Middle East.

Climate change meant that the Levant area (in the Eastern Mediterranean) became the ideal site for settlers. As the region became temperate and annual (rather than perennial) plants like wild wheat and barley began to grow that produced large seeds rather than thick wooden stems or casings to protect them from the elements. The Natufian tribes of that region were traditionally hunter-gatherers but the ever-increasing proliferation of this vegetation made settlement an attractive proposition. However, steps would have to be taken to ensure they did not drain the area of resources.

Opinion differs as to whether the decision to try rearing crops was pre-meditated, and many believe that it was a one-off experimentation rather than a strategy designed to provide them with a regular form of sustenance. However, the combination of climate change and increasingly settled populations meant that this dabbling with crop-development was inevitable. The technology began to improve and these tribes began to rear livestock, which similarly thrived in the Levant region, and tended to renewable crops. The nomadic culture by which the human race lived would forever be altered. The first step towards human society as we know it today, with its vast towns and cities, all started with agriculture.

Origins

- **Circa 9600 BCE:** Climate change and edible plants
- **Circa 9000 BCE:** Tribes turn to sedentism
- **Circa 9000 BCE:** Increase in domesticated animals

Legacy

- Irrigation and evolving agricultural technology
- Ever-growing communities
- Intensive farming leading to climate change

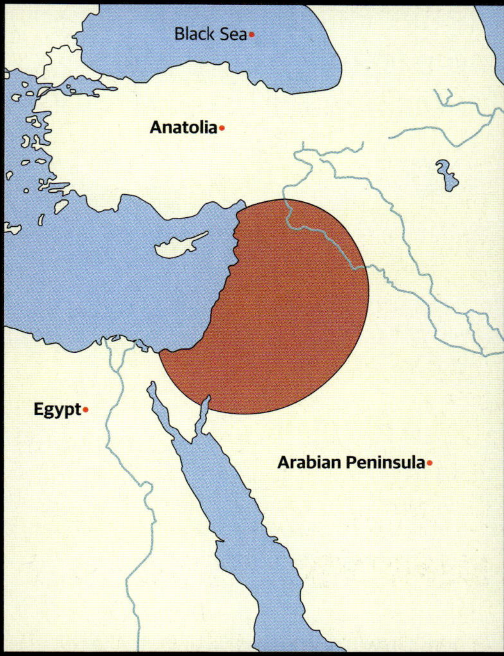

4 JULY 1776

A SUPERPOWER IS BORN

The Declaration of Independence, all began with a single document

A 2011 survey showed 51 per cent of Americans favoured Queen Elizabeth II. Had the poll been taken 237 years ago the results would have been different.

In early 1776 a political pamphlet titled 'Common Sense' was circulating the colonies. Its author, Thomas Paine, didn't pull any punches when it came to his views of King George III: "How impious is the title of sacred Majesty applied to a worm, who in the midst of his splendour is crumbling to dust."

A few months on, Thomas Jefferson penned a more formal statement, calling for a split from Britain. Adopted by a majority in Congress on 4 July, and agreed by all 13 colonies, it sparked a New York riot, during which the statue of George III was toppled. The final engrossed declaration wasn't signed till 2 August, but America continues to celebrate the day it first voted for 'Life, Liberty and the pursuit of Happiness' at the Second Continental Congress.

There are thought to be 26 surviving copies of the original Declaration in existence today, 21 owned by various US institutions. One was even found in the British National Archives in 2009.

Origins

- Britain passes the Stamp Act, ushering taxes on colonies **22 March 1765**
- The Boston Tea Party takes place in protest of the Tea Act **16 December 1773**

Legacy

- Framework for the French Declaration of Rights of man and of the Citizen **1789**
- Polarised slavery, leading to the American Civil War

'Life, liberty and the pursuit of happiness' at the Second Continental Congress

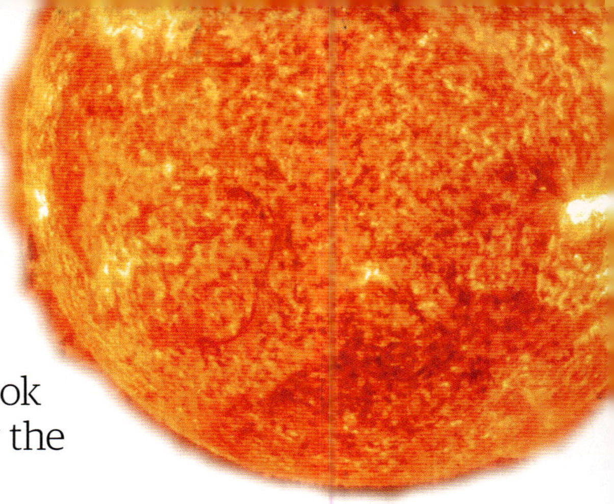

The Sun becomes the centre of the solar system 1543

After years of fearing controversy, Copernicus decided to finally publish his theory of heliocentrism in the last year of his life. His theory that the Earth revolves around the Sun, took more than a century to be accepted, and Galileo was tried by the Inquisition for heresy in 1663 after agreeing to it.

NEWTON DEFINES GRAVITY 1687

Newton's story about how his interest in the mechanics of gravity was piqued by observing an apple dropping from a tree during a garden stroll may have been exaggerated. However, that interest led to his defining the term Universal Gravitation in his work *Principia*, published in 1687.

TELEPHONE IS INVENTED

1876

The telephone is one of the most important inventions of the modern era, which makes the story behind its invention all the more controversial. Alexander Graham Bell was officially credited as the inventor because he got his patent filed hours before a strikingly similar patent by Elisha Gray, but some believe he stole a critical line from Gray's patent to get his approved first. Either way, Bell is widely regarded as its inventor.

THE FIRST OLYMPICS

776 BCE

In honour of Zeus, father of all the gods and men, the ancient Greeks held the first Olympic Games at the sanctuary of Zeus in Olympia. Only Greek men could enter, there were far fewer events than there are today, and many participated completely naked. They were held every four years until 394 CE, when the Romans banned them for years in their campaign of Christianity.

THE PILGRIM FATHERS LAND

NOVEMBER 1620

The Puritan Pilgrim Fathers believed that Satan's grip on England was strengthening. So they set sail on the Mayflower for Virginia to create a new community. They landed near Cape Cod after being blown off course after 65 days at sea, and founded the historic Plymouth Colony on the site of a deserted Native American settlement.

THE TET OFFENSIVE LAUNCHES

30 JANUARY 1968

The tide of the war in Vietnam was irreversibly turned when the North Vietnamese forces mounted the multi-pronged, well-planned Tet offensive, beginning with five separate assaults. Although the first phase was repelled, it was a death blow to America's already-diminishing confidence in their ability to win the war.

MAO PROCLAIMS THE REPUBLIC

1 OCTOBER 1949

20 years of Chinese civil war were ended by Chairman Mao's defeat of Chiang Kai-shek. The country then established itself as a communist nation. American fears grew, strengthened by the knowledge that they had tried to intervene and failed. Diplomatic relations between the two nations would only be resumed with Richard Nixon's visit to China in 1972.

1905

THE LAWS OF PHYSICS REWRITTEN

"Politics is for the present, but an equation is something for eternity"

Part of Albert Einstein's special theory of relativity published in 1905, $E=mc^2$ is by far his most well-known legacy. Despite its straightforward appearance, it deals with the complex and interchangeable relationship between mass and energy. The equation was born from a discrepancy between the work of earlier physicists – like Isaac Newton, Galileo and James Clerk Maxwell – and unravels why the speed of light is constant, as well as the concept of space-time. Einstein completely blew apart the once widely accepted notion of a 'clockwork universe'.

$E=mc^2$ was preceded by several other ground-breaking papers and the clerk-turned-science-superstar then went on to demystify many other physics conundrums, including general relativity in 1916. While universally lauded as one of modern history's greatest minds, he remained humble: "I have no special talents. I am only passionately curious," he said.

Origins

- Ole Roemer measures the speed of light **1676**
- Émilie du Châtelet suggests energy is proportional to mv2, not mv (as proposed by Isaac Newton) **1740**

Legacy

- Better understanding of the Big Bang
- 3D medical PET scans
- Rise of nuclear power

BENZ INVENTS THE CAR

1885

German engineer Karl Benz is credited as the creator of the first petrol-powered automobile. However, the Benz Patent Motorwagen was more of a tricycle with the vital part of his invention – his patented two-stroke petrol engine – attached to it.

CHINA'S LAST EMPEROR FALLS 1912

Emperor Pu Yi succeeded to the throne at two years old in 1908. Aged five, he was forced to abdicate by the Xinhai Revolution that turned China into a republic. Strangely, he was permitted to keep his title and many of his privileges. He fled after World War II and, when recaptured by China, became gardener at the Beijing gardens.

Mandela is freed 1990

Having just avoided execution, Nelson Mandela was tried by the South African government for sabotage, treason and violent conspiracy in 1964 and sentenced to life imprisonment. He served over 25 years of his sentence and was released in a dramatically different political environment in 1990. He then went on to become leader of the ANC and abolished apartheid in 1994.

HEROES & VILLAINS

The story behind some of the most controversial, loved and hated figures from throughout history

10 Murderous Kings

A blood-curdling countdown of history's deadliest monarchs

In this day and age it's quite difficult to imagine the sheer power that kings and queens once wielded over their subjects. In many ways these monarchs were more similar to modern dictators than the rulers that we know today. Murder was often a means to a political end, while crimes of passion would rarely be met with any immediate consequences.

Although the kings had ultimate power, it was a power they were forced to fight for - often using fear, war and murder, among other methods, to stay at the top. The position of king was a precarious one and, driven by this fact and an unhealthy dose of paranoia, certain monarchs left a bloody trail through history.

But beyond paranoia, what drove them to such bloodshed? Several of these kings earned their place on this list with their military campaigns. War was a show of strength, a display of dominance. With an almost-constant state of conflict, territories were lost and won with great frequency, which, of course, meant that they had to be reclaimed. The glory of a kingdom was not just determined by its size necessarily, but by a king's unwavering belief that the lands at stake belonged by right to the throne. Look at Edward I's brutal campaigns in Wales and Scotland, or Charles II of Navarre's ludicrous notions of what belonged to him - both of whom feature in this roundup of deadly royals.

Murder was often the simplest way to ensure that anyone plotting against the king was removed. Even with the introduction of the Magna Carta in England in 1215 and the emergence of Parliament, the monarch's essentially free rein to end the lives of their subjects remained. Flimsy evidence could be put forward to prove a case for treason and conspiring against the monarch, as Henry VIII demonstrated on several occasions. Meanwhile, with the whole country watching, any hint of rebellion would have to be squashed quickly and brutally, as Louis I of Aquitaine did to great effect.

In other cases, the reason behind a king's bloodthirsty nature would now be attributed to some form of mental illness. Purity of the bloodline comes with a price, as lineages would abruptly end with offspring suffering from deformities, congenital illnesses and insanity.

Whether through violent fits of rage or cold calculation, these ten kings ensured that the pages of history books dedicated to them were written in blood, but which of them takes the crown as the deadliest?

The Massacre of St Brice's Day in 1002 led to all Danes in England being put to the sword

"He issued an order that all Danes in England should be executed, calling it 'a most just extermination'"

REIGN 978-1016

COUNTRY ENGLAND

WORST CRIME
MASSACRED ALL DANES IN ENGLAND

10 Aethelred II

Aethelred's tenure as king of England led to the inglorious epithet of Aethelred the Unready. However, a better translation of the moniker would be 'ill-advised', as it is generally agreed that the counsel Aethelred received was little and poor.

Although he was too young to have been complicit in the murder of his older brother (Edward the Martyr), who was killed after having been on the throne for only two and a half years, the crime was carried out by those loyal to him in order that the younger sibling would take his place. This meant that there was a lot of mistrust surrounding the young monarch and, as the reputation of the murdered boy grew after his death, it would become increasingly difficult for Aethelred to unite his subjects.

And the necessity for a united British army was urgent with a renewed threat from the north. The Danes had recommenced raids along England's coast, breaking the treaty they had made with Aethelred's father, Edgar. After the English suffered a serious defeat at the Battle of Maldon in 991, Aethelred began paying tribute to the Danes in return for peace. However, the Danes were hard to appease and had restarted hostilities by 997.

Finally, in 1002, Aethelred reached breaking point and took drastic action. On 13 November he issued an order that all Danes in England should be executed, calling it "a most just extermination". It was an indiscriminate attempt at a show of strength that claimed the life of Danish leader Sweyn's sister, Gunhilde, and Sweyn invaded in retaliation, leading to Aethelred's downfall.

WARMONGERING	☆★★★★
INSANITY	☆☆★★★
POLITICAL MURDERS	☆★★★★
PERSONAL MURDERS	☆☆☆★★

09 Louis I

REIGN	814-840
COUNTRY	AQUITAINE
WORST CRIME	HAD HIS NEPHEW KILLED

Louis the Pious was, in many ways, as sensible a leader as his nickname would suggest. His father, Charlemagne, appointed him King of Aquitaine at the tender age of three. He became King of the Franks and Emperor of Rome upon his father's death in 814 and decided that, in order to avoid any diplomatic issues, any of his unmarried sisters would be packed off to nunneries.

When Louis nearly died in an accident in 817, he decided to ensure that, should he suddenly expire, there would be a neat plan of succession to set out who ruled what in the Frankish empire. He confirmed that his nephew Bernard would remain the king of Italy, but the will described his son Lothair's position as 'overlord', implying that Italy would be submissive to him. Needless to say, the wording of this document did not please Bernard and, spurred on by rumours that Lothair was to invade, he set about preparing a rebellion. However, word quickly reached Louis I of Bernard's plan and the king immediately took an army to confront his errant nephew. Bernard was shocked by the speed of the king's reaction and went to try and negotiate, before being forced into surrender. It's here that Louis' place in this list of murderous kings is assured...

He sentenced his nephew to death, before deciding that he should be blinded instead – a punishment that was apparently merciful. However, the procedure was not entirely successful. As a result, while Bernard was indeed blinded, he spent two days in unbearable pain before dying anyway. Three civil wars would follow but the legacy of this killing would haunt the deeply religious ruler for the rest of his life.

WARMONGERING	☆☆★★★
INSANITY	☆★★★★
POLITICAL MURDERS	☆☆☆★★
PERSONAL MURDERS	☆☆☆☆★

08 Charles II (SPAIN)

REIGN	1665-1700
COUNTRY	SPAIN
WORST CRIME	BURNED HERETICS AT THE STAKE

The reason for Charles II's reputation as a bloodthirsty king is very much rooted in his heritage. He was the last of the Habsburg line – a lineage that was so devoted to preserving the purity of its bloodline through inbreeding that it eventually led to a man like Charles. Disfigured, infertile and cursed to spend his life suffering from various illnesses, the king was in a similar amount of mental anguish.

Charles II's condition was no secret among the European court. He was just three years old when the throne became his and his mother, Mariana, became queen regent designating much of the work of governing the country to advisors.

His mother remained regent long after Charles could have taken kingship himself, but it was decided that such a move would be unwise. A struggle for power began when Mariana was exiled, and Don Juan José (Charles's half-brother) took responsibility for the country and the king.

Charles's illness was grotesquely misunderstood at the time – interpreted as a sign that the king was probably bewitched; he would even undergo an exorcism in the final years of his life.

His worst crime was the 1680 auto-de-fe (display of public penance and executions) in Madrid, during which many heretics were burned. Charles II attended the trial and burnings, though the executions were probably ordered by someone else. A blood-soaked reign but a misunderstood one.

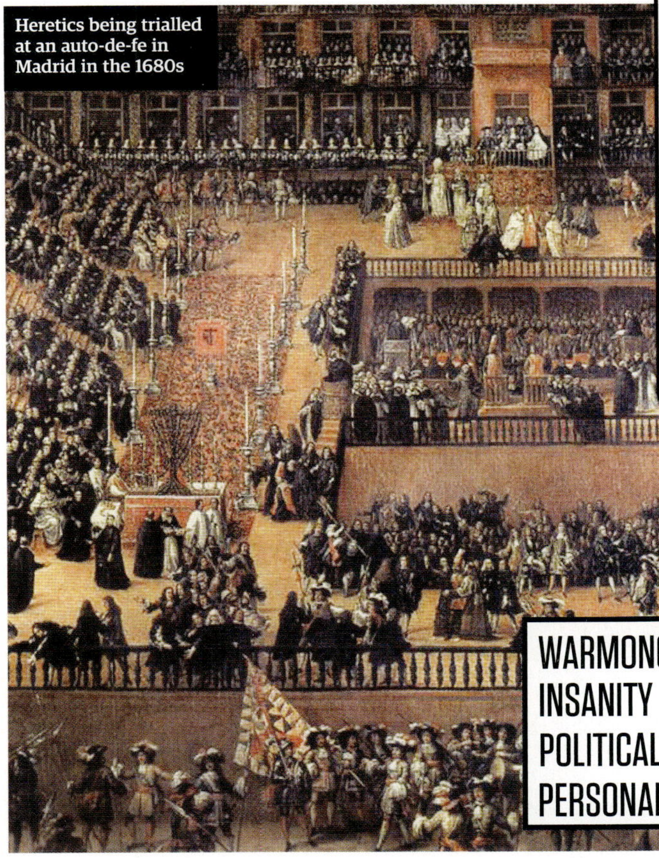

Heretics being trialled at an auto-de-fe in Madrid in the 1680s

WARMONGERING	☆☆★★★
INSANITY	☆☆☆☆☆
POLITICAL MURDERS	☆☆★★★
PERSONAL MURDERS	☆★★★★

07 Charles II
(NAVARRE)

Charles II believed that the kingdom of Navarre was far too small for a man with such a noble lineage as his and spent his life trying to wheedle his way to a more important status. He ordered the assassination of the Constable of France in 1354 and made a deal with the English, forcing the French King John II to make peace.

John grew tired of his treachery and finally arrested him in 1356, only for Charles to be broken out in 1357. When John II agreed to a peace treaty with the English, Charles II freed all the prisoners in Paris. With the city on the verge of revolution, Charles U-turned and took the opportunity to lead the aristocracy at the Battle of Mello and the subsequent massacre of the rebels.

He blindly swore patriotism and honour while consistently reaching out to the opposition in the hope of a better deal. His meddling in the war between Castile and Aragon proved disastrous and he staged being captured to avoid having to participate. Towards the end of his life he tried to convince English king Edward III to invade and overthrow Charles V, as well as being involved in two attempts on Charles's life. When his scheming with Gascony against Castile went wrong, Navarre was invaded in 1378 and he was forced to agree to an alliance with Castile and France. He burned to death in 1387, allegedly when the sackcloth filled with brandy he was bathing in caught fire.

REIGN 1349-1387

COUNTRY NAVARRE (SPAIN/FRANCE)

WORST CRIME
MURDER, TREACHERY AND COWARDICE

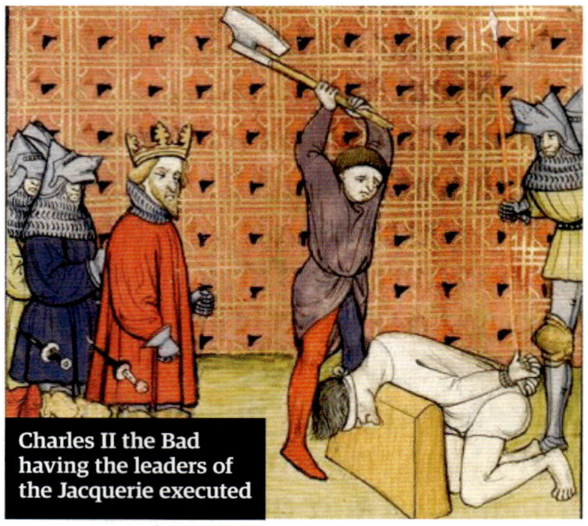

Charles II the Bad having the leaders of the Jacquerie executed

WARMONGERING	☆☆☆☆★
INSANITY	☆☆★★★
POLITICAL MURDERS	☆☆☆☆☆
PERSONAL MURDERS	☆☆☆☆☆

06 Herod I

"He ordered that his wife be executed if he didn't return from an expedition"

There are many who would claim that King Herod committed his most heinous deed with the Massacre of the Innocents. However, the story of the slaughter of all boys in Bethlehem under the age of two is only found in the Bible; there are no historical records from the time detailing such an atrocity. Herod's more frequently documented crimes were much more personal.

In fact, Herod was an excellent ruler of Judaea. Having obtained the position after being forced to flee Galilee when the Palestinians had reclaimed their land, he strengthened his kingship when he divorced in order to marry Mariamne, which pacified a leading sect of Jewish priests (the Hasmoneans). However, as time went by, it became clear that Herod was not well.

REIGN 37-4 BCE

COUNTRY JUDAEA

WORST CRIME
KILLED HIS WIFE AND CHILDREN

He was prone to fits of mental instability, which made his fierce love for his wife all the more dangerous. At one point, before leaving for a political expedition, he ordered that Mariamne should be executed if he didn't return from this expedition because he couldn't face the idea of her being with another man. His jealousy was exploited by his sister, Salome - who despised Mariamne - to convince Herod that his wife was plotting against him. Mariamne was executed in 29 BCE, and Herod - believing that their two sons, Alexandros and Aristobulus, would try to take revenge for their mother - had both their children killed in 7 BCE. Two years later, Antipater - Herod's only son by his first wife - was also executed for the same reason.

Massacre of the Innocents

WARMONGERING	☆★★★★
INSANITY	☆☆☆☆★
POLITICAL MURDERS	☆☆★★★
PERSONAL MURDERS	☆☆☆☆☆

05 Richard I

The man dubbed 'Lionheart' spent most of his life fighting. He first took up arms against his father, Henry II, in 1173 and continued to aggressively pursue the throne until Henry's death in 1189, when some quite reasonably suggested that Richard had driven the king to his grave.

Blood was spilled on the same day that Richard took the crown, when the barring of Jewish figures from the coronation was misinterpreted as an order to instigate violence against all of London's Jews. Richard ordered the executions of those who took part, but the instances of copycat 'Christian' violence would set the tone for a king who was desperate to join the Crusades.

Together with Phillip II of France, who had assisted Richard in his fight for the throne, England joined the Third Crusade. Spending the bulk of his father's treasure chest to raise a new army, Richard set off for the Holy Lands in 1190. He blazed a bloody trail through Sicily and Cyprus before arriving at Acre, Israel, in 1191.

Following the successful siege of the city, he ordered the execution of 2,700 Muslim prisoners. The crusade eventually ground to a halt and Richard was forced to retreat in 1192, only to be captured in Vienna by Leopold V. Once ransomed, he discovered that his brother, John, had given Normandy back to King Phillip in his absence.

In 1196, Richard built castles in Normandy to fortify his presence. He continued his war against Phillip until 1199, when he was struck by an arrow from the nearly undefended Châlus-Chabrol chateau. The wound turned fatally gangrenous – an undignified end for the warrior king.

REIGN 1189-1199
COUNTRY ENGLAND
WORST CRIME
WAR CRIMES OF THE CRUSADES

WARMONGERING	★★★★★
INSANITY	★★☆☆☆
POLITICAL MURDERS	★★★☆☆
PERSONAL MURDERS	★★★★☆

REIGN 1272-1307
COUNTRY ENGLAND
WORST CRIME
HAMMERING THE SCOTS

04 Edward I

When Edward I came to the throne he had a very clear goal in mind: to take back what he saw as English land which had been stolen. Upon Henry III's death, Edward returned to England from the Crusades and started planning a military campaign in Wales. Beginning with a successful invasion in 1277 he executed the Welsh leader, Llewelyn, in 1282 and Llewelyn's brother, David, a year later in response to rebellions.

The war in Wales had a devastating effect on the nation's finances. This was compounded when Edward responded violently to French King Philip reclaiming the territory of Gascony by sailing to attack in 1297, later returning to quell the Scottish rebellion. Edward intervened to such an extent that the Scots allied with the French and attacked Carlisle. Edward invaded in retaliation, beginning a brutal and lengthy conflict that earned him his nickname, Hammer of the Scots.

WARMONGERING	★★★★★
INSANITY	★★★☆☆
POLITICAL MURDERS	★★★★★
PERSONAL MURDERS	★★★★☆

03 Erik XIV

WARMONGERING	★★★☆☆
INSANITY	★★★★★
POLITICAL MURDERS	★★★☆☆
PERSONAL MURDERS	★★★★★

While many kings can lay claim to ordering the deaths of hundreds - even thousands - during the course of their reign, not many can say they committed murder with their own hands. The king of Sweden Erik XIV suffered from mental instability, but not to an extent that made him incapable of ruling. He strengthened Sweden's position in northern Europe by claiming territory in Estonia, leading to the Seven Years' War of the North between 1563 and 1570. Although his military campaigns were successful Erik's mental state was rapidly deteriorating and evidence points towards schizophrenia.

He became paranoid, eager to believe rumours of treason. He even executed two guards for 'making fun of the king'.

REIGN 1560-1568

COUNTRY SWEDEN

WORST CRIME

STABBING A NOBLEMAN TO DEATH

But it would be the Sture murders that would break him. Believing that the noble family would make a play for the throne, Erik began persecuting the Stures - specifically Nils Sture. In 1567, one of Sture's pages was tortured until he told Erik what he wanted to hear. Following a trial, death sentences began to be issued but the king remained indecisive. Finally, he visited the Stures at the castle in Uppsala (north of Stockholm) where they were imprisoned, to tell them that they were forgiven. When Erik left he discovered that a rebellion was underway, led by his brother, John. It was only a few hours later that Erik returned and stabbed Nils Sture before ordering the execution of the others.

02 Henry VIII

English king Henry VIII's voracious nature and hot temper have become the stuff of legend. He is renowned for being a man of ferocious appetites - in all aspects of life - and he was prepared to use any means necessary to quell his opposition.

Shortly after ascending to the throne, Henry married Catherine of Aragon, as his father, Henry VII, had wanted to secure an alliance with Spain. At the time he executed Edmund Dudley and Richard Empson - two of his father's advisors - on the grounds of treason. This was to become something of a pattern for Henry. From Thomas More to Thomas Cromwell, anyone who Henry perceived as either a threat to the throne or to his secession from the Catholic church was liable to find themselves with their head on the block.

REIGN 1509-1547

COUNTRY ENGLAND

WORST CRIME

EXECUTING ALL WHO OPPOSED HIM

However, he's most notorious for his list of spouses, driven by his desperation for a male heir and straightforward lust. The annulment of his marriage to Catherine of Aragon was prompted by a combination of the two as Anne Boleyn had already caught his eye. As we all know, Anne Boleyn did not last long before facing the executioner's axe - having been dubiously accused of infidelity, treachery and incest. Anne was followed by Jane Seymour, who died in childbirth; Anne of Cleves, who Henry soon separated from; and then the unfortunate Catherine Howard. Henry accused Catherine of being unfaithful with her secretary, Francis Dereham, while she claimed that Dereham had raped her. Despite her protests, she was sent to her death. Fortunately for his last wife, Catherine Parr, he died before she too could fall out of his favour.

The exact number of executions ordered by Henry VIII has not been conclusively agreed upon, but it is generally believed to be between 57,000 and 72,000. As a gruesome aside, he also made 'death by boiling' a legitimate form of execution.

> "Anyone perceived as a threat was liable to find themselves on the block"

Anne Boleyn in the Tower of London portrayed just before her execution under the orders of Henry VIII

WARMONGERING	★★★★☆
INSANITY	★★☆☆☆
POLITICAL MURDERS	★★★★★
PERSONAL MURDERS	★★★★★

01 Leopold II

Desperate to establish a colony overseas, Belgian king Leopold II turned to Africa and the potential riches of the Congo. To circumvent his own parliament, he created a dummy organisation called the International African Association, which he claimed would act in the interests of philanthropy and scientific research with a view to converting the citizens to Christianity. It was all completely legal and it gave the monarch the freedom to act however he wanted in the land under his control.

Its stated aim could not have been further from the truth. What had attracted Leopold to the Congo, in addition to the notion of creating an empire, was the tremendous supply of rubber in the area. He would spare nothing in order to get what he wanted. Despite having promised that he would protect the people of the Congo from slavers, Leopold promptly and brutally turned the country into a slave state.

The treatment of the workers was savage and uncompromising. Leopold allowed some missionaries into the Congo in order to allay the fears of foreign powers who believed he might be doing exactly what he was doing, and reports began to reach Europe about the maiming and executions of the men and women working on the plantations, as well as of the mass dumping of corpses.

It's impossible to know exactly how many people died during Leopold's rule of the Congo but the estimated figure is in the millions. The atrocities led to the establishment of the first human rights movement and Leopold was finally compelled to give up the Congo to the Belgian parliament in 1908.

REIGN 1865-1909

COUNTRY BELGIUM

WORST CRIME
FORMING A SLAVE COLONY IN AFRICA

WARMONGERING	☆☆★★★
INSANITY	☆☆☆★★
POLITICAL MURDERS	☆☆☆☆☆
PERSONAL MURDERS	☆☆☆☆☆

THE MYTHS OF ROBIN HOOD

Hero, archer, lover, poacher, murderer, thief, vagabond... The story of Robin Hood has taken many forms through the ages, but is there any truth in the legend?

Robin Hood; maybe you've heard of him? Medieval lovable rogue-type chap with green tights, good with arrows (and women), lives in a hideout in Sherwood Forest with a band of jolly outlaws who fleece greedy travelling rich folk of their cash under the threat of violence, before sending them packing. His generosity to the downtrodden is renowned and he's loved by the common folk, hated by the wealthy and powerful and he's a devil with the ladies, if you know what we mean - especially high-born damsels trapped in their metaphorical towers (or actual towers, depending on the story). He doesn't see eye-to-eye with corrupt authority figures either but don't think that Robin Hood is anything but a loyal and patriotic Englishman: everything he does, he does for his country and the rightful king, Richard I of England, who's off fighting a noble crusade against evil heathens, thousands of miles away.

A depiction of a wedding between Robin Hood and a coy looking Maid Marian, presided over by King Richard I

Robin Hood and his Merry Men: the original story has been sanitised by numerous generations

MYTH ONE

THE FAIR MAIDEN

Who was Maid Marian and was there any truth in her legend? When did she first enter the stories?

Maid Marian is more a complete fabrication than an embellished character. As a love-match and soul mate to Robin Hood, she popped onto the scene sometime in the 16th century and was likely derived from a 15th-century character: the Lady of May Day. This popular festival was a yearly tradition in the Middle Ages but it took several generations of storytelling before Marian and Robin were brought together. In fact, the increased popularity of the story of Robin Hood was probably brought about by three plays that are known to have been written for the May Day festivities: *Robin Hood and the Sheriff*, *Robin Hood and the Friar* and *Robin Hood and the Potter*. It is small wonder really, that some bard would eventually pen a romance between the dashing rebel and the fictional May Day queen.

No one blindly believes the story of Robin Hood as we know it today, but long periods of English history have had a funny habit of recycling these tales until it's hard to tell fact from fiction, or what the original truth was - if it wasn't a complete fabrication to begin with. Like a giant, generational game of Chinese whispers, the legend of Robin Hood has been passed along the popular media of the times with a bit of embellishment added here, something considered dark, unflattering or politically unsavoury removed there. And so, via the 20th century's communication revolution, it has boomed into world fame. In the last few decades we've been adding our own tint to this rose-hued tale of the arrow-slinging rebel, like the stories of Russell Crowe's disaffected soldier, Kevin Costner's noble Prince of Thieves and Errol Flynn's jubilant swashbuckling rogue. If we're going to sort some fact from fiction here, we have to unravel the Hollywood-spun Batman of the Middle Ages back to where it began, sometime in the 12th century, and look at the direct origin of today's tale.

The legend himself, if not the tales, can be traced to the time of King John of England, who was born in 1166 and reigned from 1199 until his death in 1216. These ballads and stories were born and cultivated out of an era of social upheaval. The end of King John's reign saw the English barony revolt and the signing of the Magna Carta, which was the first step along a long road to the breakdown of the ancient feudal system of government. While characters like Maid Marian appeared in tales from a later date, some of Robin's band of 'Merry Men' can be clearly identified at this time, but things get a lot murkier when it comes to the titular hero.

According to one of the more recent theories backed by, among others, historian David Baldwin, Robin Hood's real identity was that of a 13th-century farmer called Robert Godberd, whose escapades were far from the sugar-coated tales we see today. The crimes him and his band of outlaws around Nottinghamshire and nearby counties were accused of were of the brutal era

MYTH TWO

WHO WERE THE MERRY MEN?

Where did they come from and what were the skills that made them an important member of Robin Hood's gang?

LITTLE JOHN

Character: Burly lieutenant
Special skill: Staff-swinging
He's one the first men to be recruited into Robin Hood's band in modern stories and he was one of the first mentioned in the ballads of yore, too. Little John was a loyal, intelligent and, of course, strong man in poet Andrew of Wyntoun's lore. He was the only one of the Merry Men supposed to be present when Robin died and he's thought to be buried in Derbyshire.

WILL SCARLET

Character: Vain swordsman
Special skill: Wielding blades
There's been much confusion over William Scarlet's character and his plethora of names over the centuries, with one bard even including both a Scarlock and a Scarlet character in his work. He was still the youngest of the Merry Men in medieval versions of the Robin Hood story, but he liked to dress in finery and was also the most able swordsman, besting even Mr Hood himself.

MUCH THE MILLER'S SON

Character: Wily boy
Special skill: Poaching
This sneaky character has fallen into obscurity in favour of other characters in modern adaptations of Robin Hood but Much, or Midge as he's also known, appears in the oldest of the known Robin Hood ballads. A poacher caught killing a deer on the Sheriff's land, he escaped punishment and became an outlaw in his gang.

FRIAR TUCK

Character: Drunken holy man
Special skill: Holding his drink
If the legend as it appears today is to be taken at face value, Friar Tuck is a boozy and wily character who still has his heart in the right place. His character is thought to derive from a certain 15th-century Robert Stafford from Sussex, and he entered the story of Robin Hood's exploits at the same time as Maid Marian did, during the May Day festivities in the 15th and 16th centuries.

"In the last few decades we've been adding our own tint to this rose-hued tale of the arrow-slinging rebel"

in which he lived: burglaries, arson, assaulting clergymen and murdering travellers. The nature of their law-breaking has slowly been eroded throughout history to suit an increasingly gentile audience, compared with a medieval population accustomed to violence and who found Godberg's activities entirely palatable. Godberg and his fellow brigands were in defiance of a tyrant who had an iron grip on the extensive forested regions of Nottinghamshire. King John enforced the enormously unpopular Forest Law, which allowed the royal court exclusive access to vast swathes of hunting grounds, with utter ruthlessness. Thus, morally speaking, Godberg's actions were justified by the common man as necessary for the greater good of the people.

There are a number of other recorded Robin Hood-type characters with similar names and lives that span a period of 150 years or so during this time. The earliest is Robert Hod of Cirencester, a serf who lived in the household of an abbot in Gloucestershire. He murdered a visiting dignitary early in the 13th century, fled with his accomplices and was subsequently outlawed by King John's reviled minister Gerard of Athee. Four other Robert Hods existed in 1265 at the Battle of Evesham during King Henry's time. Each became fugitives and outlaws for various reasons, including robbing travellers and raiding an abbey in Yorkshire, which could explain how the character of Friar Tuck eventually made his appearance in later tales. Later versions, namely two Robyn Hods, appeared respectively as an archer in a garrison on the Isle of Wight and as a man jailed for trespassing in the King's Forest and poaching deer in 1354. The name Robert was a common one around this time, while the surname Hod or Hode likely came from the old English word for a head covering. It's also possible his surname was derived from the story of 'Robin of the Wood'.

With the array of similar characters and names of people who existed at this time it's not surprising that historians have trouble pinning the character's origin on any one man. The earliest surviving ballads of the Robin Hood story don't even elaborate on his exploits: they make no mention of the troubles of the time, Robin Hood's cause or the years he was active, simply that he was an outlaw who lived in and around Sherwood or Barnsdale. To further confuse things, there are numerous accounts of outlaws in the 13th and 14th centuries adopting the name of Robin Hood and Little John, which suggests the story had achieved some popularity even then, although adopting the name of a famous outlaw – fictional or otherwise – was common among criminals at this time.

Robin Hood and his men capturing and tying the abbot of Saint Mary's to a tree

This Robin Hood had no spouse or family, no land and certainly no title. No reason is given for his criminality and his characteristics were likely drawn from some real-life outlaws of the time. One of the most telling aspects of these stories is the language they were written in: up until 1362, when Parliament decreed that English was to be used in court, French was widely spoken in the country – whereas even the earliest stories of Robin are in English, which helps establish a date.

By the 14th and 15th centuries, the tales of Robin Hood had gained some fame as they were disseminated in the traditional May Day festivities, while his story had begun to be written into plays and ballads. There's no mention of the folk hero living at the time of King John, but he can be found in the 15th-century stories of *Robin Hood and the Monk, The Lyttle Geste of Robyn Hode, Robin Hood and Guy of Gisborne, Robin Hood and the Curtal Friar* and *Robin Hoode his Death*. The plays *Robin Hood and the Friar* and *Robin Hood and the Potter* were written specifically for the May Day Games in 1560 and were based on earlier ballads of the same name. During this period, his Merry Men began to accrete together from various sources as

> "There are numerous accounts of outlaws in the 13th and 14th centuries adopting the name of Robin Hood and Little John"

Robin was embellished with details like so many layers of varnish. Word of the character had began to spread beyond the counties of the midlands and in the late-15th century, he is referred to in plays written as far afield as Somerset and Reading. He was well known even to the famous womanizing, warmongering king of England, Henry VIII, and his royal court. The young monarch's idea of celebrating May Day involved walking into Queen Catherine of Aragon's chambers with his nobles, "apparelled in short cotes of Kentish Kendal, with hodes on their heddes, and hosen of the same, every one of them his bowe and arrowes, and a sworde and a bucklar, like outlawes, or Robyn Hode's men," according to *Hall's Chronicle* by Edward Hall, a 16th-century scholar.

By the late-16th century, the Merry Men had acquired a friar, Robin had a love interest and he'd also gained nobility. Playwright Anthony Munday wrote two plays on the outlaw, *The Downfall of Robert Earl of Huntington* and *The Death of Robert Earl of Huntington*, in which Robin (Robert) has clearly been lofted into high society. Or at least, it was his position to lose: in the plays, Munday makes Robin an earl in the reign of Richard I who is disinherited by the king. Fleeing into the Greenwood, he is followed by the daughter of Robert Fitzwalter, one of the leading barons who rallied against the king, where they fall in love and she changes her name to Maid Marian. King John, angry that his would-be bride has been stolen from him by an outlaw, pursues her in the second play and poisons her at Dunmow Priory.

The idea that Robin was a fallen noble and some kind of love triangle existed between King John, Maid Marian and Robin still endures in some stories today. But by introducing a lover and giving him blue blood, the Robin Hood of the 16th century makes the transition from a brutal and often murderous outlaw in defiance of the monarchy to a more domesticated hero, a protagonist the ruling classes could admire and relate to - someone with just cause against an evil ruler. His status as an outlaw had been relegated to a trait that added an element of drama to the story, rather than one that defined it.

From the 16th century onward, with the advent of the printing press, the story of Robin Hood becomes more refined and much more familiar. Across the next few centuries, the character and the stories would pick up traits

Maid Marian being rescued by Robin Hood

MYTH THREE

THE EVIL VILLAIN?

King John was a real person who raised taxes for Richard's foreign wars. Has history treated him unfairly?

King John was indeed a real person who lived at the same time Robin Hood was purported to be in and around Nottinghamshire, shaking up the status quo. By today's standards, he was a decadent, warmongering, self-serving tyrant who ruled over a turbulent period in British history. He is commonly regarded as a cruel king but the truth of it is that he was a leader of his generation. Him and his predecessors, the Angevin monarchs, operated with relative impunity under the authority of divine majesty: the king was above the law and could therefore do whatever pleased them. King John was a mercurial chap with a penchant for electing men outside the ranks of his barons to the royal court, favouring lesser nobles from the continent and spurning his own, powerful English nobles closer to home, whom he eyed suspiciously for signs of treachery. It was this, in part, that led to the signing of the Magna Carta, the seminal charter that led to constitutional law in England. His barons were sick of his arbitrary rule and insisted that, as a part of the Magna Carta, no free man could be punished by any other law than the law of the land. Of course, the Magna Carta never limited the king's powers in practice and King John only signed it to mollify his barons, but it remains the single most significant act of his reign. But this would have been lost on Robin Hood, the common serfs and farmers of these feudal times who as a general rule, would have feared the king and hated likes of his Forest Law, which would have been mercilessly enforced.

Robin Hood and Little John - two popular names adopted by rogues and criminals in the 13th century

MYTH FOUR

FRIEND OF THE POOR?

Was Robin Hood as generous as the tales depict him?

If Robin Hood and his Merry Men did exist in the time of King John, it's highly unlikely they would have embarked on the scale of philanthropy portrayed in the modern tale. This idea likely came from an early medieval ballad involving Richard at the Lee, a knight who had fallen upon hard times. His lands were to be forfeited to an abbot because he couldn't repay a loan to the abbey, so Robin gives him money to pay his mortgage. Historian John Paul Davis goes further as to suggest that Robin Hood stole from the rich and lent to the poor, as a kind of medieval loan shark. In his book *Robin Hood: The Unknown Templar*, Davis says that Hood loaned Richard a sum of £400, before stealing it back off the abbot once Richard has paid the abbey back. Victorian-era author Howard Pyle and 20th-century films undoubtedly had a big hand in transforming Hood from a devious bandit into the philanthropist he is today. So did someone named Robin Hood steal from the rich and give to the poor? It is possible, yes. Did he have their best interests at heart? That's as clear as the legend itself.

> "16th-century Robin Hood makes the transition from a brutal and murderous outlaw in defiance of the monarchy"

and themes that generations to come would adopt when turning to their own adaptations. The 18th-century Robin Hood sees him encounter farcical situations. For example, the ballads of the time talk of a series of tradesmen and professionals getting the upper hand with the hapless outlaw, while the Sheriff of Nottingham is the only one to be bested by Robin. Robin dresses up as a friar in *Robin Hood's Golden Prize* and cheats two priests out of five hundred pounds - nearly $16,000 (£10,000) in today's money - before he's caught and summons the Merry Men with his horn.

The Victorians, notorious for enamelling history with their own style and values, weren't shy about leaving their mark on Robin Hood either. By the mid-19th century, the cost and efficiency of printing books was such that they had become available to the masses. US writer and illustrator Howard Pyle took the traditional folk tale of Robin Hood and adapted it to his own children's version, serialising it into short stories called *The Merry Adventures of Robin Hood*, which became enormously popular. His green-tights vagabond was a moral philanthropist who would go on to spawn a whole century of the people's hero that took from the rich and gave to the poor. By the time author TH White came along, the story of Robin Hood was among the world's most well known.

White took it a step further and, as an author made famous by his Arthurian novels, brought Robin Hood and his Merry Men into his novel *The Sword In The Stone*, which was made into an anthropomorphic Disney film a quarter of a century later.

The late-20th century and the booming phenomenon that was cinema brought with it numerous adaptations, most of which aren't remotely faithful even to the 16th-century versions. The Sean Connery and Audrey Hepburn film *Robin and Marian* made much of the romance but for the first time, cast King Richard as a less-than-benevolent character. The *Robin of Sherwood* television series went as far as to add a Muslim character in the form of Nasir the Saracen, a trend the famous Kevin Costner film followed through Morgan Freeman's Azeem.

The character of the lovable rogue has international appeal, so almost every country has its own version of Robin Hood: in Wales, Twm Siôn Cati is likened to Hood as a high-ranking highwayman driven to robbery as an income by his Protestant faith under a Catholic monarch. Ukranian rebel Ustym Karmaliuk made his name in the 19th century for robbing the rich and distributing the proceeds of his crimes to the poor, and over a millennium before Robin Hood came to the fore, Boudicca, queen of the Iceni, defied the Romans when they forcibly took control of her lands and people. She led a successful revolt that destroyed a Roman legion and the Roman capital before it was put down. Almost every generation has a story that is similar to Robin Hood, illustrating the very human desire and need to have a figure who stands for right against wrong, light against dark.

Given that nearly a millennium has passed since the first tale of Robin Hood was told, in addition to his murky origins that even 13th-century bards cannot agree on, it's unlikely any historian will be able to settle on who Robin Hood and his Merry Men were exactly, or what little truth there is to their deeds. As far as history is concerned, the Robin Hood legend has become a victim of its own popularity, obscured by generations of storytelling taking it firmly into the realms of fantasy.

JAZZ
DANCING
CHALMERS

Public enemy number one

AL CAPONE

Arriving in Chicago as a minor league mobster, Al Capone helped build an empire of prostitution, bootlegging and murder that made him a notorious household name

The needle skipped as the gun barked twice in the killer's hand, the record player screeching into the silence of the restaurant's corridor as its owner crashed to the floor, blood pooling out onto the polished tiles.

Giacomo 'Big Jim' Colosimo, his body cooling from its exit wounds, had recently left his wife, filing for divorce and skipping town to marry a 19-year-old cabaret singer. His ex-wife, Victoria Moresco, or one of her brothers, was the prime suspect in this crime of passion, but the police knew enough to pay a visit to two of Colosimo's associates - the genial Johnny Torrio and his sidekick, the disquieting Alfonse Capone, three nasty scars on his cheek contorting as he smiled. "Big Jim and me were like brothers," claimed Torrio. "Mr Colosimo and me both loved opera", added Capone. "He was a grand guy."

Colosimo's murder on 11 May 1920 is still regarded as unsolved, but perhaps it's a crime that Chicago Police Department chose to leave that way. For nearly a decade Colosimo had ruled Chicago through hard graft and intimidation - running over 100 brothels with his wife - and extorting protection money from most of the city's illegal gambling dens, the profits snaking through the entire city, supplementing the meagre wages of the cop on the street corner and boosting the bank account of the city's two-time mayor, William 'Big Bill' Hale Thompson.

Chicago was a rough town. Booming in the early 1920s thanks to heavy industry and cheap labour, the Windy City was a Wild West frontier town with chimney stacks instead of cacti and bullet-riddled Model-T Fords in lieu of horses. "She was vibrant and violent," wrote local journalist Robert St John, "stimulating and ruthless, intolerant of smugness, impatient with those either physically or intellectually timid."

Capone had arrived in Chicago from New York in 1919 to work for his old friend Torrio, who had earned Colosimo's trust by chasing off a rival extortion racket and stuck around as the boss's second in command. Capone soon put the feared reputation he had enjoyed back home to work as a debt collector, seeing first hand how Colosimo's operation held a stranglehold over the underworld; gambling dens who refused to pay up for Big Jim's protection would either find themselves the subject of a convenient police raid or - worse still - a visit from Capone, who was more than happy to break a few legs and mess up a card table with a swing from his baseball bat.

Capone in New York

Born in 1898 in a run-down district of Brooklyn to Italian immigrants Gabriele and Teresina Capone, Al Capone's life of crime began early, brawling with street gangs and running errands for mobsters. One, a young rising star called Johnny Torrio, would loom larger in his life later on.

Capone soon found work with Frankie Yale (born Francesco Ioele), a vicious thug with links to Torrio. Working as a barman in Yale's bar, the Harvard Inn – a notorious haunt of prostitutes and gangsters – Capone got the vicious scars on his face when he leered at one mobster's sister "Honey, you got a nice ass and I mean that as a compliment, believe me." The furious Frank Galluccio called Capone out and slashed him three times across his cheek with a knife. He needed 30 stitches, but he was lucky the hoodlum had been drinking because Galluccio was aiming for his jugular. In the bar he also picked up syphilis, which eventually caused his death, but may have affected him even earlier. Neurosyphilis attacks the brain and the spinal column, and can cause violent mood swings, delusions and megalomania.

Johnny Torrio

Even after handing control over to Capone after he was shot Torrio was still involved in organised crime and became a close associate of Lucky Luciano and other mob bosses.

Compared to the claustrophobic Big Apple, where half a dozen gangs butted heads over a block at a time, Torrio and Capone found Chicago fertile for expansion, as the only thing that stood in their way was their own boss. In January 1920 the rules of the game changed again as the 18th Amendment to the US Constitution came into effect. Also known as the Volstead Act, which prohibited the production, transportation and sale of alcohol – but not the consumption – Prohibition meant a huge swathe of the population were suddenly transformed into potential customers. Torrio and Capone saw that this was a revenue stream with the potential to dwarf even prostitution and racketeering, but to their dismay Colosimo was having none of it. When Colosimo was conveniently removed from the picture, John 'The Fox' Torrio became the boss of the Chicago Outfit, and by his side stood Al Capone.

With Torrio's blessing, Capone set about covertly reopening breweries and distilleries that had been closed by the Volstead Act, setting up an ambitious distribution network to the city's mean speakeasies with the help of his older brothers Ralph and Frank Capone. "Nobody wanted Prohibition," he said. "This town voted six to one against it. Somebody had to throw some liquor on that thirst. Why not me?"

The loyal Ralph was put in charge of one of the Chicago Outfit's legal enterprises, a soft-drink bottling plant which earned him the nickname 'Bottles', while Frank honed a reputation for savagery that overshadowed even Al's. Estimated to have been responsible for 300 deaths, Frank infamously advised his little bother that, "you get no talk back from a corpse."

It was happening under Johnny Torrio's command but there was no doubt that bootlegging was Al Capone's kingdom, and he was soon to pay for it in blood as 1923 saw the downfall of Chicago's sticky fingered mayor, 'Big Bill' Thompson. The Democrat William Emmett Dever was voted in on a pledge to sweep the gangs

How America swam with booze

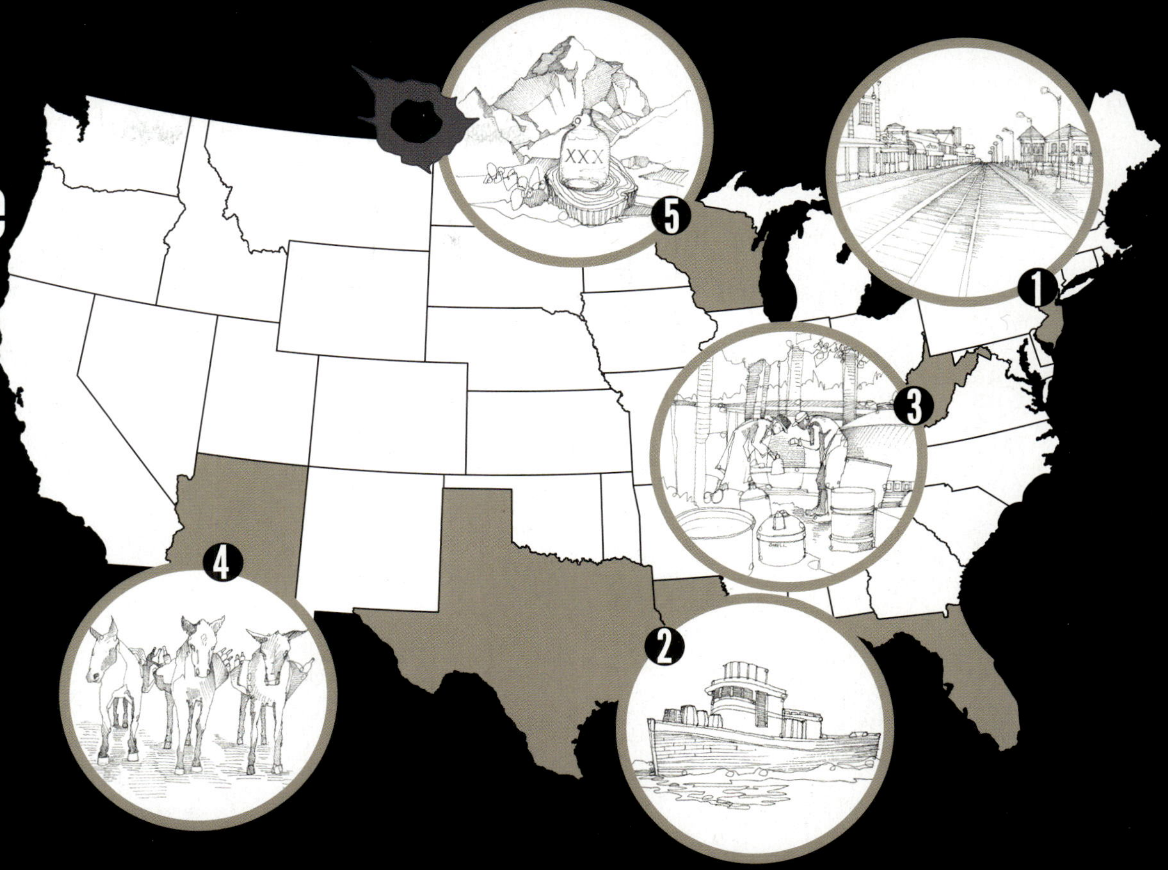

1. WHISKY ON THE BOARDWALK

Ships laden down with whisky from Canada would anchor off the coast of New Jersey, well beyond the maritime limit patrolled by the US Coast Guard. Smugglers would sail out to pick up the crates of booze and New Jersey's vast coastline became something of a free-for-all, with rival gangs hijacking each other's shipments. The hedonistic boardwalk resort of Atlantic City became the major gateway with the town's Irish-American racketeer Enoch 'Nucky' Johnson taking a major cut before it moved onward to Capone in Chicago or other mobs in New York and Jersey City.

2. RUM FROM THE CARIBBEAN

With Prohibition, Cuba emerged as a hedonistic getaway from the newly 'dry' US to the Bacardi-soaked Caribbean. Traffic flowed both ways, however, with 'rum runners' smuggling rum from Cuba, Jamaica and the Bahamas into South Florida, Texas and Louisiana.

In Texas, Galveston became the major entry point, supplying the rest of Texas and much of the Midwest. Dubbed the 'Free State of Galveston', brothers Sam and Rose Maceo ruled the local vice trade and successfully held off competition from Capone and New York boss Albert Anastasia.

3. A LAKE OF WHISKY

Although Ontario had its own temperance laws, they didn't ban distilling alcohol – leading to a flow of hooch across Lake Michigan and up the Detroit River from Windsor to Detroit. With illegally obtained papers saying their final destination was Venezuela, they would quietly off-load their cargo in Motor City instead. Detroit had been 'dry' well before Prohibition and the Purple Gang tightly controlled the rum-running trade and were major suppliers to Capone's Chicago Outfit.

4. MULES FROM MEXICO

Mass smuggling of US goods into Mexico was turned completely on its head thanks to Prohibition. Now home-made tequila and mescal was smuggled in the opposite direction by mule in groups of three or four, often crossing rivers at night, or by truck and car along dusty and isolated roads.

Texas's 1,300km (800mi) Mexican border was simply too wide be to adequately policed, and cat-and-mouse chases between the smugglers and Texas Rangers became the stuff of legend.

5. MOUNTAIN MOONSHINE

While champagne, gin, rum and whisky were available to those with the cash to cover its dangerous distribution, the poorer had to be taken care of too and moonshine cut the costs significantly.

Rural communities in the Appalachian Mountains and the Midwest had a tradition of home brew, but now a market opened up for their moonshine.

Stills could explode and quality control was poor and potentially life-threatening – but moonshiners often expanded their operations into barn-sized breweries.

from the city, and Torrio entrusted Capone with an urgent relocation to Cicero – the fourth largest city in Illinois – just outside of Chicago and the legislative reach of 'Decent Dever.' While Torrio and Capone had ruled their criminal empire largely as Colosimo had – with money in the right pockets and threats whispered in the right ears – the takeover of Cicero was an overt display of force, as Capone set about rigging the mayoral election for the mob's pet politician, Joseph Z Klenha.

On the eve of the 1924 mayoral election, Frank Capone burst into the office of the Democrat candidate for Cicero with some of his thugs, beating the hopeful to a pulp with their pistol butts, trashing his office and firing their revolvers into the ceiling as a preamble for the next day's audacious takeover. As cold, grey 1 April dawned, Capone hoods stormed into the polling stations to screen voters, snatching their ballot papers from them to ensure they were ticking the right box. Election officials with the stones to intervene were dealt with; a Democrat campaign worker was shot in the legs and dumped in a cellar, two other men were shot in the street and another had his throat cut.

Eventually, a desperate judge bussed in 70 Chicago police officers, deputised on the spot into the Cicero Police Department, to restore order. As the rain started to fall, Frank Capone found himself in a firefight outside a polling station. Opening fire on an approaching police car, he was gunned down by the startled cops, but it was too late – the town belonged to the Chicago Outfit. Frank got a funeral fit for war hero, with $20,000 worth of flowers placed around the silver plated coffin and over 150 cars in the motorcade. Despite the appalling bloodshed in the takeover of Cicero, Al Capone had been something of an enigma to the press.

However, as he got his hands dirtier and dirtier and frequently acted unstably – a possible consequences of syphilis contracted back in New York – his name was beginning to be heard outside of darkened back rooms where shady men made deals. A few weeks after Frank's body hit the pavement, small-time burglar 'Ragtime' Joe Howard was

St Valentine's Day Massacre

A step by step account of the day when seven men were gunned down in cold blood

STEP 1

GIVING THE NOD

Mobster and boxer 'Machine Gun' Jack McGurn, a survivor of an attack by the rival North Side Gang, approaches Al Capone in his Miami winter home with a plan to take out the North Side leader, George Clarence 'Bugs' Moran and his lieutenants.

STEP 2

THE SET-UP

On 13 February 1929, McGurn has a booze hijacker approach Moran about selling him some top-end whisky for the bargain price of $57 a case, they arrange to meet in the morning. He adds the whisky is stolen from Detroit's Purple Gang – suppliers to Capone's mob.

STEP 3

THE LOOK-OUTS

McGurn stations lookouts – the brothers Harry and Phil Keywell, both members of the allied Purple Gang – in an apartment opposite Moran's headquarters, a nondescript garage behind the offices of SMC Cartage Company at 2122 North Clark Street.

STEP 4

THE TRAP CLOSES

On 14 February at 10.30am, the North Side Gang gather at their garage HQ, expecting a shipment of Old Log Cabin Whiskey. McGurn's scouts think they spot Moran arriving – it's Albert Weinshank, wearing the same-coloured coat and hat as his boss.

STEP 5

THE AMBUSH

Four gunmen in a stolen police car – two of them wearing police uniforms – burst in. Believing this to be a routine raid, the six members of the North Side Gang and two of their associates surrender and allow the 'policemen' to remove their weapons.

STEP 6

THE LUCKY ESCAPE

Moran and Ted Newberry arrive late through a side street in time to see the police car pull up and wait it out in a café. Spotting another mobster, Henry Gusenberg, they warn him off, while a fourth survivor also arrives late. He notes down the car's license plate and skedaddles.

Murder weapon

Fitted with either a 20-round box or the iconic 50-round circular drum, the Thompson Submachine Gun could fire between 800 and 900 rounds a minute, allowing its wielder to spray his enemy with the entire magazine in a matter of seconds. Though retailing for $200 at a time when a car cost $400, it used ubiquitous .45 ammunition and could be easily broken down for transport and reassembled in under a minute. Effective at a range up to 45 metres (150 feet), the Tommy gun was perfect for close-range firefights across streets and the marble counter of the speakeasy. It quickly became a cultural symbol of gangsters in the 1920s, so much that when the police started recruiting their 'G-men', they made sure to equip them with Tommy guns of their own.

Victims

Four unfortunate victims of the massacre

John May

Not a member of the North Side Gang, May was a mechanic who worked on their cars and occasionally as muscle. May was trying to stay out of trouble, but the demands of seven children left him with no other option but to take work from the mob.

Peter Gusenberg and Frank Gusenberg

Hitmen for the North Side Gang, the Gusenberg brothers entered the criminal underworld in their teens. They took part in a drive-by shooting of Capone's HQ in 1926 and killed two of his allies in 1928.

Adam Heyer

Moran's business manager and North Side Gang accountant, Heyer owned the lease on the gang's headquarters. Described as a snappy dresser, Heyer had been in prison twice – once for robbery and once for running a confidence game.

Police investigation

The hunt for the killers

Frank Gusenberg lived on for hours despite being riddled with wounds, but sticking stubbornly to the mob's code of silence he refused to admit he'd even been shot, let alone who'd done it, before he died. The Chicago Police Department quickly announced that they believed Capone associates John Scalise, Alberto Anselmi, Jack McGurn and Frank Rio were responsible, but the case floundered due to lack of evidence and McGurn skipped town with his moll.

In frustration, the police began its retaliation efforts by shaking down Detroit's Purple Gang on the basis that Moran's mob had recently been hijacking their liquor shipments. On 22 February, the burnt remains of the police Cadillac were found, but it was impossible to pin it on either Capone or the Purple Gang, while the two murder weapons later turned up in a police raid on the Michigan home of bank robber and hitman Fred 'Killer' Burke in November that same year.

Burke, who led a vicious gang that Capone called his "American boys", was finally arrested in March 1931, attempting to rob a bank in Kirksville, Missouri, and died in prison in 1940 from diabetes. Having killed a Michigan police officer, the Chicago police were unable to extradite him to Illinois and his role in the St Valentine's Day Massacre went unexamined.

Meanwhile in a completely unrelated case, the FBI had finally pinned down the ruthless Barker-Karpis gang of bank robbers and kidnappers, when one of their members – Byron 'Monty' Bolton – confessed to the St Valentine's Day Massacre and implicated Burke. Having no jurisdiction over the case, the FBI suppressed the information but it finally leaked to the press, adding to the already considerable confusion and the mystery of the entire case.

THE MASSACRE

STEP 7

The two fake cops line the men up against a wall. Suddenly the two plain-clothes assassins open fire with Tommy guns while the others join in with a sawn-off shotgun and .45 handgun – spraying each man with at least ten bullets across their head and torso.

THE COVER-UP

STEP 8

The men in uniform lead the two plain-clothes assassins back to the police car with their hands raised, as if they'd been arrested. Neighbours, peering out of the windows, alerted by the rattle of gunfire, assume the villains have been apprehended.

Suspects

Who might have pulled the trigger?

John Scalise and Alberto Anselmi

John Scalise and Alberto Anselmi

Capone's most feared hitmen, the Sicilian-born 'murder twins' were believed responsible for the death of North Side Gang boss – and Moran's predecessor – Dean O'Banion in 1924, as well as a failed attack on Moran and the murder of two police officers in June 1925. Both were sent to prison, but released a year later.

Frank Rio

One of Capone's most loyal and dependable bodyguards, Italian-born Rio had been arrested twice, once for handling stolen furs and once for the daylight robbery of a mail train but intimidation and bribery of judges helped him escape conviction, earning him the nickname 'Slippery' Frank Rio.

"His revolver levelled at Torrio's skull - the gun clicked on empty and the would-be assassins fled"

enjoying a drink in a bar, when two men entered. Witnesses, who quickly forgot all the other details, recalled him say a friendly "Hello Al" before he was shot point blank – four rounds into his cheek and two into his shoulder. Nobody saw anything, nobody recognised the man, but the police knew who was responsible and so did the press, so for the first time, Capone's mugshot appeared on the front page.

In private, Capone's gang whispered that Howard had stuck up Jack 'Greasy Thumb' Guzik for $1,500, boasting he had "made the little Jew whine." Guzik was Capone's trusted money man, responsible for regular payoffs to cops and judges. Soon the name 'Scarface' began to stick, needling away at Capone's vanity – he never allowed the left side of his face to be photographed – and he began to lash out at the flickering flash bulbs of the photographers.

There were far more immediate threats than damning headlines, though. The predominantly Irish-American North Side Gang run by Dean O'Banion controlled the breweries and the bootlegging in Chicago's North Side and had resisted all of Torrio's efforts to bring them to heel. Alliances and truces had dwindled and fallen apart, but the last straw came on 19 May 1924 as O'Banion finally relinquished his share of the Sieben Brewery to Torrio. As soon as Torrio and his boys – joined by their allies in Little Sicily's 'Terrible Gennas' – showed up, a conveniently timed police raid swept in and the boss was left with a $5,000 fine and a nine-month jail sentence. "Deany was all right," smirked Capone, who took over the day-to-day running of the mob while Torrio served his sentence. "But like everyone else, his head got away from his hat."

One day while O'Banion clipped chrysanthemums in his flower shop, Schofields, Mike 'The Devil' Genna, John Scalise, Albert Anselmi and Frankie Yale strode in. As O'Banion and Yale shook hands, Scalise and Anselmi fired two bullets into his chest and two into his throat. As he lay on the floor in a pool of blood and petals, he was shot in the back of the head for good measure. He had been dealt with.

George Clarence 'Bugs' Moran took over the North Side Gang and nursed their grudge, moving the headquarters from Schofields to the garage that would become the site of the shocking St Valentine's Day Massacre in 1929, the culmination of a brutal and bloody five-year gang war between the Chicago Outfit and the North Side Gang.

Upon his release Torrio kept a low profile – safe in the knowledge that with Capone in the hot seat, he'd be less of a target. For all of the Fox's wiles, he just hadn't reckoned on how personal this war had become. Returning from a day shopping with his wife on the morning of 24 January 1925, gunfire lit up the street from a blue Cadillac lurking on the curb, shredding shopping bags to confetti. Blood mingled with the groceries from a litany of wounds as Johnny Torrio stared at the sky, the shrieking of Anna Torrio strangely distant. As Bugs Moran stood over him, blocking the crisp winter sun, his revolver levelled at Torrio's skull – the gun clicked on empty and the would-be assassins fled.

Capone's ascendancy was immediate as Torrio underwent emergency surgery. Capone slept by his mentor's bedside – the men of the Chicago Outfit standing guard around the clock, eying each disinterested nurse and flower-clutching day visitor suspiciously. "It's all yours, Al," said Torrio eventually. "Me? I'm quitting. It's Europe for me."

With the Fox quietly returning to Italy, Capone moved his headquarters into Chicago's luxurious Lexington Hotel, taking over the

Victims of The St Valentine's Day Massacre

> "Capone moved into his study where petitioners waited anxiously for favours and his patronage"

Five facts about Scarface

- Capone's specially-outfitted, bulletproof Cadillac was seized by the US Treasury Department in 1932. It was later used by the government as President Franklin Roosevelt's limousine.
- Even though he is synonymous with Chicago, he only lived in the city for 12 years of his life.
- Allegedly, he had never heard of Eliot Ness, the government agent sent to bring him to justice.
- The man who helped America swim in booze during Prohibition's favourite drink was Templeton Rye whisky.
- His men carried out most of the deaths he is responsible for, but Capone is still thought to have killed more than a dozen men personally.

fourth and fifth floors where he held court like an emperor, surrounded by mobsters and prostitutes. A concrete vault was installed in the basement and a secret staircase hidden behind a mirror in one of his bathrooms, just one part of a web of tunnels that would allow him a quick escape. Rising late most days, he took his time pouring over the morning papers like a statesman, before dressing himself in expensive finely tailored suits. Early afternoon, Capone moved into his study in another suite where petitioners waited anxiously for favours and his patronage. Nobody talked about the "Free Kingdom of Torrio" anymore. No, now the press called Cicero the "Capital of Caponeland."

Capone began to court newspaper men, handing out expensive cigars and inviting them to lavish parties, where the lord of the Chicago underworld played billiards with boxers, baseball players and the notoriously corrupt mayor of Chicago, Big Bill Thompson, miraculously re-elected in 1927. "Public service is my motto," Capone explained to attentive reporters in December 1927. "99 per cent of the public in [Chicago] drink and gamble and my offense has been to furnish them with those amusements. My booze has been good and my games on the square."

Already the public had some sympathy for the bootleggers and Capone took hold of the notion and twisted it into the spectre of Robin Hood, portraying himself as heroic outlaw giving the people what they wanted.

The bigger Capone's business became, the more intricate and vulnerable the network of mobsters, bribes and alliances required to sustain it. It got to a point where the endemic corruption of Chicago's law and government simply couldn't be ignored. In the wake of the shocking St Valentine's Day Massacre, Herbert Hoover was elected US president on an anti-corruption platform. His first move was to dispatch Prohibition agent Eliot Ness and a handpicked team of incorruptible 'Untouchables' to clean up Chicago's streets by raiding Capone's speakeasies and stills, and more importantly, it transpired, a team of IRS agents headed by accountant-turned-lawman Frank J Wilson with a mandate to turn over Capone's finances for something that would stick in court.

"Every time a boy falls off a tricycle, every time a black cat has gray kittens, every time someone stubs a toe, every time there's a murder or a fire or

Capone with family and friends at a picnic, Chicago, 1929

Capone and Alcatraz

What was he sentenced for?

Capone was sentenced to 11 years for three counts of tax evasion (1927-9) and two counts of failing to provide tax returns (1928-9) as his lavish lifestyle and lack of legitimate income was used against him. 11 further counts of tax evasion and 5,000 violations of the Volstead Act were dropped out of fear the prosecution would be unable to get a conviction.

What was his defence?

Capone's legal team originally struck a deal with the prosecution to admit to the lighter charges and serve between two and five years so business would be able to go on as usual. However, when details leaked to the press the outrage was so great that the deal was immediately canned and the judge threw the book at him.

What happened at the trial?

The jury was suddenly exchanged for another in the court by Judge Wilkerson when the police learnt of a plot from Capone's mob to bribe them. The new jury, all from rural Illinois, were sequestered overnight to keep them out of the Chicago Outfit's reach. Wilkerson sentenced Capone to 11 years, $50,000 in fines, court costs of another $30,000 and no bail.

How was life for him in jail?

Initially, Capone served his sentence in Atlanta, Georgia, continuing to rule his crime empire by proxy, bribing guards with thousands of dollars hidden in the hollow handle of a tennis racket to be able to communicate with the outside world. He was then sent to the newly opened Alcatraz, where his link to the outside world was finally severed.

Was Alcatraz a 'hard' prison?

In Alcatraz, Capone's letters were censored, prohibited subjects and current events were removed, newspapers banned and all magazines had to be at least seven months old. He was only allowed visits from immediate family, who would be separated from the one-time king of crime by a sheet of glass.

Why was he released?

Capone was released into the care of his family on 16 November 1939 due to brain damage caused by neurosyphilis. By 1946, he was deemed to have the intelligence of a 12-year-old, suffering from delusional fits, raving about communists and plots to kill him. On 21 January 1947, Capone had a stroke and suffered a fatal heart attack on 25 January 1947, aged 48.

Alcatraz was a federal prison from 1933 until 1963

the Marines land in Nicaragua, the police and the newspapers holler, 'Get Capone!'" raged Chicago's premier gangster in his penthouse. "I'm sick of it."

As the gangster was having a tantrum, one of the men tasked with bringing him to justice was having second thoughts. "Doubts raced through my mind as I considered the feasibility of enforcing a law which the majority of honest citizens didn't seem to want," Ness admitted in his autobiography. "I felt a chill foreboding for my men as I envisioned the violent reaction we would produce in the criminal octopus hovering over Chicago, its tentacles of terror reaching out all over the nation. We had undertaken what might be a suicidal mission."

While Capone wallowed in fine silks and syphilitic megalomania in his penthouse, Ness and his Untouchables began nipping at his heels – shutting down 18 stills and arresting 52 bootleggers in a single night. In the first six months alone, Ness' daring raids had cost the Chicago Outfit an estimated $1,000,000, as well as some of loyal lieutenants, who now languished in jail for violations of the Volstead Act. He shrugged off Capone's clumsy attempts at bribery, as well as two assassination attempts.

It was only ever an irritant, taking chunks out of his income and his pride – but to a mobster as egotistical as Capone, such defiance drove him into a rage. It was a fury Ness gleefully exploited – parading captured vehicles outside his hotel and taunting him on the phone. However much Ness might have damaged his ego, the real danger to the man who made the streets of Chicago swim in booze and blood came from fraud investigator Frank J Wilson as he poured over reams of paperwork.

In May 1927, the US Supreme Court's 'Sullivan decision' had reversed a bizarre legal loophole that meant gangsters were legally exempt from having to register illegal income on their tax returns, on the basis that it would violate their Fifth Amendment rights. Manly Sullivan, a Chicago bootlegger whose trial lent the decision its name, received a landmark conviction for tax evasion.

That same year, the Chicago Outfit's income was an estimated $108 million. Capone simply had to be next. Facing a possible 34-year jail term from Wilson's tax case and Ness's Prohibition case, the former would stick and the latter wouldn't, but that scarcely mattered. It was the end of Capone's empire of crime, brought down not by gunfire, violence and police raids, but by the simple, dry truth of the balance sheet. The reign of Chicago's public enemy number one was over.

Marcus Tullius Cicero

Strategist, philosopher and man of the people, Cicero's dramatic career coincided with the fall of a republic and the rise of an empire

Marcus Tullius Cicero peeked out of his covered litter to check if he was being followed. He was sweating, his heart was pounding and he looked nervous. It was not the first time he was on the run from the authorities. The Roman Republic he had dedicated his whole life to protect had betrayed him once again and this time there would be no reprieve. Out of the corner of his eye, he saw two armed soldiers strolling towards the slaves carrying the litter. They called him by name and told the slaves to stop; Cicero knew he had only moments to live. He regarded the men solemnly and declared: "There is nothing proper about what you are doing, soldier, but do try to kill me properly." He bowed his head out and waited for the killing blow.

With no influence within the senate, forum or any connections to the patronage network of the Patrician, Cicero's family languished in obscurity before he came of age. Residing in the town of Arpinum, Cicero attended schools to improve his lot and his father insisted he should make something of himself within Roman politics. He learned Greek and studied the philosophies and teachings of Plato and Archimedes; in Roman culture this knowledge was required to be considered capable of leading Rome's political and military elite. He was a diligent student, even visiting Greece to discover the secrets of their philosophical ideals. As he gained a reputation in the provinces as a skilled litigator, he also wooed the crowds gathered at public court hearings with his oratory skills, and became famous as a man who could win any legal case he took on.

Cicero was more than aware of his enemies. At the consular elections in 63 BCE he wore armour underneath his toga

Representing landowners and provincial merchants gave Cicero a firm understanding of the law but wasn't enough for his burgeoning ego. Therefore, when he was asked to prosecute a case involving Gaius Verres, a greedy Roman governor who had oppressed and intimidated the people of Sicily, he saw an opportunity to ascent to the place where he had always wanted to go; Rome. He was taking an awful risk though as Verres had hired Rome's foremost lawyer to defend him, Quintus Hortalus. If the young and inexperienced Cicero lost against him he would be finished. He diligently prepared his case, spending hours working on every inflection of his voice and action of his body to make sure he came across as the best orator ever heard. He knew only the best would do, as the case was going to the Forum in Rome, the centre of imperial Roman justice.

The preparation paid off. Not only did he win the case, he was guaranteed a place as a magistrate in the Roman cursus honorum, one of the most respected levels of government. He continued to fly through the ranks of public office, thriving on the adventure that encompassed life while working high-profile cases. He fell in love with the glamour of addressing the people from the plinths of the Roman Forum.

Public speaking was one of the finest skills a Roman citizen could have, and Cicero was considered its greatest orator

"The Roman Republic he had dedicated his whole life to protect had betrayed him once again"

Only the senate could grant a triumph, which held great esteem and was coveted by all of Rome's great men

Life in Cicero's time

Rome the conqueror

While Rome's power was not at its height during Cicero's lifetime, it was still a dominant force in the Italian peninsula and beyond. Its influence stretched from the muddy fields of Gaul, modern-day France, to the grain-rich plains of the Egyptian Nile.

Slaves and free Romans

Roman society was based around the distinction between Romans who had the right to own property and influence the political system and slaves who had no rights at all. Slaves were used in every part of Roman life, from domestic servants to labourers in mines. As was expected for a man of his standing, Cicero himself owned a number of slaves.

The Republic

Before the great emperors of Rome stood the Roman Republic, a political system dominated by the senate and its consul leaders. While the Republic looked democratic and free on the surface, in reality only the elite were allowed to serve and the whole political process was shamelessly corrupt.

Class struggle

Class division was split between the Patrician, the ruling elite, and the Plebeian, all other Romans. While the ruling families maintained control over the senate throughout this period they lived in constant fear of the ferrocity and fickleness of the plebeian 'mob', which had to be appeased regularly.

The gods and man

Religion played an important part in the daily lives of Romans and their pantheon of gods and goddesses were seen to have a direct influence on the lives of Rome's citizens. Strange cults and colourful religious ceremonies were a constant feature of the bustling city streets.

Marc Antony's oration over the body of Julius Caesar, both of whom were enemies of Cicero

Pax Romana

Despite Rome's apparent stability throughout this period, the Roman Republic and its political system was going through immense upheaval. The senate was becoming unable to curtail the ambitions of powerful Roman leaders who commanded vast armies. One of them, Gaius Julius Caesar, had been ruling Rome as joint consul with Pompey Magnus but feared a plot concocted by Pompey to overthrow his authority within the senate. In short order, their conflict threw the whole of Rome and its dependencies into a disruptive conflict that pitted Romans against Romans. As this was happening the senate struggled to maintain a role for itself within the city and was constantly being overruled by men like Caesar who was holding a lethal trump card – an army capable of sacking the city. Public officials often found themselves behind developing events. When Caesar was assassinated, Mark Antony became the dominant force within the city. When Caesar's adopted son Octavian, who also called himself Caesar, took over the city and Antony fled, Antony's supporters found themselves on shifting sand. For senators like Cicero, this was a dangerous time and picking the wrong side during these insurrections could spell doom if the opposing side regained power. There was also the constant threat of political assassination, a method not uncommon in Roman society for removing political enemies.

Cicero reached the peak of any Roman's career when he was elected consul, the highest office attainable. As consul he utilised his oratory skills to put down a conspiracy of rebellion against him, convincing the mob to condemn the men involved as traitors. He condemned them to death, reasoning that the situation was dangerous enough and that the tide of public opinion swelling around him would be protection against not affording the accused a trial. Declaring his verdict he spoke one word to the crowd: "Vixerunt" ("They are dead"), which was received by rapturous applause from the people. In reality this was a risky tactic: in the cruel political game of Rome, operating outside the law in public office spawned enemies and sure enough, when his tenure ended, a group of political enemies introduced a law punishing those who had condemned Roman citizens without trial. Cicero had been outmanoeuvred. The mob had turned against him, the new consul wasn't sympathetic and he was exiled.

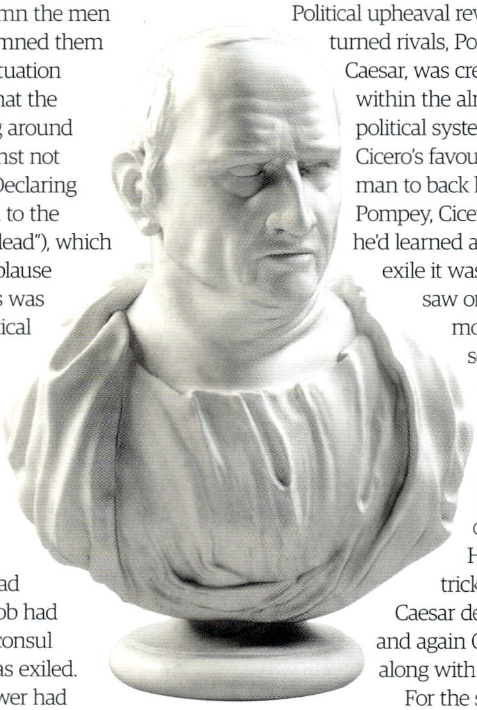

Cicero's dramatic rise to power had been cut short. He wrote at length to his noble friend Titus Atticus about his woe: "Your pleas have prevented me from committing suicide. But what is there to live for? Don't blame me for complaining. My afflictions surpass any of those you have heard earlier." He couldn't see how he would ever command power again.

So, in 57 BCE, when Roman leadership changed once again and Cicero was given a reprieve it was as if his prayers had been answered. He boarded a ship from his Greek residence and prepared to re-enter the cut-throat world of Roman politics.

All was not well in the Republic on his return home. Political upheaval revolving around two friends turned rivals, Pompey Magnus and Julius Caesar, was creating dangerous divisions within the already fractious Roman political system. While Caesar courted Cicero's favour, looking for a respectable man to back his grievousness against Pompey, Cicero decided to play safe. If he'd learned anything during his years in exile it was to back a winner when he saw one. Pompey had more men, more support in the senate and seemed to hold the support of Rome's mob. He threw in his lot with Pompey as the man who would see the Republic restored and reward Cicero with power and influence once Caesar was defeated.

However, fate played a cruel trick on Cicero. Defying the odds, Caesar defeated Pompey in open battle and again Cicero was exiled from Rome, along with Pompey's dilapidated forces.

For the second time Cicero was on the run from his homeland and his future looked bleak. His return to Rome came after Caesar, looking to shore up a very unsettled senate, decided to pardon him. Instead of punishment, Caesar praised Cicero, commenting on his oratory skills: "It is more important to have greatly extended the frontiers of the Roman spirit than the frontiers of the Roman empire." But flattery did not sway Cicero over to Caesar's side and what he found when he returned to Rome affronted

Defining moment

Gaius Verres' case 75 BCE

One of the most celebrated cases of Cicero's career is his prosecution of the corrupt Sicilian governor Gaius Verres, a tyrant who brutalised his Roman subjects. After hearing Cicero's reputation as an excellent orator, the Sicilians petition Cicero to prosecute Verres on their behalf. After some debate, Cicero takes the case to Rome and promptly wins against Verres's expensive lawyer through his superb oratory skills. With the gathered crowd cheering whenever Cicero speaks his relationship with the people is sealed. This early success is the foundation upon which his political career is built.

Timeline

106 BCE

Birth of Cicero
Cicero is born into an equestrian order family in Arpinum, outside of Rome. While his father is a man of means, Cicero's family is not considered part of the ruling elite.
106 BCE

Precursor
Cicero joins the army as a precursor under the leadership of Strabo and Sulla. He serves during the War of Allies between the Republic and several Italian cities.
90 BCE

Philosopher
Cicero becomes fascinated by Greek philosophy. Roman society dictates that knowledge of Greek is mandatory for those in power.
87 BCE

Praetor of Rome
Cicero becomes a Praetor and a famous magistrate of the law. Praetor is also a military position but he shows very limited interest in the military.
66 BCE

Real power
Cicero is made consul of the Roman senate, one of the most powerful positions in Rome. The consul is leader of the senate and has full veto power. While consul, he uncovers a conspiracy to overthrow him by Catiline. The decision to condemn the traitors to death without a trial will come back to haunt him.
63 BCE

The assassination of Julius Caesar, 44 BCE. Caesar tried to bring Cicero into his inner circle while he was working within the political system

"He had made another critical error by trusting the young man who was now calling himself Augustus Caesar"

his sensibilities. Caesar was ruling the Republic like a tyrant, changing tradition to fit his own political needs.

Unsurprisingly, Caesar made many enemies and, in yet another explosion of ruthless violence, Caesar was murdered on the senate floor during the religious festival of the Ides of March. Cicero decided to play this latest development more subtly than the Pompey fiasco. He neither supported nor condemned the assassination in public, although he wrote a private letter to one of Brutus's supporters, saying: 'How I could wish that you had invited me to that glorious banquet on the Ides of March.'

With Caesar dispatched and Brutus's conspirators looking for a man to rally around, Cicero once again became a man of power and influence, perhaps only bested in this respect by Mark Antony. Antony's affiliation with Caesar was well known, and a source of intense jealously for less-connected men like Cicero. Cicero regarded Antony as little more than a political opportunist, profiting on the death of his master. He publicly denounced him, writing orations against him and making scandalous remarks about his sexuality to friends. But Antony held an army at his command, which outweighed the mere words of a skilled orator. It appeared as if Antony was set to stay in Rome until Octavian, Julius's adopted son and heir, returned to the capital. Cicero supported him as a liberator from the brutish Antony, claiming that he was a man of honour, and endorsed his fight against Antony. In a pitched battle, Octavian defeated Antony, who fled to Gaul. Again, Cicero made a judgement call and assessed that Antony was finished, his flight from Rome retribution for his brash behaviour. But Cicero was proved wrong once more. Surprisingly, Octavian made peace with Antony in order to steal power away from the hostile senate and, along with Marcus Lepidus, declared a Triumvirate - a type of military Junta - to rule Rome.

His works were discovered in the 14th century and influenced how the Renaissance rulers governed

Cicero did his best to swallow his burning resentment at the destruction of the Republic and ingratiate himself with Octavian, but it was too little, too late. He had made another critical error in judgement by trusting the young man who was now calling himself Augustus Caesar. Suddenly designated a public enemy, Cicero faced two options; stay and face a show trial or run. The man who was later described by Quintilian as 'eloquence himself', bolted into the night, with nothing but the toga on his back, hunted by the people he helped bring to power. As he raced for the safety of Greece, one of his brother's slaves betrayed him to Mark Antony's spy and he was apprehended within striking distance of the coast.

In the great marketplace of Rome two armed soldiers strolled up to the front doors of the Forum carrying a large, heavy sack. They opened it and pulled out its contents, a dismembered head and two hands covered in congealed blood. One of the men began attaching the head to the door, forcing the rotting jaw open and pulling out the tongue, pinning it across the putrid skin to make the mouth look as if it was speaking. In a final grotesque display, Cicero's last address to the people was nailed to the Forum for all to see.

Defining moment
Betrayed by Octavian
November 43 BCE

Octavian Caesar, the adopted son and heir apparent to Gaius Julius Caesar, returns to Rome. Cicero makes overtures of friendship to the young man now calling himself Caesar. Mark Antony is forced to flee the city into the mountains. This is a short-lived victory for Cicero and the Republic, as Octavian is unwilling to share power with the 'fools' in the senate. He betrays Cicero and makes a separate deal with Antony. With Octavian and Antony now working together, Cicero finds himself out of favour and isolated.

43 BCE

Exiled
After falling out of favour with the new consul and his tribunes, Cicero is forced into exile and retreats to Greek Thessalonica, falling into deep depression.
58 BCE

Return to Rome
Invited to return to Rome by Titus Milo, Cicero eagerly accepts the opportunity to revive his political career in the Republic and returns to Rome.
57 BCE

Outlaw
Cicero finds himself on the wrong side of public opinion by backing Pompey rather than his rival, the popular Gaius Julius Caesar. He is subsequently forced to flee from the city with Pompey's soldiers.
49 BCE

Ides of March
Caesar is murdered on the senate floor by Brutus, a Pompey supporter. While Cicero is not present at the assassination he privately supports Brutus's actions.
44 BCE

Cicero vs. Mark Antony
In the following power vacuum, Cicero and Mark Antony become Rome's dominant figures. Unfortunately, there is little love lost between the two and they frequently clash.
February 43 BCE

Death of an orator
After seeing that Octavian Caesar and Mark Antony have betrayed him and he is now on their 'most wanted' list, Cicero flees Rome but is caught and summarily executed.
December 43 BCE

JFK LIFE & LEGACY

50 years after his death, John F Kennedy still inspires and fascinates the world

Election night, Tuesday 8 November 1960. John 'Jack' Fitzgerald Kennedy waited for the voting results to come through on the television, his family sat around him in the living room of his brother's home in Hyannis Port, Massachusetts. The endless television interviews, broadcast debates, rallies and travelling had taken their toll on his health, he hadn't had a proper meal or a good night's sleep in two weeks, and now he was beyond exhausted. The endless lectures from his father, Joe, about image and how it didn't matter who you were, only what people thought you were, had started to grate on him. Even his wife Jackie, normally a source of comfort, was starting to unsettle him - when more favourable results came in and she said, "Oh bunny, you're president now!" he quickly turned his head away from the television screen and looked at her with his tired eyes, replying "No... no, it's too early yet".

After the "longest night in history," as Jackie would later describe it, the call came in the following morning. Nixon had admitted defeat and sent a congratulatory telegram to Kennedy. It was one of the closet elections in American history; the final tally being 34,227,096 to 34,107,646 of the popular vote, with 303 to 219 of the electoral vote going to the young pretender. The bare facts say it was hardly a ringing endorsement of Kennedy, but given the experience and relative popularity of Nixon, it was a spectacular victory. Against the advice of his closet supporters, Kennedy visited Nixon in Florida on 14 November. Kennedy wasn't impressed. He silently listened to Nixon dominate what was meant to be a friendly conversation about the last few months, and wondered how a man like this had nearly won the presidency. As he clambered back onto his helicopter after it was over, he turned to an aide and said, "It was just as well for all of us he didn't quite make it!"

Kennedy's presidency would go down in history as the dawn of a new era. He changed the face of politics by courting the media and creating his very own cult of celebrity, inspiring hope through his charm and freedom through his liberal policies. He gave the US a renewed self-confidence through his tough reputation abroad, and after his brutal assassination in Dallas his legacy would live on.

At the start of Kennedy's long fight for Democratic nomination in 1957, a reporter said that Kennedy was Washington's 'hottest tourist attraction'. It was widely rumoured he had an 'in' in *Life* magazine because of all the positive press he received there, and the *American Mercury* hailed him as the "perfect politician". Others were less

JOHN F KENNEDY

American, 1917-1963

Brief Bio

John 'Jack' F Kennedy was born into a rich Irish-American Catholic family from Brookline, Massachusetts. He served in the Navy during World War II, commanding a patrol boat in the Pacific that was destroyed by enemy fire. He married Jackie Bouvier, a rich and well-established Catholic socialite in 1953, and ascended to the presidency in 1961. He would only serve two years of his term before he was assassinated in 1963.

convinced. "He'll never make it with that haircut," commented a prominent politician from New York.

It was true that Kennedy had his critics, but it was his deep connection with the media, getting his name in the public domain and making sure that through his family connections it stayed out there in the best possible light, that made his political campaigns in the Fifties a success. The media was enamoured with his good looks, beautiful wife and young family. He represented the American dream, descended from Irish immigrants and doing well through America's bounty to become a senator in the most powerful country in the world. He was the equivalent of an A-list celebrity on Capitol Hill, and he didn't mind the status, as he himself remarked, "This publicity does one good thing: it takes the Vice out of Vice-President." This wasn't to say that he was a shallow man who simply enjoyed the press for his own vanity; the press shots of him and Jackie with their children in Hyannis Port may have been doctored to fit the idyll of the perfect American family, but they do portray a genuine sentiment of love.

One of the most compelling stories that illustrates his character was not caught on camera, however. During his tenure in office, an aide was showing a group of disabled children around the White House when their wheelchairs prevented them from joining the rest of the tour group. Kennedy, late for a meeting, spotted them and came over to the children. The aide recalled: "He crossed the lawn to us, insisted on being introduced to each child and either picked up each limp, paralysed hand to shake it, or touched the child on the cheek. He had a different conversation with each child... the child's face radiated a joy totally impossible to describe." Kennedy's natural charm was rooted in compassion - something that the press could project, but not create.

The power over the press he possessed even allowed him to overcome the prejudices sections of American society held due to his Catholic upbringing; one writer remarked, "The stereotype of the Irish Catholic politician, the pugnacious, priest-ridden representative of an embittered, embattled minority, simply does not fit the poised, urbane, cosmopolitan young socialite from Harvard." This was put to the test when he was nominated as the Democratic candidate for the presidency. He knew he would need something more than his easy smile, good looks and friends in the print media, as these alone would not be enough against a seasoned politician like Nixon; he would need something that would allow him to reach millions and captivate them with his personality. He needed the power of television.

Kennedy's time would come during the first live television debates in September 1960, a contest that was watched by over 60 million people. Kennedy had taken a tour of the television studio beforehand, where his aides had worked out how the lighting, sound and shooting angles would benefit him; everything would have to be perfect if he was to shine on the box. Both candidates were offered the services of a CBS make-up artist - not that Kennedy needed it, as his skin looked tanned and healthy after campaigning in California. Nixon, on the other hand, looked pasty and sweaty, having only just recovered from a knee injury, but declined the make-up services. Ultimately, he got one of his aides to apply some make-up on minutes before the broadcast to cover up his stubble, but coupled with his pale complexion, it only made him look ill and dirty. Kennedy received coaching from consultants to allow him to practice rebuking Nixon's comment

ONE OF MY SONS WILL BE PRESIDENT

Joe Kennedy famously made the above claim about his sons. He was a man who expected a lot from his family - after all, they were Kennedys, and thus destined for greatness. Born in 1888, Joe grew up in a well-established Catholic family from Boston. He worked in Hollywood as a film producer and then entered politics as part of the Franklin Roosevelt administration. He later became ambassador to Britain, famously saying the country was "finished" in 1940. He was renowned for his political connections, using them to see his children established among the elite of American society after the war. It was also rumoured that he had unofficial connections with the Mafia, using them as he used everyone else: to get more power and influence. He was a domineering and harsh father, especially when his family didn't meet his high standards, and infamously had his daughter Rosemary lobotomised because of her violent personality. He also 'vetted' husbands for his daughters, ensuring they all married into families that would benefit the family. His affairs with other women were legendary, estranging him from his wife, Rose. He was a pessimist and isolationist, weighed down with old prejudices of the Protestant-dominated middle class. Jack was none of these things, outgrowing Joe's outdated beliefs.

> "Not everyone was convinced by Kenendy. 'He'll never make it with that haircut,' commented a prominent politician from New York"

JFK: President, statesman and American hero

while maintaining eye contact with the audience straight down the lens.

Nixon was confident he could wing it, with one commentator noting afterwards that, "Nixon was addressing himself to Kennedy - but Kennedy was addressing himself to the audience that was the nation." Kennedy chose a suit that contrasted well with the background of the set, while Nixon's blended horribly into the backdrop. Kennedy was prepared and ready; Nixon looked nervous and tired. The result was a popular victory for Kennedy, with one newspaper editor commenting, "The [television] medium is good to Kennedy and most unkind to Nixon. It makes Kennedy look forceful. It makes Nixon look guilty." Emphasising the differences in perception television offered, the majority of those who heard the radio debate thought Nixon had won, while those who watched on television were inclined in favour of Kennedy.

Kennedy was the first presidential candidate to properly utilise the power of the media and the idea of looking 'right' to connect with audiences through the medium of television, and it paid out in dividends. Subsequent presidents and their PR teams would never forget it. To this day, the presidential debates are given the highest priority, with PR consultants spending hours coaching and teaching respective nominees when to smile, when to laugh and how to look, even down to the shoes and ties they're wearing. It was Kennedy's stunning victory and his associations with the press before and after the 1960 election that subsequent presidential campaigns modelled themselves on. The image of the man who would lead the American people was now just as important as the man's politics. But of course, looking right was

Senator John F Kennedy and Vice-President Richard Nixon during the second televised debate

Spectators line the streets of Ireland to catch a glimpse of Kennedy

Presidential nominees Kennedy and Nixon smiling for the cameras prior to their first televised debate

HOW AMERICA WAS WON

The presidential election of 1960 was one of the closest in American history. Richard Nixon, Kennedy's opponent, was able to gain significant control over the American Midwest, a traditional Republican stronghold, and in California and Florida, which carried with it a large number of votes in the electoral college. Kennedy, however, seized control of Texas, a state with a large number of voters, through his running mate Lyndon B Johnson and the industrial heartland of America in the Northeast with the help of his father through his political connections with influential industrialists. One of the major battlegrounds was Chicago, Illinois, which held a large amount of supporters for both Kennedy and Nixon. Controversies would emerge later about Democratic mayor of Chicago, Richard Daley, rigging the Illinois vote for Kennedy after a conversation he had with Joe Kennedy and, apparently, the Chicago outfit. In the end, Illinois was won by a paper-thin margin of 8,858 votes.

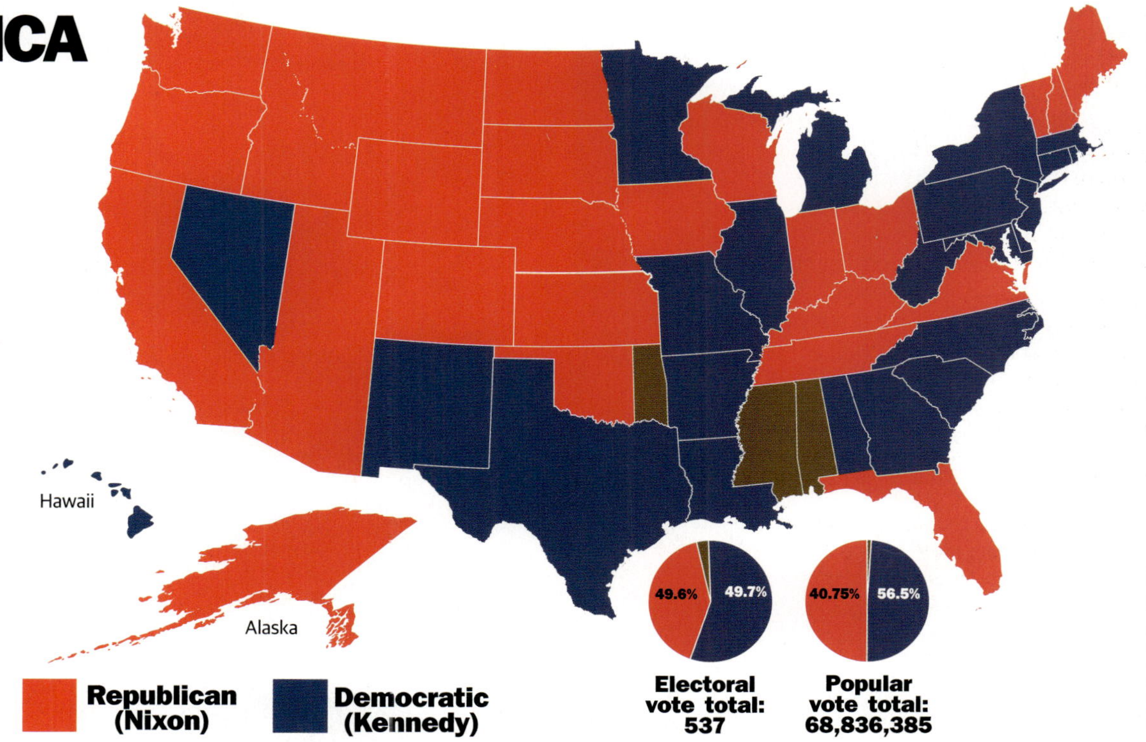

only part of the story; Kennedy had to have the right policies to fully tap into the pool of voters. As influential columnist William V Shannon wrote, "Month after month, from the glossy pages of *Life* to the multicoloured cover of *Redbook*, Jack and Jackie Kennedy smile out at millions of readers; he with his tousled hair and winning smile, she with her dark eyes and beautiful face... But what has all this to with statesmanship?" Ostensibly, the answer could be found in his hard-nosed Cold War rhetoric, but there was another issue burning through America in the Sixties that Kennedy could not afford to ignore: the fight for civil rights.

By 1960, the civil rights movement under Martin Luther King Jr was worrying the southern states, who were holding firm on segregation and humiliating the political community in America as a whole in the process. How on earth could a country that claimed to be the leader of the free world still instigate a policy that restricted, oppressed and otherwise degraded American citizens based on their skin colour? It was a question that was becoming urgent, with the broadcast media reporting all the sit-ins and protests of black citizens in the deep south to an anxious American public; the very people Kennedy would have to get on his side if he was to take the presidency and keep hold of it.

As the election loomed in the autumn of 1960, Kennedy was still looking weak on the civil rights issue. He was certainly more liberal than his opponent, but he didn't have anything of substance to beat him with. By coincidence, King was arrested on 19 October - a month before the election - while taking part in a sit-in protest. Kennedy pounced on it as an opportunity. He phoned the shaken Mrs King, saying "I want to express to you my concern about your husband. I understand that you are expecting a baby, and I just wanted you to know that I was thinking about you and Dr King." It galvanised black voters, with King's father saying, "He can be my President, Catholic or whatever he is. It took courage to call my daughter-in-law at a time like this. He has the moral courage to stand up for what he knows is right." King himself was unconvinced. Despite these words, he was still not pushing civil rights; he was playing the political game. It was just words - words enough to capture the presidency, but words nonetheless.

King would call Kennedy's bluff in August 1963 after Kennedy's inaction, marching on Washington with thousands of supporters. Kennedy begged him not to, fearing the marchers would turn violent. But march they did, black and white, the largest demonstration to ever come to the capital, with King at the front of the huge procession, proudly proclaiming, "I have a dream that one day this nation will rise up and live out the true meaning of its creed: we hold these truths to be self-evident that all men are created equal." Kennedy looked on open-mouthed; the rapture of the crowd hanging on King's every word was beyond impressive. He immediately invited King and his inner circle to the White House, offering

John F Kennedy in uniform, 1942

John and Jackie on their wedding day in 1953

The Kennedy family relax at their home in Hyannis Port

Deep in thought while in transit in the 1960 US Presidential campaign

With Martin Luther King and other delegates from the rally in Washington DC

Over 200,000 protestors marched along the Capitol mall in Washington on 28 August 1963

"He had created an atmosphere where change, when it came, would seem no longer an upheaval"

refreshments and a promise to get things moving where he could on civil rights. It was probably a combination of Kennedy's own moral scruples and King's loud insistence that finally got civil rights on the right path, but inaction would still dog Kennedy's record on the agenda.

To say that Kennedy was a mere political opportunist would be grossly unfair, however. He was a man of principles, and the treatment of black communities in the deep South sickened him. However, it is a myth that he was a radical activist of the civil rights movement; he was far too pragmatic for that. Actively supporting the civil rights movement more than he did would have destroyed his support in the South and make what Nixon would later call the 'silent majority' everywhere else uneasy. His presidency did not bring solid change, and his successor Lyndon B Johnson would do far more, but it was a rallying cry for a new beginning. By meeting King and publicly endorsing the ideal of civil rights for all, even if he did not actively support the campaign in practice, would give civil rights the national platform it needed and Kennedy's own celebrity endorsement to bring civil rights to the top of the national agenda. As Arthur Schlesinger, a social commentator in the Sixties observed, "He had quietly created an atmosphere where change, when it came, would seem no longer an upheaval, but the inexorable unfolding of the promise of American life." Kennedy would not go eyeball-to-eyeball with civil rights, but he would with Communism. It was the realms of foreign affairs where he would make his stand, where there could be no comprise, and where the legend of Kennedy's confrontation with the Soviets would change the world forever.

Communism was not only objectionable as far as Kennedy was concerned, but a moral evil. It stood against everything he believed about human rights and human dignity. The Communist leadership were godless, their state control oppressed its own people and their vast armies oppressed the people of the globe; it was to be despised. When he made his inaugural address he spoke of not daring to "tempt them with weakness. For only when our arms are sufficient beyond doubt can we be certain beyond doubt that they will never be employed." This was the hard line of the Cold War warrior – create the biggest conventional and nuclear arsenal available to scare the Communists into never attacking the free world, and Kennedy believed in it completely. He would go on to talk about the need for reconciliation, but warned against negotiating "out of fear." He had followed the line of Theodore Roosevelt, the man who flexed American muscle at the turn of the century: tread softly on the international stage, but carry a big stick. Rhetoric would turn to action when Kennedy gave the green light to the ill-fated Bay of Pigs operation, later to be known as the 'undeniable fiasco'. It was the first major military undertaking of his presidency, but the plan was ill-conceived and deeply flawed from the beginning. Even Kennedy talked about plausible deniability of the whole affair by its end. The plan was for the CIA to land thousands of military-trained Cuban exiles onto the Cuban mainland and, by proxy, try to enact a coup. It relied on Castro not being in full control of Cuba, although unfortunately for Kennedy he was. As the invasion party landed, Cubans loyal to Castro bombed and machine-gunned the exiles into the sea, causing horrendous casualties. CIA chiefs pleaded with the president to allow the US air force to support the exiles, and initially Kennedy was inclined to agree, saying, "I'd rather be called an aggressor than a bum." Soviet interest in the affair would cool his aggression, and after tense diplomatic negotiation he shied away from further intervention with US air support in case the Russians were "apt to cause trouble." It was seen as a betrayal by the CIA and the Cuban exiles, who were left without adequate air cover and died in their hundreds on Cuban beaches. Neither the CIA nor the exiles would forget it.

Kennedy meets with US Army officials during the Cuban Missile Crisis of October 1962

FIRST LADY

Jackie Kennedy was a woman of intelligence, beauty and money; a true American socialite. She was born into one of the wealthiest Catholic families in America, and her father, John Vernou 'Black Jack' Bouvier, owned land and capital throughout the Northeast. She met Jack through her work as a photographer in Washington DC, marrying him on 12 September 1953 after a whirlwind romance. In many ways she set the tone for future First Ladies.

Like her husband she courted the media, making sure she always dressed immaculately and remained on message for press interviews. But she also made the position her own, and was a force for change in the White House, seeing to it that the unique furniture, ornaments and pictures within its rooms were preserved and catalogued, where before they had either been lost or neglected by previous occupants. She established the post of White House Curator, and created the White House Fine Arts Committee to protect the treasures inside its walls. She could also speak several foreign languages, which she would use to her advantage on goodwill missions abroad. Her charm and grace enamoured foreign dignitaries, and after one trip to Paris, Vienna and Greece, Clark Clifford, advisor to the president sent her a congratulatory note saying, "Once in a great while, an individual will capture the imagination of people all over the world. You have done this… through your graciousness and tact." As her celebrity status spread, she received so much fan mail that it required 13 people to process the letters. Often they were deeply personal, with a girl from Indonesia writing, "I've seen pictures of you. I am studying English because I admire you so much." Another from a Japanese girl said, "My mother tells me not to slump so that I will grow up to be tall and queenly like you." She became so popular that her husband often joked that it was Jackie people wanted to see. She always put her family first, ensuring that her children were well-cared for and educated, saying to a reporter, "If you bungle raising your children, I don't think whatever else you do well matters very much."

The failure of the Bay of Pigs invasion did not temper the attitudes of the president or his closest advisors; quite the contrary. The disaster convinced the Kennedy administration that the Communists needed to be taken seriously, as anymore failures would risk goading aggressive Communist intentions. In the highly pressurised environment of the White House, straight-talking, hard-ball attitudes and the concoction of the 'red menace' frequently turned strategy into personal vendettas against the Communist leadership for the Kennedy family. Bobby Kennedy, Jack's younger brother and Attorney-General for the American government, would take the Bay of Pigs disaster as a personal slight against him. Castro had made the Kennedy family (and the US) look weak, and now he was going to "get him" by any means necessary, even commissioning a plan for an exploding seashell to be planted at Castro's favourite diving spot to take his head off. Conversely, Jack didn't order a full invasion of Cuba, nor any provocative move in that region until it was absolutely necessary. In a famous comment made to an aide about the prospect of an American invasion of Cuba, he said; "The minute I land one marine we're in this thing up to our necks. I can't get the United States into a war and then lose it, no matter what it takes. I'm not going to risk a slaughter".

But Kennedy's caution was still infused with the influence of manful bravado inherited from his patriarchal family and the hawks in his own government, who were ever-ready to go toe-to-toe with the Communists. Ultimately, his refusal to 'blink' during the blockade of Cuba brought the world to the brink of nuclear war: for 13 days in 1962, he held the fate of billions in his hands in order to prove to the Russian Premier Khrushchev that when it came to American security there could be no compromise. As with the Bay of Pigs, it was also intensely personal. Kennedy felt deceived by the Soviets, who were talking to him about nuclear disarmament while installing medium-range missiles on the Cuban mainland. He called the Soviets "barefaced liars" and hurled expletives whenever he heard the names of Castro or Khrushchev during meetings in the run up to the blockade. They had made him look foolish and soft on the Communist problem, and the blockade represented the most he could do to confront them without tipping the world into a nuclear holocaust.

Rational thinking gave way to zero-sum thinking on the nature of the international Communist threat after the Cuban Missile Crisis, even if by this point impartial evidence suggested that Communism was not only far weaker, but also hopelessly divided among its global constituents. To Kennedy, however, ever-ready to fight the good fight, the threat was still real and it was engulfing south-east Asia. He ordered more military advisors

Kennedy looks deep in thought as he awaits developments in the Cuban crisis that could have escalated to nuclear war

President Kennedy presiding over a meeting with senior White House officials during the Cuban Missile Crisis

into Vietnam, as well as the creation of a new fighting force designed to combat Communist insurgents at grass-roots level: the Green Berets .

He publicly endorsed the Diem regime in South Vietnam led by Ngo Dinh Diem, despite private reservations about their effectiveness and cruelty to their own people. As the war intensified, Diem, a stanch Catholic, was drawing ever more criticism from his own people, the majority of who were Buddhist. After brutal crackdowns on the Buddhist community at the beginning of 1963, monks set themselves on fire in the middle of a busy street in Saigon in protest. The response by one of Diem's closet advisors, his sister-in-law Madame Ngo Dinh Nhu, was heartless. She told a CBS film crew that the Buddhists had just "barbecued" themselves, and next time she would provide the mustard. For Kennedy, a man who lived shoulder to shoulder with the media, this was a disaster. The regime that America was supposed to be protecting was in fact a cruel dictatorship. Kennedy's troops remained in Vietnam even after the brutal events of 1963 as Diem's regime may have been harsh, but as far as Kennedy's administration was concerned, at least it wasn't Communist.

The memory of Kennedy's legendary stand-off with Communism would linger in the halls of the White House after his death. No future president would dare look weak in front of the Communist lest they appeared weaker than Kennedy, prompting a military invasion of Vietnam by Johnson and a perception that any failure to contain Communism throughout the globe was a de-facto failure of the current American administration. Debates about whether the Vietnam War would have been conducted differently if Kennedy had been at the helm continue to endure. Kennedy balked at appearing weak in front of the Communists, but he was a far more able negotiator than his successors and, it is said by some, would have brought Vietnam to a peaceful conclusion far quicker and with less casualties. But part of Kennedy's success was due to his international grandstanding. His image as young, energetic and tough chimed well with the mood of a US that wanted a nation that was assertive and cut away from the stagnation of the Eisenhower years and the defeats under Truman. It is unlikely that he would have ordered a full withdrawal at Vietnam, but part of his enduring persona has, like the issues surrounding civil rights, created a myth that things would have been very different - and a lot better - had he survived.

The bleak days of November 1963 would haunt America forever. Kennedy's funeral took place on 25 November, three days after his assassination. As his funeral procession made its long march up to St Matthew's Cathedral, it was accompanied by Black Jack, a riderless horse symbolising the loss of a great leader. When his casket was brought out after the service, foreign dignitaries including Charles de Gaulle of France and thousands of American citizens watched in silence. Troops of the United States Navy brought the casket down the steep steps, and as it reached the bottom Jackie Kennedy knelt down and whispered to her son, John Jr; "John, you can salute your daddy now and say goodbye to him." Author William Manchester noted, "Of all of Monday's images, nothing approached the force of John's salute... it was heart-wrenching." In summing up the day's events, columnist Mary McGrory wrote of "grief nobly borne." Kennedy's final resting place was the Arlington National Cemetery - as befitting an American hero.

On hearing of Kennedy's death, British Prime Minister Harold Macmillan said that Kennedy embodied "all the hopes and aspirations of this new world." His influence continues to be felt; Barack Obama's 'Hope' campaign for a new beginning in the US was influenced by Kennedy's own in 1960. Kennedy was a man that could be admired, followed and respected. His death shocked everyone, and his boundless potential and hope for a better and more peaceful world was lost forever, along with the man that he might have become.

Kennedy signs the Nuclear Test Ban Treaty in the White House Treaty Room on 7 October 1963

President and Mrs Kennedy with leaders of the Cuban Invasion Brigade

THE OTHER WOMEN

MARILYN MONROE

The Marilyn Monroe affair was probably the most infamous of Kennedy's relationships during his time in government. The two met through Peter Lawford on four separate occasions, one of which, it is claimed, resulted in sexual relations. Her raunchy rendition of *Happy Birthday* during Kennedy's 45th birthday celebrations and the dress she was wearing at the time, described as "flesh with sequins sewed onto it," left little to the imagination.

JUDITH CAMPBELL

Long the subject of repeated denials and cover-ups, until revelations in the Seventies revealed that Kennedy indeed had an on-off affair with Campbell, who was also linked with Mob bosses Sam Giancana and John Roselli. It was one of the most enduring affairs Kennedy had, and he was aware of the risks to his political career of sleeping with a woman with connections to the Mafia, but carried on.

GUNILLA VON POST

The Von Post affair started just after Kennedy was married. Von Post was a Swedish socialite, meeting Kennedy on the French Riviera after her aristocratic family sent her there to brush up on her French. A passionate affair ensued, with graphic love letters and lustful liaisons occurring throughout the Fifties. The tryst was so serious that Kennedy reportedly considered leaving Jackie for her, but feared his father's reaction.

THE ONE THAT GOT AWAY... SOPHIA LOREN

In a rather embarrassing episode, Sophia Loren, one of the most iconic film stars of the age, turned Kennedy down, and in no uncertain terms told him and his lackey to leave her alone during a dinner at the Italian Embassy in Washington in the late Fifties. This was despite Kennedy's gallant offer to include her female interpreter in a night of passion so that she didn't feel left out.

"Her story appealed to his love of astrology and fortune-telling and besides, he desperately needed any help he could get"

Joan of Arc

The teenage martyr who led the French army and put the fear of God into the English

A young woman whose faith led her to challenge kings and inspire armies, Joan of Arc's devout belief that God had appointed her to lead the French to victory against the English drove her from the village of her birth and onto the battlefield. In her brief time she became a national figurehead, a symbol. It was an image she cultivated and encouraged and one that would ultimately lead to her death.

Flames secured Joan's martyrdom, just as they provoked her fierce patriotism. Jehanne D'Arc, or la Pucelle (the Maid) as she came to be known, was born in 1412 in the village of Domrémy, located across the river from Burgundy territory. The Burgundians, allies of the English, regularly attacked French territory. In July 1428, Joan's family fled a raid and returned to find the enemy had burned their town, fields and church. Joan had heard angelic voices since the age of 12 or 13, urging her to remain pious, but now they gave her a specific mission. The voices of Archangel Michael, St Catherine and St Margaret directed her to go into France and find her king, the Dauphin Charles.

> She claimed to have her first vision at the age of 12, when St Catherine, St Michael and St Margaret appeared to her in a field

The alliance between England and Burgundy had kept Charles from claiming the French crown. His enemies not only occupied Paris, but also held the city of Reims, where coronations took place. The crown would have to wait however, as the French city of Orléans was currently in the grip of a protracted siege. Orléans needed help and Joan believed she was the one to deliver it. On 13 May 1428, the sixteen-year-old arrived in Vaucouleurs and begged Robert de Baudricourt, the captain of the garrison, to give her a military escort to Charles' court at Chinon. Baudricourt replied that she should be taken home and beaten. However, Joan would not be deterred and returned in January the next year.

She claimed she was the subject of a prophecy from 1398, about a maid who would "deliver the kingdom of France from the enemy." Baudricourt turned her down again, but her efforts were gaining traction. She gained favour with local nobility, particularly the Duke of Lorraine. Although Joan refused to attempt to cure his gout, the Duke agreed to give her a small escort and in February she travelled in men's clothes to Chinon, where she was presented to the court.

Charles was cautious but curious. Taking advice from a mad heretic could be devastating to his campaign, but her story appealed to his love of astrology and fortune-telling and besides, he desperately needed any help he could get. Joan immediately picked him out from the crowd and pledged her allegiance: "Most illustrious Lord Dauphin, I come and am sent from God to give assistance to you and the kingdom." He was impressed, but ordered she be tested before giving any official credence to her claims. One of the key figures in these trials was Yolande of Aragon, one of the true powers behind Charles and an intelligent strategist. After Joan's maidenhood was proved, she faced questions from clergy and theologians and passed with flying colours. Whether or not they truly believed in her voices was irrelevant. Charles now had a messenger of God, and Yolande raised a convoy for this messenger to lead.

Joan of Arc at the Coronation of Charles VII

Life in the time of Joan of Arc

The Black Death

From 1348 to 1350, the Black Death ravaged England, claiming the lives of some 1.5 million people. Carried by fleas, in turn carried by the rats infesting London, the bubonic plague spread through overpopulated towns and cities. England's economy and resources would feel its effects for decades to come.

Emissaries from God

Joan of Arc was not the first woman to claim the heavenly host had spoken to her. Hildegard of Bingen (1098-1179) railed against corruption in the clergy, St Clare of Assisi (1194-1253) claimed to be able to hear and see Mass on the wall of her room when she was too ill to move, and Catherine of Siena (1347-1380) travelled Italy urging states to make peace with Rome.

From bows to cannons

As the Hundred Years' War raged on through the decades, the technology of warfare began to change. The English longbows at Agincourt in 1415 were the difference between victory and defeat, but as open battles were often replaced by lengthy sieges, cannon fire became a deciding factor. By the siege of Orléans both sides deployed cannons.

Heresy trials

The definition of heresy covers a great deal of sins, but the term boils down to denying any established Christian dogma. In the Middle Ages, heresy trials became more common and the Catholic Church aggressively pursued any enemies. This continued into the 16th century, with Copernican scholars accused of heresy.

The Bavarian Hussites

Czech religious reformer Jan Huss was burned at the stake in 1415 for heresy. After his death, the Hussite movement was born, separating itself from Rome. The Hussites declared that communion should be given with bread and wine, they believed in poverty of the priesthood, punishment of sinners and freedom of preaching. The Pope announced a crusade against them in 1420.

Edward III, one of the instigators of The Hundred Years' War, crosses the Somme

The Hundred Years' War, 1337-1453

After William the Conqueror defeated Harold at Hastings in 1066 and claimed the English throne, English and Norman territories were combined. It was inevitably difficult to keep control of the taken land. By the reign of English King Edward III in 1327, only Gascony and Pontieu remained. When the French King Charles IV died heirless, Edward believed his mother and Charles' sister Isabella was the next in line, meaning the crown should be his. The French disagreed and chose Charles' cousin Philip. A furious Edward refused to pay homage and when Philip confiscated his lands in Aquitaine in retaliation, Edward declared war.

The Edwardian era of the Hundred Years' War lasted until 1360. The English captured Philip's successor, King John II, but a compromise wasn't reached until the Treaty of Brétigny, in which Edward agreed to abandon his claim in exchange for Aquitaine and Calais. War resumed in 1369 when Charles V of France responded to Edward the Black Prince refusing his summons by declaring war. Charles successfully reclaimed many of the territories his predecessor lost, and the Black Prince's son Richard II would make peace with Charles VI in 1389. After the truce had been repeatedly extended, war resumed in 1415 when Henry V invaded, leading to decades of conflict during which the English would take Paris and claim kingship. They would not be driven out until the Battle of Castillon in 1453, the official end of the Hundred Years' War.

In April 1429, Joan rode out, holding her white standard and wearing a suit of armour commissioned by Charles. She announced that her sword would be found in the church of Sainte-Catherine-de-Fierbois, hidden behind the altar. It was an old gift to the church from the crusades, and the discovery was treated as a miracle. Her pious conduct became renowned; she forced her soldiers to stop taking the Lord's name in vain and expelled prostitutes from their camps. She dictated letters to the English, instructing them to leave France or face the wrath of God. A canny propagandist, the Dauphin ensured these letters were copied and widely distributed.

However, Joan was still an untested military leader. She arrived at Orléans eager for battle but had not understood that her forces were there as support, nothing more. Although frustrated, she managed to get her men into the city, past the English troops and was rewarded with the adulation of the citizens. They may have been pleased to see her but her impatience to attack was at odds with her fellow commanders' strategy. In her frustration she hurled insults at the English from the battlements.

When an attack was decided upon on 4 May 1428, Joan was not even told by the commanders and woke up as the fight was in progress. She arrived just in time to rally her troops and inspire them to capture their target: the small fortress of Saint-Loup. It was their first victory and Joan's confidence grew. She dictated a fearsome final letter to the English, ordering them to leave, and on 6 May another attack was mounted. Joan led the attack herself, routing the enemy. She advanced again the next day, claiming to be the first to storm the ramparts at Les Tourelles, where she took an arrow to the shoulder but stayed in the fight. The French commanders credited her for inspiring the troops to victory. Orléans hadn't just been relieved; the English had been routed.

Joan sent many letters to English and Burgundian troops but she was illiterate and had to dictate them

With Orléans free, Joan wanted Charles to proceed immediately to Reims but the Dauphin was more cautious. He wanted to clear the Loire valley and began raising money for the campaign. It would be a month before Joan would see combat again.

Technically, the young Duke of Alençon led the army but he was a firm believer in the young female warrior and frequently deferred to her. They swept quickly through the English resistance and laid siege to Beaugency. The English surrendered without realising a relief force was on its way, a force the French promptly set off after. They met at Patay on 18 June, where the ill-prepared English were decimated, with over 2,000

"She dictated a fearsome final letter to the English, ordering them to leave, and on 6 May another attack was mounted. Joan led the attack herself, routing the enemy"

Defining moment
First vision 1424

At just 12 or 13 years old, she first claims to hear the voices of angels speaking to her. At first, the voices tell her to 'govern' her conduct. If she feels she had not behaved properly, the voices would admonish her. They also tell her to reject the marriage her family had arranged for her. Joan soon identifies the main voice as Michael, the archangel who led the battle against Satan in the Book of Revelation. As Joan grows older, Michael's messages continue to advise her toward piety, but gradually grow more political. Finally, Michael and the other voices, those of St Catherine and St Margaret, tell her to travel to France and begin her mission.

Timeline

1412

Birth of a warrior
Joan is born to a farming family in the town of Domrémy. She never receives formal education or learns to read and write, instead learning about religion from her mother Isabelle.
1412

Domrémy burns
The territory across the river from Domrémy is Burgundian, and a raid into French territory proves a defining moment for Joan. Her family flees to Neufchateau and returns to find the enemy having burnt their town.
1428

Journey to Vaucouleurs
In 1428 Joan's voices tell her to travel to France and talk to the dauphin Charles. She travels to Vaucouleurs to demand an escort, beginning a series of attempts ending in success after convincing nobles that she is the fulfilment of a prophecy.
May 1428

Audience with the king
Joan is granted a meeting with the Dauphin Charles, who sees value in her for his military campaign to free Orléans. Joan immediately identifies him in a room full of people and impresses him with her fervour.
6 March 1429

The sword is found
After convincing the clergy and theologians of her maidenhood and her gift, Joan is allowed to lead a force to Orléans. She announces that her sword can be found in the church of Saint Catherine-de-Fierbois.
April 1429

dead and all but one senior officer captured. Joan played little part in it but by this point that mattered not, as her legend only grew stronger. By now, Charles was ready to head for Reims and the coronation. He led a grand procession, entered the city on 16 July and was crowned the next day. She was desperate for the king to attack Paris but he chose to leave Reims instead, only to be barred from crossing the Seine by English troops. Joan was ecstatic as she saw the only answer was an attack on Paris.

After skirmishes throughout August and a truce with Burgundy, on 8 September Joan finally led the Paris attack she had been itching for. She stood on the moat, demanding surrender, but the only reply she received was an English arrow through her leg. After hours of bombardment, her men reached her under the cover of darkness, but she was determined to continue the fight the next day. However, once Charles saw the number of French casualties he ordered her to return to his side.

The attack had failed and Joan's usefulness was suddenly in doubt. She needed a victory to restore her reputation but in November 1429 failed to take the castle of La Charité after a long siege. When she returned to court, Charles gave her hereditary nobility but made sure she stayed with him, frustrating Joan. It was her duty to be on the battlefield expelling the enemy from her home soil, not rotting in court.

By 1430, the English were preparing a full-scale invasion of France to reclaim their recently lost territory. When the city of Compiègne refused to surrender, Joan rode to support them without Charles' authorisation. On 23 May she led an attack from the city, but the English reinforcements cut her off at the rear and she could not retreat. She was pulled from her horse and forced to surrender to the Burgundians. She testified that constant sexual harassment was the reason she remained in men's clothing while the voices in her head told her not to escape. Defying them, she leapt from the tower but was injured and recaptured.

Joan dressed in men's clothes, claiming the spirits told her to. She also wore her hair short, but this is often not depicted in portraits

The English needed to make an example of Joan and the Parisian theologians wanted to try her for heresy, idolatry and witchcraft. She needed to answer for the way in which she had circumvented the church by claiming to receive her instructions from her 'voices' while her ability to inspire followers had to be stopped. If she were convicted by a foreign power the damage to Charles' reputation would be severe, so the French court paid the Duke of Burgundy £10,000 for her.

Joan of Arc was burnt at the stake in 1431

Six rounds of questioning took place between 21 February and 3 March 1431, with nine more between 10 and 17 March, conducted in her cell. Joan never changed her story. On 24 May, she was taken to the scaffold and told that if she did not abjure, she would be given to the secular authorities that would carry out her death sentence. Joan wavered as the sentence began to be read out. In front of the crowd, she recanted and was sentenced to life imprisonment and to wear women's clothes.

Two days later Joan changed her mind. Demanding she be allowed to attend mass, Joan was found in men's clothes, claiming the voices had told her that her abjuration was treason. Now the only possible outcome was execution. On 30 May she was allowed to make her confession and take communion before she was taken to the Old Market in Rouen and tied to the stake. She was given a small crucifix and a Dominican priest held a parish cross high so she could see it even as the flames began to lick around her. The young warrior who had led her country to such great victories over the English cried out, "Jesus!" repeatedly before leaving this world. The king she had helped crown, Charles VII, not once tried to help Joan. She was a tool that had stopped being useful. Still, the legend of Jehanne la Pucelle only grew stronger with time. In 1456 the sentence was annulled and in 1920, Joan of Arc was canonised by Pope Benedict XV. She is now a saint.

Defining moment

Siege of Orléans 29 April-8 May 1429

Joan arrives at Orléans amid great fanfare from the citizens of the city but is met with indifference by her fellow commanders. She is determined to mount an attack as soon as possible but is told they would wait for a relief effort. She is so poorly regarded by the other generals that when a sortie takes place, she's not told beforehand. Instead, she races out and joins the attack just in time to rally the flagging troops, ultimately claiming a fortress. This will be the first in a series of victories that would liberate Orléans and confirm her status for many as a heaven-sent hero.

Charles is crowned
After swiftly clearing the Loire region of English resistance, Charles finally travels to Reims where he is crowned King Charles VII of France. The coronation fulfils another part of Joan's voices' prophecy.
17 July 1429

A failed siege
Following Charles' coronation, Joan is convinced that Paris will fall. However, the siege fails as 1,500 men fall to the English bombardment, with Joan herself wounded, having to be pulled from the battlefield under nightfall.
8 September 1429

Capture
While leading an unsanctioned relief effort of Compiègne, Joan decides to attack the Burgundian troops surrounding the city. She is cut off by the English and pulled from her horse while trying to escape.
23 March 1430

Trial
Needing to regain superiority, the church interrogates Joan, telling her she can abjure or face a secular court that will execute her. She retracts her statement, only to change her mind days later, stating she'd rather die than deny what she knows to be true.
9 January-24 May 1431

Burned to death
Having recanted her abjuration, Joan is sentenced to be burned at the stake. A Dominican priest holds a cross up high enough for her to see from the flames. She calls out "Jesus!" several times as she burns to death.
30 May 1431

1456

Late justice
Charles orders that Joan's trial be investigated, a proceeding taking roughly six years to complete. Finally, in 1456, the original verdict is annulled, deciding the process had been unjust.
1456

WILLIAM SHAKESPEARE

English, 1564-1616

Brief Bio

Born in Stratford-upon-Avon to glove maker John Shakespeare and landowner's daughter Mary Arden, William Shakespeare had three children with his wife Anne Hathaway. He moved to London in the late 1580s to pursue an acting career, becoming a prominent and prolific playwright and poet, producing an average of two plays a year until 1611 before retiring to Stratford.

Rebel with a cause SHAKESPEARE

He may be England's most celebrated writer, but did Shakespeare hide codes and double meanings in his work to subvert the establishment during a time of religious turmoil?

Two guards grabbed him tightly and dragged him down a stone corridor, his shackled legs meaning he was unable to keep up the frantic pace they had set. He was determined to show no sign of weakness and tried to concentrate on the senses around him, such as the rats scurrying by his feet, the insects crawling on the walls and the warmth on his face from the burning torches that illuminated the short path.

How had things come to this? He was Robert Southwell, born into a good family and a man who devoted his life to God, being ordained a priest in 1584 in Rome. But what had been one of the best years of his life had also turned into one of the most bitter when later the same year, the 'Jesuits, etc Act' had ordered all Roman Catholic priests to leave England. They were given 40 days' grace to do so and many of his friends had hurriedly scrambled their belongings together and fled the island nation for friendlier shores. These were difficult times to be a Catholic in England.

Pain ripped through his body as the guards swung him around a corner and flung open a new cell door for him. Looking at the horrible conditions his mind raced back. Damn that Henry VIII, he thought. Damn him and his desire for a male heir and his lust for Anne Boleyn that had seen him turn his back on the Catholic faith he had been brought up in. And damn that German monk Martin Luther whose actions had led the Protestant Reformation that had swept through Europe and ultimately been adopted throughout England.

Southwell was levered inside the cramped, dank space. He recognised it from the descriptions of others whose fate had brought them here; it was Limbo, the most feared cell within Newgate Prison, inside a gate in the Roman London Wall. The door closed and the guards walked away. His heart beating wildly with fear, he reflected on his decision to leave Rome in 1586 to travel back to England to work as a Jesuit missionary, staying with numerous Catholic families, thus becoming a wanted man.

Eventually, the door swung open and he was dragged out of his cramped cell. He could barely stand as he was taken to trial, hauled before Lord Chief Justice John Popham and indicted as a traitor. He defiantly laid out his position, admitted to being a priest and his sentence was passed. He was, Popham said, to be hanged, drawn and quartered. After being beaten on the journey through London's streets he was forced to stand. His head was placed in a noose and he was briefly hanged. Cut down while still alive, his bowels were removed before his beating heart was dragged from his body and he was cut into four pieces. His severed head was held aloft. This was England in the late-16th century - Queen Elizabeth's religious compromise wasn't without its share of pain and suffering.

This was the world William Shakespeare lived n as he wrote his great works. He had moved to ondon from Stratford-upon-Avon in 1587, leaving behind his young family to pursue a career as an actor and a playwright with the troupe Lord Strange's Men. He had married Anne Hathaway in 1582, when he was 18 and she was 26, and together they had three children, Susanna, Hamnet and Judith. But the ure of the stage had been too strong to ignore.

It had not taken Shakespeare long to make a name for himself. His first play, *Henry VI, Part 1*, written n 1591, made its debut a year later. It was successful enough to make fellow playwrights jealous. One of them was Robert Greene, arguably the first professional author in England. Unlike Shakespeare, he was university educated and urged his friends not to give Shakespeare any work, calling him an 'upstart crow.' Shakespeare was unmoved by such words. It would be, academics conferred later, a sign he was making his mark.

By 1594, he had written more plays and seen both *Venus and Adonis* and *The Rape of Lucrese* published. He dedicated them to his patron Henry Wriothesley, the Earl of Southampton. He liked the Earl. Southampton was from a long Catholic dynasty and he appreciated poetry and theatre. When the theatres re-opened in 1594 following an outbreak of bubonic plague, he was keen to invite the Earl along. After all, Shakespeare's new troupe, Lord Chamberlain's Men, was becoming popular, with them even invited to perform in the royal court of Queen Elizabeth I. Shakespeare had also bought shares in Lord Chamberlain's Men and was becoming a powerful and influential figure.

The Reformation had changed England's approach to religion, moving the country away from its Catholic roots and into the arms of Protestantism. But it had not been as peaceful a transition as is sometimes painted. Protest leaders who encouraged more than 30,000 priests, gentry and commoners to demand a return to Catholicism in 1536 had been executed. Two years later, reformers had banished the cult of saints, destroying shrines and banning the population of England from making pilgrimages. Riots in 1549 were repressed in the most vicious of ways – the reformers would hang priests from church towers and lop off the heads of laymen who refused to obey the new order.

All this affected the Bard; he wasn't writing in a bubble and nor were the actors who performed his work. Clare Asquith states in *Shadowplay: The Hidden Beliefs and Coded Politics of William Shakespeare*: "Shakespeare's family are thought to have been Catholics [...] his early years would have echoed to angry discussions of the impact of fines and imprisonments, the liberties taken by the Queen's commissioners, the wreckage under Edward and the wicked errors of the old King."

Speaking out against the establishment was hard – not least for those who wanted to keep their heads. Anyone wanting to put across another point of view had to be smart and Asquith believes the man who would go on to be England's most celebrated poet and playwright rebelled and devised a secret

"Queen Elizabeth's religious compromise wasn't without its share of pain"

code, inserting messages and double meaning into his writing. It isn't as outlandish as it may sound; cryptology had been used since ancient times and there were examples of secret codes being used in this time period. For example, it is known that Mary, Queen of Scots used a cipher secretary called Gilbert Curle to handle her secret correspondence. It wasn't entirely sophisticated, though, so her plot to overthrow Elizabeth was soon uncovered – Catholic double agent Gilbert Gifford intercepted letters that had been smuggled out in casks of ale and reported them to Sir Francis Walsingham, who had created a school for espionage.

For Catholics, certain words and key phrases stood out. For example, 'tempest' or 'storm' were used to signify England's troubles, according to Asquith. So Shakespeare may well have been convinced he could change people's view of the world by writing on an entertainment and political and religious level.

First he had to work out exactly what message he wanted to put across. Philip II of Spain, who had married Mary I, felt England's Catholics had been abandoned and there had long been a promise that, if the Catholics bided their time, help would come. Relations between Spain and England had declined to an all-new low. This culminated in the sailing of 122 ships from Spain in 1588 with the aim of the Spanish Armada being to overthrow Elizabeth I and replace the Protestant regime.

The Spanish Armada tried to overthrow Elizabeth I's rule in England with a massive naval assault

The sacking of Antwerp in 1576, a major event in the Eighty Years' War

"Their plan was to blow the building sky high, taking parliamentarians and King James I with it"

The Gunpowder Plot was a politically and religiously charged conspiracy to blow up the Houses of Parliament

Catholics felt James I was guilty of. "My own theory is that Shakespeare, though not an outright rebel, used his increasingly privileged position to address the court and the crown, both Elizabeth, and James, on the issue of religious toleration", Asquith asserts. "He protested against the persecution and injustice perpetrated in the name of the monarch, and pleaded for religious toleration."

Such an assessment revises the prevailing thinking that Shakespeare wrote universal plays and avoided any topicality. Some literary scholars remain hostile to the idea that the playwright was involved in the volatile religious issues of the day, but could he really have ignored what was going on around him? It's plausible that he wanted to do more than merely shake the literary world; he wanted to influence politics and religion, to affect his society.

When he sat at his desk, overlooking the squalid, filthy conditions of London, William Shakespeare may have been looking out at a more enlightened nation than ever before, but is was still a city and a country where the screams of religious and political prisoners filled the corridors of cramped jail cells as torturers extracted forced confessions. This sobering reality was a stark reminder of the perils of religious divisions that continued throughout Shakespeare's life. Was it a society that he rebelled against in his own way? The final and definitive answer to that, like some of the great man's work, is unfortunately lost to the ages.

SHAKESPEAREAN THEORIES

He didn't really write the works

The authorship of Shakespeare's work has been the subject of debate for decades. With no original manuscripts, no mention of him even being a writer in his will and a command of Latin, Greek and other languages that would belie his apparent poor education, many believe that Edward de Vere, the 17th Earl of Oxford was the writer rather than the small-town boy from Stratford. And if not him, then one of 80 other historical figures that have been mentioned over the years, such as Marlowe.

He didn't even exist

Some scholars believe that the Shakespeare revered today as a playwright was actually a fictional character. They believe that the few documents relating to him were actually for a man called William Shaxper or Shakspere who was born in 1564, married and had children but became an actor and remained in such a role until his retirement. Certainly, Shakespeare's death appears to have been unmarked. Had Shakespeare been such a prominent playwright, there would surely have been many documents mourning his passing, critics say.

He was an Italian

Those who argue Shakespeare was not quite who he claims he was are called anti-Stratfordians. One of their theories is that Shakespeare – or Michaelangelo Florio Crollalanza – had moved from Sicily to London, fearing the Holy Inquisition. The family name of Crollalanza was translated and became Shakespeare. Sicilian professor Martini Iuvara claims to have proof and mentions the Sicilian play *Tanto Traffico Per Niente* written by Crollalanza. It can, he claims, be translated into *Much Ado About Nothing.*

Lord Chamberlain's Men, Shakespeare's famous troupe, performed for Queen Elizabeth I

The Armada was defeated but it had succeeded in creating further religious and political divisions, so the authorities were on even greater alert. Within this world Shakespeare got to work and, at first, kept things simple. "My reading is that the early plays were light, comical, critical and oppositional, written for Lord Strange's Men", asserts Asquith. The earliest plays addressed political reunion and spiritual revival. Their plots related to divided families, parallels for an England cut in two.

Asquith believes the Bard placed certain markers in his texts that signalled a second, hidden meaning. He would use opposing words such as 'fair' and 'dark' and 'high' and 'low': 'fair' and 'high' being indications of Catholicism while 'dark' and 'low' would indicate Protestantism. Asquith takes this as reference to the black clothes worn by Puritans and to the 'high' church services that would include mass as opposed to the 'low' services that didn't. If this theory is true - a matter of some debate - then it enabled Shakespeare to get specific messages across, using characters to signify the two sides and by using words commonly associated with Catholic codes. For example, according to the theory, 'love' is divided into human and spiritual and 'tempest' refers to the turbulence of the Reformation and Counter-Reformation and the Bard used his own terms to disguise a message that was pro-Catholic.

At the same time, Shakespeare was operating in establishment circles. "He was drawn into the orbit of the court and wrote elegant pleas for toleration to Elizabeth, in the elaborate allegorical language she was used to", says Asquith. But England was becoming more violent again. Shakespeare's patron, the Earl of Southampton, rebelled against Elizabeth I, becoming Robert, Earl of Essex's lieutenant in an attempt to raise the people of London against the government. The Essex faction had ordered a performance of the 'deposition' play *Richard II* just before the rebellion and Shakespeare's company had their work cut out afterward denying complicity. The plan ended in failure in 1601, but in that same year, Shakespeare wrote *Hamlet*, encouraging action against unjust rule. "His more critical work supported the cause of the Earl of Essex against the [William] Cecil regime", says Asquith. If this is true, then Shakespeare really was one of the defining rebels of the period.

Critics have said for decades that the writer was against populist rebellions and supported authority and the rule of law, "but with the recent reassessment of the extent of dissidence at the end of Elizabeth's reign, Shakespeare's Elizabethan work begins to seem more oppositional", Asquith argues.

"What if the authority he upholds was not that of the breakaway Tudor state, but of the European church against which Henry VIII rebelled?" she asks. "What if he sympathised with the intellectual Puritan reformers, who felt secular monarchs like the Tudors had no business assuming spiritual authority over individual conscience? What if he, like so many contemporaries, opposed the destruction of the old English landscape, from the hostels,

"He devised a secret code, inserting messages and double meaning into his writing"

RELIGIOUS COMPROMISE?

With the untimely death of King Edward VI in 1553, struck with fever and cough that gradually worsened, Mary I ascended to the throne and set about calling a halt to the Reformation. She swung England firmly back towards Catholicism, causing reformers to run scared and flee. Among those displaced was civil servant William Cecil, his relief of a lucky escape palpable as he heard of the 273 Protestants burnt to death under Mary's reign. Terror had been brought on the Protestants but Cecil had the ear of Elizabeth, who he had known for years. She had embraced the Church of England, so much that she had been imprisoned for two months in the Tower of London by her half-sister Mary, who feared she was part of a plot to depose her.

When Mary died in 1558, Cecil wanted to return to a Protestant England. Queen Elizabeth succeeded the throne since Mary had born no child and Cecil became her advisor. Within the year, a uniform state religion had returned. Elizabeth was confirmed as Supreme Governor of the Church of England.

The Act of Uniformity in 1558 set the order of prayer in the *English Book of Common Prayer*. Crucifixes and candlesticks were to be allowed, although new bishops protested. But Protestants who had fled returned and wanted their religion to be supreme. Cecil ensured Catholics would be excluded from public life although he allowed them to worship as long as they did not threaten the queen and did so discreetly. Catholics who rose would be dealt with in the most serious of ways.

The religious upheaval before and during Elizabeth I's reign saw many people executed

CODEBREAKING THE BARD'S PLAYS

Claire Asquith on the secret codes she believes are imbued within Shakespeare's works

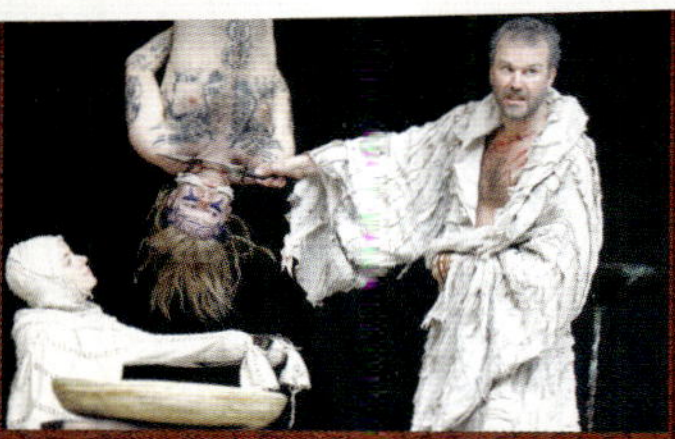

TITUS ANDRONICUS

Synopsis: Written between 1588 and 1593, the play is set in the latter days of the Roman Empire. Bloody in the extreme, the play explores the life of a fictional Roman general, Titus, caught in a vicious circle of revenge with the queen of the Goths, Tamora.
Rebel? Shakespeare appears to be pleading for calm among England's dissidents, having written a play that highlights suffering and repression while arguing the case against a violent rebellion. The message, claims Asquith, is very much about biding time, waiting for help in the guise of a promised invasion and, as such, it mirrored the rhetoric of Catholic leaders who stressed England would be saved via diplomacy or invasion rather than an internal uprising. "It is a gory portrayal of just the kind of state atrocities conducted in the mid-1590s, and in the previous reign as well. Yet it discourages equally bloody revenge", says Asquith.

TAMING OF THE SHREW

Synopsis: Written between 1590 and 1592, the courtship of Petruchio is at the heart of the play. It shows his attempts to tame the wild Katherina, a girl he loves but is rebuffed by until he manages to win her over.
Rebel? Displaying evidence of the 'high-low' opposition language that Shakespeare used to refer to Catholics and Protestants, Katherina is "brown in hue." Her sister is called Bianca, meaning 'white' and she is the respectable one of the two. This paints Katherina to be like a reformer and in need of being brought into line. Asquith says the "oddly political language" used by the chastened shrew is "meant to alert us to the play's secondary level." For those accustomed to finding deeper meanings, the message would have been obvious, according to her. She says: "The play shows England as a warring family, the monarch helpless to stop vengeful puritans baiting afflicted Catholics."

KING LEAR

Synopsis: The tragedy is set in the court of an ageing monarch. He wants to pass the monarchy to his three daughters and asks them to prove they love him the best but one cannot so he splits it between two before falling into madness.
Rebel? Lear's actions caused a tumbling effect as various people were banished, reunited, imprisoned and heartbroken. Asquith claims this is an "unvarnished dramatisation of the state of James' England, a final attempt to awaken the King to the intolerable humiliations and sufferings of his Catholic subjects." She tells us the message within is clear: "If you exile true Christian spirituality – and both puritans and Catholics were exiled – the country descends into amoral anarchy." She adds: "It is worth noticing that though he discourages mob-led rebellion, he includes nine invasions in his work, and they are all portrayed as positive events."

THE WINTER'S TALE

Synopsis: Suspicious that his childhood friend is his pregnant wife's lover, Leontes accuses his wife of infidelity and having an illegitimate child. Having ordered the newborn baby to be abandoned, he is later reunited with her, much to his delight.
Rebel? With the play believed to have been written in 1611, this was one of Shakespeare's later plays and it appears to contain a strong message: "After all the post-reformation trauma, the spirituality that was lost turns out to have been secretly preserved", says Asquith. As with *The Tempest*, *Pericles* and *Cymbeline*, *The Winter's Tale* started with suffering and ended with happiness. It showed a transition that could put past remorse to bed, highlighting the possibility that evils can be defeated and overcome and that a true home can be found for spiritualism if it is wanted. It would have encouraged the audience to keep the faith and not give up hope.

colleges, monasteries and hospitals to the rich iconography of churches to local roadside shrines and holy wells?"

It can be argued that the Bard personified England itself so that he could explore just why the ideas behind the Reformation had taken hold, presenting it as gullible and deluded, willing to turn its back on spiritual heritage, with the play *Two Gentlemen Of Verona* cited as evidence of this. The more elaborate plays retained the puns, wordplay and double meanings so beloved of audiences in Elizabethan times, but Asquith notes that some of Shakespeare's characters came to be increasingly dramatic and allegorical; they had a hidden spiritual meaning that transcended the literal sense of the text.

When King James assumed the throne in 1603, Catholics had assumed that he would lend them greater support than Elizabeth, given that his mother was a staunch Catholic. But that was not to be and Shakespeare must have been well aware of a growing political and religious resentment against the monarchy, with a feeling of rebellion growing. His plays in this period became more cynical, which some have speculated was a consequence of the world he was living in.

Matters came to a head with an explosive event in 1605. Guy Fawkes, Thomas Wintour, Everard Digby and Thomas Percy hired a cellar beneath the Houses of Parliament for a few weeks, gathering gunpowder and storing it in their newly acquired space. Their plan was to blow the building sky high, taking parliamentarians and King James I with it. But their cover was blown and Guy Fawkes was taken away to be tortured into confession, the deadly rack being the instrument said to have broken him. He was sentenced to be hanged, drawn and quartered. At around the same time, Shakespeare wrote *King Lear*, *Othello* and *Macbeth*, all plays warning against unjust rule, which many Catholics felt James I was guilty of. "My own theory is that Shakespeare, though not an outright rebel, used his privileged position to address the court and the crown, both Elizabeth, and James, on the issue of religious toleration", Asquith asserts. "He protested against the persecution and injustice perpetrated in the name of the monarch, and pleaded for religious toleration."

Such an assessment revises thinking that Shakespeare wrote universal plays and avoided any topicality. Some scholars remain hostile to the idea that he was involved in the volatile issues of the day, but could he really have ignored what was going on around him? It's plausible that he wanted to do more than merely shake the literary world; that he wanted to influence politics and religion.

Sat at his desk, overlooking the squalid conditions of London, Shakespeare may have been looking at a more enlightened nation than ever before, but is was still a place where the screams of religious and political prisoners filled the corridors of cramped jail cells as torturers extracted confessions. Was it a society that he rebelled against in his own way? The definitive answer to that, like some of the great man's work, is unfortunately lost to the ages.

ANCIENT CIVILISATIONS

Uncover the history of some of the world's most revolutionary early societies, and how they formed our world today

宮本無三四

MARK ANTONY

Rome/Egypt, 83-30 BCE

Brief Bio

Marcus Antonius was born in 83 BCE and, as a young man, was known as something of a playboy in Rome. But after fighting alongside Julius Caesar on the battlefield, he quickly established his military prowess. After Caesar's assassination, he formed a power trio with Marcus Lepidus and Octavian, but his growing love of the Egyptian queen Cleopatra would prove to be his downfall.

CLEOPATRA VII

Egypt, circa 69-30 BCE

Brief Bio

Cleopatra was the daughter of Ptolemy XII Auletes and Cleopatra V. Born in Alexandria in 69 BCE her bloodline propagated a series of brother-sister marriages that were frequently corroded by family violence and murder. After a tumultuous reign, Octavian of Rome invaded Egypt and ended her rule. Rather than face the humiliation of defeat, Cleopatra committed suicide.

THE LAST PHARAOH AND THE FALL OF ANCIENT EGYPT

Cleopatra VII remains an icon of both the ancient and modern world. Today, she continues to captivate and puzzle historians, remaining one of history's most enchanting and enigmatic figures.

The alliance of Mark Antony and Cleopatra changed the face of the world. A coalition which began as a political statement soon evolved into a tumultuous, and later tragic, love affair.

Despite her florid reputation, Cleopatra took only two lovers - both were rulers of Rome. Cleopatra recognised Rome as the leading power of the ancient world. Egypt, rich in gold and grain, provided the material resources to fuel that power. Both affairs had begun with a political agenda. They had enabled the queen to establish a secure and profitable union between Rome and Egypt. Despite this, however, events took an unexpected turn when she met the younger general. Cleopatra and Mark Antony fell in love, embarking on a passionate and unpredictable relationship that brought both riches and remorse. Their partnership, as lovers and politicians, both immortalised and destroyed a dynasty - it brought to a close 3,000 years of pharaonic rule.

Long before her meeting with Mark Antony, the queen had borne a child to her first Roman lover, Gaius Julius Caesar and she had named the child Caesarion - 'little Caesar'. In doing so, Cleopatra had secured for herself an enormous power base, for Caesar had no heir. Despite its material wealth, Egypt had suffered years of famine that had weakened the reserves of her granaries and her people. The country was in eclipse. Her allied states had also felt the grip of Rome tightening around their throats. Alexandria had long been important to Rome. As a gateway to the East, it was a major port with a large cosmopolitan community. It was renowned for its libraries, culture and trade. Egypt also had an abundant source of grain with which it fed its imperial army. On the other hand, the Romans regarded the Egyptian people and their religion with suspicion - its cults, along with its strange animal-headed gods, were an abomination to the refined Roman senses.

In 30 BCE, a love affair between a powerful queen and a respected military leader caused scandal in Rome and ultimately brought about the end of a dynasty

While her alliance with Rome continued, Cleopatra - and her throne - remained secure. For this reason, Cleopatra courted Rome and its leading figures. From the beginning, Cleopatra was an enigma to a man like Mark Antony. Having grown up in Rome, he was familiar with upper-class women who were cloistered in the home and whose only role in life was to be that of good wives and mothers. The women of Rome were largely regarded as vessels of chastity; Cleopatra was the antithesis of a Roman woman.

Growing up in a highly political and dangerous household where life was precarious, she was descended from a long line of rulers - all named Ptolemy - who could trace their line to Alexander the Great. In order to keep their bloodline pure, female rulers often married their brothers. This practice brought outward strength but inner conflicts; during her early life Cleopatra witnessed brutal power struggles within her own family. Indeed, as her power grew, she had no choice but to execute her rival siblings.

Cleopatra had to live by her wits. She was a highly educated woman with a sharp mind and a keen instinct. She spoke several languages, including Egyptian - making her unique among her peers. She was a cultivated woman, a patron of the arts and devoted to books. Despite her later reputation as a femme fatale, she was not considered beautiful. It was said she had a charismatic presence, was a fine conversationalist and had a sweet, seductive voice - a trait she may have cultivated as a child. Most importantly, Cleopatra was a survivor; she knew that in order to sustain her throne, she needed to control the might of Rome, and Mark Antony could offer this.

Mark Antony and Cleopatra were as fire and water. Born in January 83 BCE, Antony was a true son of Rome. Like Cleopatra, he sought decadence and danger - he had quickly gained a reputation for drinking and gambling, and seems to have been attracted to exotic religious cults. Later, he earned fame and fortune among the militia; as the commander of a cavalry regiment he received great honours fighting with Caesar's armies in Gaul. Antony and Caesar formed a mutual friendship and a distant kinship had strengthened their alliance. As Caesar's star ascended, so too had Mark

Antony's, and when the elder man became dictator, Antony was appointed Magister Equitum (Master of the Horse) and governed Rome in Caesar's absence. Better suited to the battlefield, Mark Antony made an impetuous politician - highly volatile, his excesses in wine and women became the topic of much public gossip, for these often included affairs with other men's wives.

After the assassination of Caesar, Cleopatra and Mark Antony fled Rome and Cleopatra returned to Egypt. With Caesar dead, her position had become tenuous. The Romans regarded a female ruler with abhorrence and she desperately needed an ally in the Senate. When revolt failed to materialise, Mark Antony returned to the Forum to find a city outraged at the atrocities that had befallen Caesar.

The assassins were executed or fell into obscurity, and it was left to Octavian (Caesar's appointed heir), Lepidus (his trusted commander) and Mark Antony to calm the storm. The three men formed the Second Triumvirate granting themselves equal powers of government.

Antony was now in a strong position. As the three men began to carve out Roman territory each assigned themselves important provinces. Mark Antony had set his heart on Cleopatra and Egypt. He sent a message to his lover asking her to meet him at Tarsus in modern-day Turkey, determined to win her support for his military campaigns.

On this particular meeting she presented herself as the embodiment of the goddess Venus. The imperial queen of Egypt arrived on a golden barge; decked in fine linen and precious gems, she was attended by servants dressed as sea nymphs. While she drifted towards Mark Antony like a creature from myth, she refused to disembark. As queen of Egypt, she expected Antony to wait on her.

Mark Antony's temper was inflamed, but so were his passions. Plutarch said of their relationship "observing Cleopatra's looks and her subtlety and tricky wit in conversation, he [Antony's agent] at once knew that Antony would never think of doing such a woman any harm, and that in fact she'd have the greatest influence over him."

Not surprisingly, Antony chose to spend the winter of 41-40 BCE with Cleopatra in Alexandria - the result of this visit was the birth of twin children, Alexander Helios and Cleopatra Selene II, whose names are linked with the dual powers of the Sun and the Moon.

Rome was greatly disturbed by this turn of events. In order to secure his loyalty, Octavian arranged a marriage between Mark Antony and his sister, Octavia - a move that infuriated the Egyptian queen. To avoid a public insult, Mark Antony stumbled into an acrimonious and dangerous union. Meanwhile, the queen of Egypt financed his army, allowing him to capture Jerusalem where he installed Herod as the puppet king of Judaea. Four years later, Antony visited Alexandria again en route to make war with the Parthians. His relationship with Cleopatra had gathered momentum and he had made Alexandria his home. Despite his union with Octavia, he married Cleopatra and they had another child.

Soon, Antony grew tired of luxurious living, exotic palaces and hunting in the Egyptian Delta; he longed for the glories of war. When Antony invaded Parthian territory with an army of about 100,000 Roman and allied troops, the campaign proved disastrous. He never recovered from the shock of defeat. Octavian took this opportunity; he demoted Lepidus, belittled Mark Antony and seized unilateral power. He reminded Rome of the menacing relationship between Antony and his abominable foreign queen. While feigning shock at the abandonment of his sister, he told the citizens of Rome that Mark Antony was now living as an Egyptian; this was regarded as an act of treason.

Antony and Cleopatra responded to the attack with theatrics. After a successful invasion of Armenia, Mark Antony infuriated his fellow Romans by holding a Triumph (formal celebration) in the city of Alexandria. Mark Antony then issued a series of proclamations known as the Donations of Alexandria when he named Cleopatra and her

"Octavian arranged a marriage between Mark Antony and his sister, Octavia - a move that infuriated the Egyptian queen"

A 19th-century depiction of Cleopatra on the River Nile

MYTH VS REALITY

Just how realistic is our modern conception of the Egyptian queen?

A modern reader's perspective of Cleopatra has no doubt been heavily influenced by the numerous works of fiction that have been released charting her life in the many centuries following her death.

Foremost among these must arguably be William Shakespeare's 1623 tragedy *Antony And Cleopatra*, a play that follows events from the Sicilian revolt of 44 BCE through to the Final War of the Roman Republic in which Cleopatra commits suicide in 30 BCE by asp bite. In this performance, Cleopatra is frequently portrayed as beautiful, power-hungry and manipulative.

So how accurate is Shakespeare's representation of the Egyptian ruler? Well, it is loosely based on a translation of Plutarch's *Parallel Lives* - a series of biographies on famous Greek and Roman men that were printed in a first edition in Florence in the early-16th century (no doubt where Shakespeare picked it up).

The one in question from which the Great Bard draws is the *Life Of Mark Antony*, which is interesting, as it does not deal directly with the pharaoh but rather with the Roman general and his relationship to her. Further, Shakespeare does not lay out events of the time as stated by Plutarch, with dates and events shifted in time and contrasting accounts of Cleopatra simplified. A good example of this is how varying accounts of her death, including death by poisoning, willing death by snake bike to the arm and unwilling accidental snakebite to the arm, is rewritten as willing death by snakebite to the breast.

Of course, Shakespeare's account of Cleopatra has been further embellished in subsequent centuries with other works of fiction such as the well-known 1963 film adaptation of her life with Elizabeth Taylor playing the lead. Aside from Taylor's questionable portrayal, this movie introduced many smaller yet pervasive inaccuracies such as Cleopatra wearing her hair in bangs. In reality, the Egyptian queen would have worn a wig of tight curls on top of her head, which would have been shaven.

THE MEN WHO RULED ROME 43 – 33 BCE

OCTAVIAN

Octavian, later known as Augustus (born on 23 September 63 BCE), became the first emperor of Rome. He ruled from 27 BCE until his death. Unlike his compatriot Mark Antony, Octavian placed great importance on Roman morality, and was more suited to philosophy than war. His rise to power was largely due to adoption by his maternal great-uncle Gaius Julius Caesar. Along with Mark Antony and Marcus Lepidus he formed the Second Triumvirate. The Triumvirate divided the Roman Republic between the three of them and ruled as military dictators. Despite his reputation as a cruel and calculating leader, Octavian brought an era of peace and prosperity known as the Pax Romana. He died on 19 August 14 CE.

Italian Gaul

Mark Antony was a seasoned campaigner in Gaul where he accompanied his kinsman Julius Caesar into battle and proved his mettle as a soldier.

Macedonia

The Ptolemies were descended from a line of Macedonians that could trace their origins to Alexander the Great.

Africa

A source of vast riches for Lepidus and Rome. It was here that the Romans found exotic animals for their gladiatorial arenas.

Alexandria

Founded by Alexander the Great, the city was occupied by the Ptolemies until the death of Cleopatra VII.

MARK ANTONY

Mark Antony was born on 14 January 83 BCE and died, aged 53, in Alexandria, Egypt. According to Plutarch his early life was spent gambling and drinking as he embarked on a series of dangerous love affairs. He was a hedonist and a womaniser whose many wives bore him a cacophony of children; his descendants included notable emperors such as Caligula and Nero. As a soldier, though, he showed promise; his bravery and determination made him popular among his men and he distinguished himself as a cavalry officer. His connections with the noble families of Rome secured his future role as a powerful but somewhat unpredictable military leader.

MARCUS AEMILIUS LEPIDUS

Lepidus, like Mark Antony, was a fierce advocate of Julius Caesar who gave Lepidus great honorary titles and a role in the Senate that was equivalent to that of a prime minister today. His career was cut short when Caesar was assassinated. In allowing Lepidus to live, Caesar's assassins made an irrevocable error of judgement. Octavian, Antony and Lepidus became the driving force of Rome - their initial aim, to cut off the head of the Senate. After they had executed many of their enemies, their alliance, in effect, heralded the end of the Republic. Lepidus ruled over Spain and Africa and, while he was abroad, Octavian began his quest for ultimate power. He forced Lepidus into exile in Circeii, Italy, where he died as an old man around 13 BCE.

Actium
The ancient battle that changed the world

The battle took place on 2 September 31 BCE, on the Ionian Sea on the border of the city of Actium. It was thought that Antony's fleet had the advantage. It boasted 500 ships - each a war galley designed with turrets. Known as quinqueremes, Mark Antony's warships each weighed 300 tons; they were especially designed to ram enemy vessels.

Commanded by his general, Marcus Agrippa, Octavian's fleet consisted of 250 ships. Agrippa launched his initial attack from the left wing of the fleet and attempted to outflank Mark Antony - the battle was brutal and prolonged. Unfortunately, many of Antony's soldiers were dying of malaria and his ships were undermanned. Therefore, Octavian's fleet was greatly encouraged. These Liburnian vessels were manned by well-trained and rested soldiers, and the ships were fast and agile. As they outmanoeuvred their enemy, the deck soldiers used fire arrows and slingshots to diminish their capability. Realising the severity of his situation, Mark Antony decided to retreat and regroup. He took advantage of a break in the enemy formation and made a dash for it. In doing so, he abandoned many of his men to their fate.

Defeated by Octavian's fleet, Mark Antony fled the battle, leaving his soldiers to die

children heirs to his conquered territories. It was, in effect, a declaration of war. Mark Antony named Caesarion the legitimate son and heir of Caesar - Octavian, of course, being the 'adopted' son of the former dictator. Octavian had no choice but to retaliate. He told the Senate that Antony had "gone native" and that he had been effeminated by the Egyptian queen. Mark Antony divorced Octavia and accused Octavian of forging Caesar's will. Rome was drawn into a civil war - which culminated in the defeat of Antony at the Battle of Actium.

After his clear victory, Octavian returned to Rome. During the 12 months that followed, he left Antony and Cleopatra to contemplate their defeat and consider their demise. Egypt's neighbouring territories were largely annexed to Rome; for this reason, Antony and Cleopatra's attempts to regroup and raise an army proved futile.

It was in August 30 BCE that Octavian finally invaded Egypt. Antony made one last valiant attempt to usurp the Roman leader, but in the end, his fate had been cast. He did what was required of all honourable Roman soldiers and fell upon his sword. In an attempt to safeguard her children Cleopatra made a tentative effort to make terms with Octavian. In his final hour, Antony was brought to Cleopatra's mausoleum and he died in her arms. Octavian allowed Cleopatra to conduct burial rituals for Antony's body. While he presented an outward show of friendship, he naturally wanted her dead. He was, in fact, in a difficult position.

Roman law dictated that Cleopatra should be treated as an enemy of the state. She should be taken back to Rome in shackles and paraded before the mob. However, a female ruler was a rare entity - the display could end up backfiring on Octavian and prove highly distasteful.

> "Roman law dictated Cleopatra should be treated as an enemy of the state, taken back to Rome and paraded before the mob"

He was relieved then, when Cleopatra took the courageous decision to end her own life. Some historians believe that she was bitten by a snake hidden in a fig basket. Others suggest that she drank wine laced with hemlock. An account of her death can be found in Plutarch's *Lives*.

'The messengers [of Octavian] came at full speed, and found the guards apprehensive of nothing; but, on opening the doors, they saw her stone-dead, lying upon a bed of gold, set out in all her royal ornaments. Iras, one of her women, lay dying at her feet, and Charmion, just ready to fall, scarce able to hold up her head, was adjusting her mistress's diadem. And when one that came in said angrily, "Was this well done of your lady, Charmion?" "Extremely well," she answered, "and as became the descendant of so many kings". As she said this she fell down dead by the bedside.'

In Rome, the son of the orator Cicero announced the deaths of Antony and Cleopatra with relish. Mark Antony was stripped of his accolades, his image erased from coinage and his statues removed. Under threat from Octavian, Iullus Antonius - Mark Antony's eldest son - later committed suicide. Concurring with Homer - that "It is bad to have too many Caesars" - Octavian also had Caesarion murdered. The remaining children of Cleopatra and Antony were spared and taken to Rome where they were adopted by Antony's family.

With the death of Cleopatra, the Sun had finally set on the Hellenistic Dynasty - and indeed on the 3,000-year rule of the pharaohs.

End of an Era

Cleopatra's surviving children were adopted by Octavia, became Roman citizens and faded quickly into obscurity. Egypt, now a Roman province, was ruled by a prefect. Greek remained the official language. While Alexandria continued to flourish, it became a site of many religious and military uprisings. In 269 CE Alexandria was claimed by yet another woman, when Zenobia, the ferocious warrior Queen of Palmyra, conquered Egypt. Zenobia - an admirer of Cleopatra - was quick to behead her detested Roman foes. She ruled Egypt until 274, before she herself was taken hostage by the Roman Emperor Aurelian; in an ironic twist of fate, Zenobia appeared in golden chains during Aurelian's Triumph in Rome.

The legacy of Greco-Roman Egypt still survives. It can be seen in a series of magnificent temples that were built along the River Nile. These include the Temple of Hathor at Dendera, where fabulous images of Cleopatra and Caesarion still dominate its walls.

The delicate amalgamation of the Egyptian and Roman cultures can be seen on many mummy portrait panels from the Greco-Roman period. Contrasts are visible in paintings and sculptures where traditional Egyptian iconography is paired with Roman symbolism. The result - a hybrid blend of the ancient and even more ancient - is now all that remains of the former bond between Rome and Egypt: Antony and Cleopatra.

A ROMAN LEGIONNAIRE

SOLDIER IN THE ROMAN ARMY, ANCIENT ROME, CIRCA 750 BCE – 476 CE

CASSIS

A HELMET AS MUCH FOR SHOW AS IT IS PROTECTION

The Roman legionnaire's helmet was made from bronze and provided protection for the whole head. The plumes on the top were usually made from horsehair or feathers, though may have only been worn for ceremonial duties.

PILUM

TAKING OUT ENEMIES FROM AFAR

Metal-tipped and with a weighted end, the legionnaire's javelin was between 1.8 and 2.1 metres (six and seven feet) long. It could be hurled to devastating effect and was accurate up to around 30 paces in some hands.

GLADIUS

THE PRIMARY WEAPON USED DURING CLOSE COMBAT

Adopted during the Punic Wars, this short sword was the legionnaire's main offensive weapon of choice. It was primarily a thrusting and slashing sword, ideal for close combat, and became part of the legionnaire's signature parry-and-stab move.

TUNIC

A LAYER OF PADDING BELOW THE LORICA SEGMENTATA

Worn underneath the armour coming down roughly to the middle of the thigh, the tunic was made out of rough wool, and was most often red or left undyed (white). The only colours not used were black (because it symbolised death) and pink, yellow and green, as they were considered feminine.

CALIGAE

THE LIGHTWEIGHT FOOTWEAR THAT WAS BUILT FOR LONG MARCHES

Despite superficially resembling sandals, these were in reality marching boots, made of leather with heavy soles. They were designed to allow air to circulate around the feet and reduce the risk of blisters during marching, although in colder locations (like Britain) woollen socks were often worn with them.

LORICA SEGMENTATA

A COAT OF METAL TO DEFLECT ATTACKS

Once only used by the highest-ranking soldiers, this form of armour eventually became standard after the Romans perfected the ability to mass-produce metal goods. Consisting of strips of iron or steel that had been heated by coal and quenched in oil or water, it was perfect for deflecting swords and arrows.

SCUTUM

A SHIELD USED FOR BOTH DEFENCE AND OFFENCE

Constructed from plywood and covered in leather, the oval-shaped shield called a scutum was over a metre (3.3 feet) in length, and proved a valuable defence against ranged weapons. Up close, it could also be used as a weapon.

SECRETS OF THE AZTECS

A civilisation now lost in time, the ancient Aztecs were masters of science and technology, creating medicines, machines and mega-structures unsurpassed on Earth

Despite being isolated within the deep, dark, unforgiving jungles of Central America, for over 300 years the ancient Aztecs defied their reputation as blood-obsessed barbarians by pioneering many of the scientific and technological advances we take for granted today. What's more, they did so across a broad range of fields, from astronomy to medicine, hoarding their acquired knowledge within huge libraries of codices that contained the secrets to the vast and impressive society they had built.

Unfortunately, much of this knowledge was lost forever when the Spanish conquistadors of Hernán Cortés brought the civilisation to their knees in the early-16th century, with these supposedly heretical texts burned en masse. Luckily, a few records of Aztec scientific knowledge survived and today historians are working tirelessly to unlock their secrets. Read on to discover some of their most impressive scientific knowledge.

Marvelous mathematicians

Buried deep within the Codex Vergara (a cadastral manuscript) lies a wealth of information about Aztec mathematics, which has now been decoded and revealed to be a vigesimal system rather than our decimal system in use today. The Aztec vigesimal system uses 20 as its base, with written dots equating to one, hyphen-style bars equating to five and various other symbols accounting for 20 and multiples thereof. According to the Vergara, as well as other codices, this system was employed for tax purposes, which was largely based on land owned, as well as for commerce, with quantities of produce traded with precision thanks to the creation of hard rules for addition, subtraction, division and multiplication. Of all the pre-Columbian peoples of Central America, the Aztecs were the most accomplished mathematicians, using a unique numbering system for arithmetic, record keeping and even in a taxation system for Tenochtitlan and the surviving lands.

Land was also measured mathematically, with a selection of algorithms utilised to calculate area, the most basic being the multiplication of length by width, while multiplying the averages of two opposite sides by an adjacent side used for irregular shapes. Land was measured in terms of 'land rods', which was the standard Aztec unit of linear measurement, measuring in at 2.5 metres

THE AZTEC CALENDAR

Understand this unique time-keeping system now

The Aztec calendar consisted of a 365-day cycle, referred to as a 'year count', and a 260-day cycle, referred to as a 'day count'. Together, these two cycles formed a 52-year century or 'calendar round' for the civilisation, with the former based on the movements of the sun and the latter based on religious belief. The year-count cycle consisted of eighteen 20-day months, with a separate five-day period at the end that was considered unlucky. The day-count cycle consisted of twenty 13-day periods referred to as trecena, with each trecena attributed to a different god.

While it is obvious that many parts of the their calendar system were inaccurate, the fact that the Aztecs could harness their advancements in astronomy and mathematics to create a calendar that was so close to an Earth year while deep in the isolated jungles of central America, is a remarkable feat. Furthermore, despite the Aztecs' religious calendar being centred on mythological deities, many of its aspects are based on scientific study of the Earth's environment and atmosphere. A good representation of the Aztec religious calendar – the cycle referred to as the day count – can be seen in the Aztec calendar stone, a massive 3.7m (12ft) in diameter, 24-ton ornate sun stone that once held great importance in the ancient civilisation of the Aztecs. The stone, which demonstrates the Aztecs' advanced understanding of geometry, is broken down into constituent parts in the diagram to the right.

the night sky for centuries and handing it down through generations in isolation from the wider world. Records show that as well as being capable of accurately tracking the movements of celestial bodies such as the Sun, Moon and other planets – which they accomplished by placing sets of crossed wooden poles along their site lines – they utilised that information to create a religious and solar calendar as well as orientate their key structures along equinoctial lines. For example, the Templo Mayor of Tenochtitlan was aligned so that on the spring equinox (21 March) the Sun rose directly between its two top-mounted shrines, with ceremonies held there in dedication of it.

From their ability to navigate by the position of the stars, through to their creation of solar calendar and onto their construction of temples in perfect alignment so that the Sun's rays shone focussed on their summit during the equinox, the Aztecs were truly expert astronomers. Astronomy was practised primarily by Aztec nobility and priests with the latter using dedicated observatories within temples to track the movements of celestial bodies.

By harnessing the knowledge of the celestial cycles, the Aztecs could also use astronomy to

Much of what we know about the Aztecs is from their own writings and records

track the length of a solar year and lunar month, as well as determine the duration of Venus's orbit and the prediction of any solar or lunar eclipses. According to depictions in Aztec codices, they also became extremely skilled at timing the appearances of comets and asteroids and often marked such occasions with ritualistic events.

Of course, the most practical everyday application of Aztec astronomy was in their construction of a calendar, which included both a 365-day annual solar calendar as well as 260-day divination calendar (for a detailed explanation see 'The Aztec Calendar' boxout). The former calendar was physically manifested in Tenochtitlan as the Calendar Stone, displayed so that all could keep track of the passing of time.

Formidable farmers

One area where the Aztecs utilised their scientific and technological ingenuity to maximum effect was in their farming practices. Living in and around large swamps and lake-heavy areas of Central America, the Aztecs designed and employed terracing and artificial island systems to ensure crops had optimal land area to grow. They built aqueducts and dug channels to ensure crops were irrigated, and crafted their own tools and basic farming machines for crop planting and harvesting. The most common crop grown by the Aztecs was maize (corn), but due to their mastery of the art many other crops such as squashes, beans, avocados and guavas were delivered. With their largest city-state of Tenochtitlan built in the middle of Lake Texcoco and housing north of 200,000 people, a large and consistent food supply was necessary for the Aztecs. Their mastery of irrigation and the chinampas construction system meant that vast fields of produce were grown all-year-round, with maize, beans, squash and much more grown with a frequency unsurpassed on the continent.

The Aztecs also harnessed knowledge of nutrition, specifically in terms of the health of soils and water when used to grow crops. Indeed, the Aztecs operated one of the most advanced crop-rotation systems ever created: their knowledge that certain crops deplete the land of specific nutrients was used to ensure soils were always cycled for a new type of produce, granting

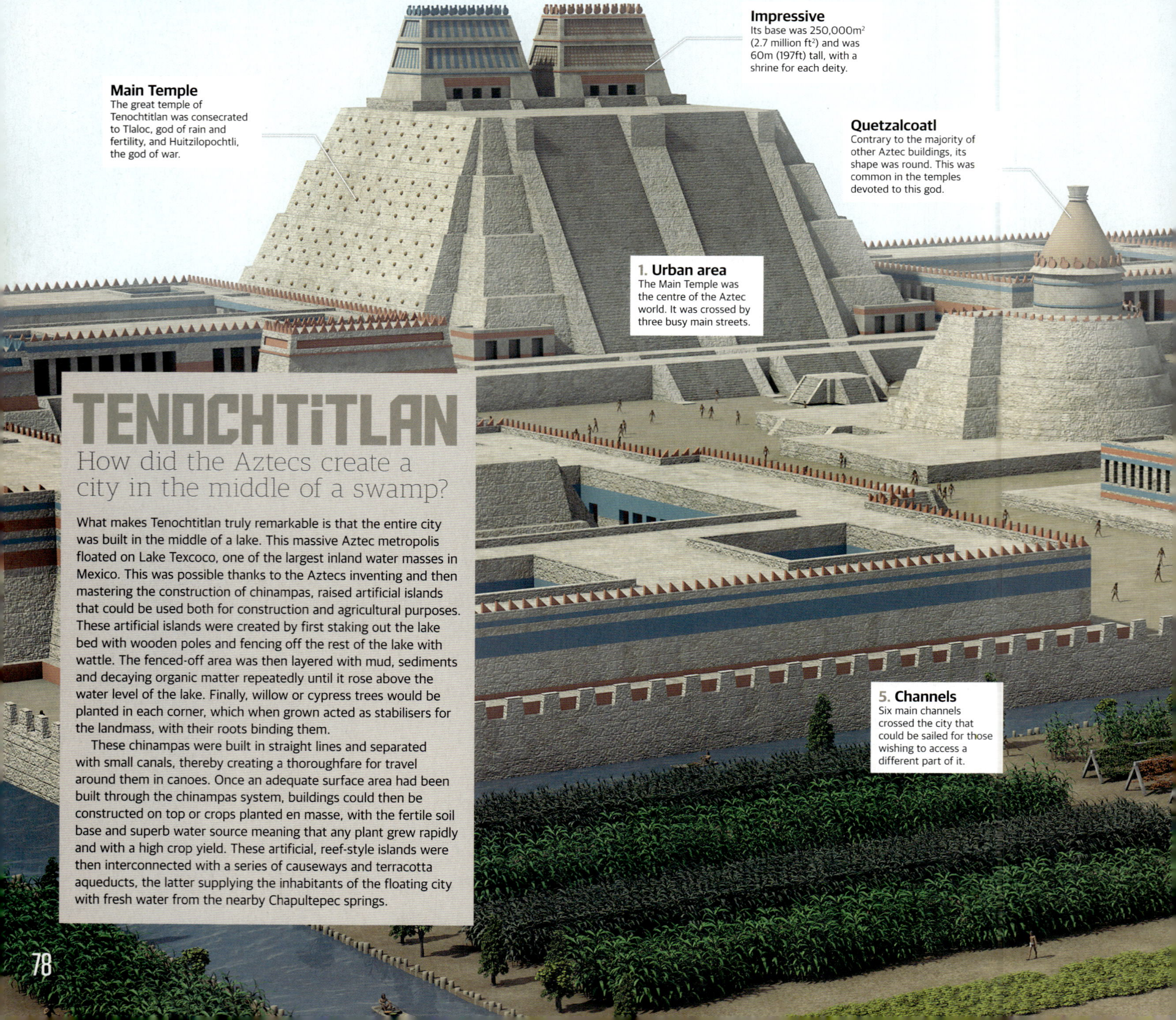

TENOCHTITLAN

How did the Aztecs create a city in the middle of a swamp?

What makes Tenochtitlan truly remarkable is that the entire city was built in the middle of a lake. This massive Aztec metropolis floated on Lake Texcoco, one of the largest inland water masses in Mexico. This was possible thanks to the Aztecs inventing and then mastering the construction of chinampas, raised artificial islands that could be used both for construction and agricultural purposes. These artificial islands were created by first staking out the lake bed with wooden poles and fencing off the rest of the lake with wattle. The fenced-off area was then layered with mud, sediments and decaying organic matter repeatedly until it rose above the water level of the lake. Finally, willow or cypress trees would be planted in each corner, which when grown acted as stabilisers for the landmass, with their roots binding them.

These chinampas were built in straight lines and separated with small canals, thereby creating a thoroughfare for travel around them in canoes. Once an adequate surface area had been built through the chinampas system, buildings could then be constructed on top or crops planted en masse, with the fertile soil base and superb water source meaning that any plant grew rapidly and with a high crop yield. These artificial, reef-style islands were then interconnected with a series of causeways and terracotta aqueducts, the latter supplying the inhabitants of the floating city with fresh water from the nearby Chapultepec springs.

GREAT TENOCHTITLAN

Towards 1325, the Aztec settled in the region of the Texcoco lake, south of Mexico valley. They built the city of Tenochtitlan on a long islet that reached a population of more than 200,000 inhabitants, the double of any European city of the time. The city was enlarged towards the nearby islands. It was divided into four neighbourhoods where the twenty clans or calpulli, that grouped the Aztec families, were distributed. Each calpulli was relatively autonomous; it had its own temples, schools and markets. Tens of canals crossed the city sailed by 50,000 reed boats every day and crossed by wooden bridges that were removed at night.

Location

The capital above the Texcoco lake

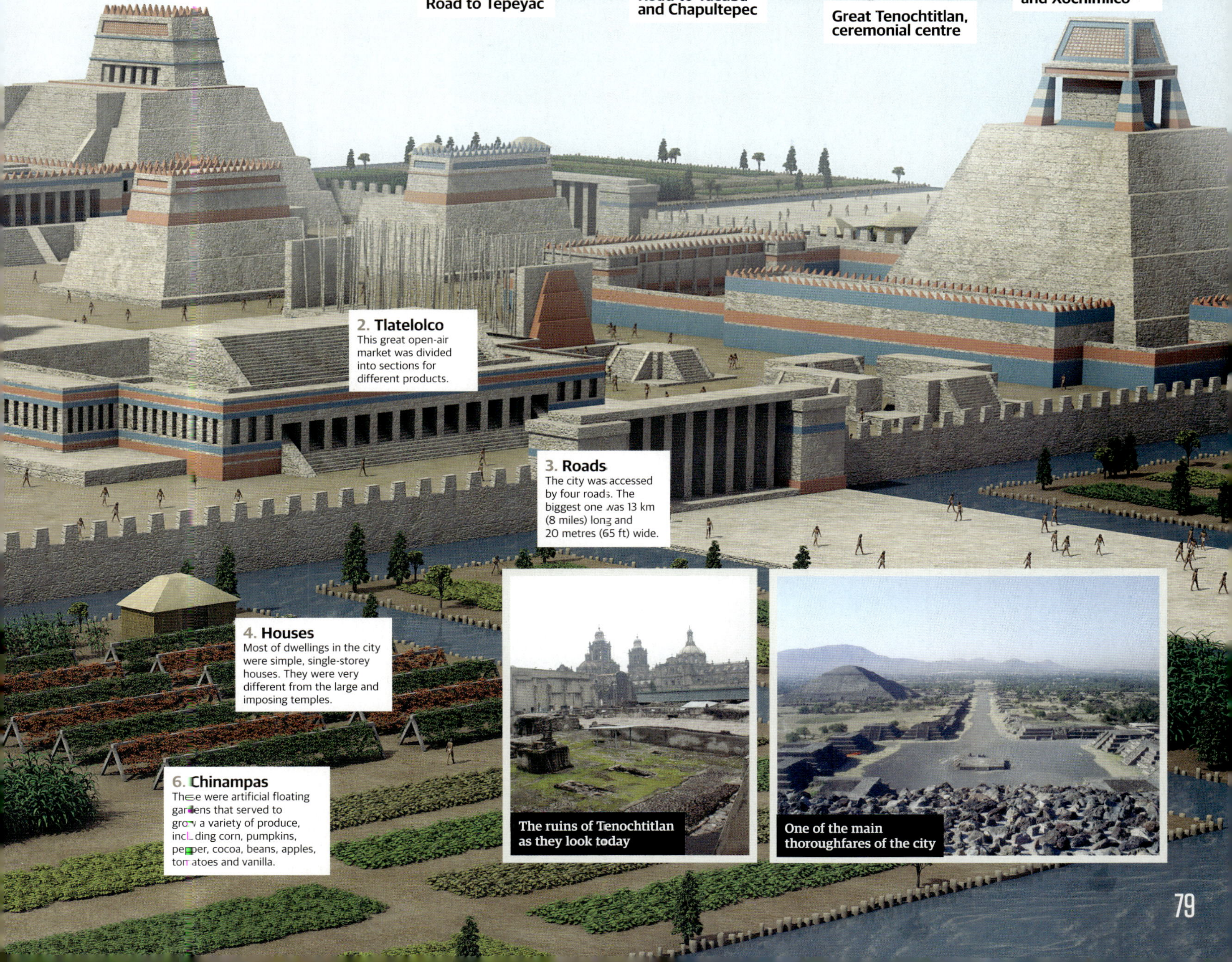

2. Tlatelolco
This great open-air market was divided into sections for different products.

3. Roads
The city was accessed by four roads. The biggest one was 13 km (8 miles) long and 20 metres (65 ft) wide.

4. Houses
Most of dwellings in the city were simple, single-storey houses. They were very different from the large and imposing temples.

6. Chinampas
These were artificial floating gardens that served to grow a variety of produce, including corn, pumpkins, pepper, cocoa, beans, apples, tomatoes and vanilla.

The ruins of Tenochtitlan as they look today

One of the main thoroughfares of the city

> "Aztecs granted prestige to the position of doctor and encouraged them to study the human body and potential remedies"

it time to recover. Further, specific crops were partnered with ones ensuring a nutritional balance within the planting area, with the combination ensuring that farms maximised crop yield for every square metre of land used. The Aztecs also grew many herbs within their systems, with these used in another specialist Aztec science; herbology.

Masters of medicine

Aztecs' understanding of medicinal science was incredibly advanced for the time. In a period where most western nations were still addressing illnesses with either prayer or misguided placebos, Aztec civilisation granted prestige to the position of doctor and encouraged them to study the human body and potential remedies in depth. Among these studies, those of plants and their medicinal effects were central, from which Aztec doctors fashioned antispasmodic medications capable of preventing muscle spasms during surgery, according to codices such as the Codex Barberini, commonly referred to as the 'Aztec Herbal.' This was primarily achieved through the use of the passion flower. Other inventions included organic paste painkillers, liquid rubber for curing earaches and ground obsidian for the sealing of wounds.

Aztec physicians became the most skilled herbalists in the world, thanks to their in-depth study of the human body and their environment. Indeed, along with the establishment of hospitals, Aztec doctors were encouraged to undertake research, studying the effects of plants grown in large communal gardens. On top of this scientific approach, Aztec doctors accrued significant general medical knowledge that today we take for granted, including that people should not look at eclipses to prevent against vision damage, steam baths could cleanse the skin and sinuses and that specific foods were better for the human body than others.These vast banks of knowledge allowed the Aztecs to scientifically and technologically surpass many of Earth's other ancient cultures, and in a fraction of the time, with the Mesoamerican peoples taking mere centuries to build a society the others – such as Ancient Egypts – took thousands of years to build.

The secrets of science that they uncovered have, on the whole, withstood the test of time, with salvaged knowledge from the ancient culture leading to further developments in their field and contributing greatly to the sciences as they exist today.

How do we know this?

Our information about the Aztecs comes from a combination of surviving Aztec documents, such as the codices Borbonicus and Boturini, which were written by Aztec priests, Spanish reports on the Aztecs from their conquest of the region in the 16th century, and excavated archaeological evidence. Of the sources, the primary Aztec codices are the most useful, with rich details about their calendar, rituals, ceremonies and tradition derived from them. Unfortunately, codices from pre-conquest Mexico are few in number due to the Spanish burning many of them when they took over, so today decoding what few codices remain is crucial to furthering our understanding.

EL TEMPLO MAYOR

How did the Aztecs build this most awesome of citadels?

Originally constructed in 1325 and then added to and extended six times afterwards, the massive Templo Mayor citadel of Tenochtitlan was surely one of the wonders of the ancient world, towering over the Aztec city state's other structures at close to 30 m (90 ft) in height. Indeed, by the time it was eventually sacked and destroyed by the Spanish conquistadors of the 16th century, the pyramid temple consisted of four steep sloped terraces topped with a great platform measuring 80 x 100 m (262 x 328 ft), with a further two sets of stone stairs leading to a pair of grand shrines. Every part of the temple was decorated with carvings and surrounding it lay a vast stone-slabbed precinct that measured 4,000 m^2 (43,000 ft^2) filled with balustrades and further decorative aspects. Not bad considering it was constructed by slaves and working-class craftsmen under the direction of a ruling class of learned architects and mathematicians.

Indeed, El Templo Mayor was arguably the culmination of the advanced construction techniques mastered by the Aztecs over their civilisation's tenure in Central America. From the sculpting of vast blocks of stone from dedicated quarries for its terraces – the Aztecs were the first culture to industrialise this process in Central and South America – to utilising scaffolds and rope lifts to transport men and tools up its structure and onto the expert craftsmanship that allowed them to carve vast ornamental dragons and mix polychrome paints to decorate the temple's exterior, El Templo Mayor became the temple of temples. Indeed, if it were not for the sudden obliteration of their society by the Spanish conquistador Hernán Cortés, who knows how much higher and more complicated their temples could have grown?

PERICLES
Greek, 495 BCE-429 BCE

Brief Bio

At once a general, statesman, orator and scholar, Pericles' rule saw Athens' Golden Age, where democracy flourished and the arts blossomed. Pericles led Athens from around 461 BCE until his death. A brilliant politician, he embodied Greek democratic ideals and was the city's longest-serving ruler until he died from plague in 429 BCE.

Top 5 facts
PERICLES

A 'FOUNDER OF DEMOCRACY'
ANCIENT GREECE, 495-429 BCE

01 PARTHENON COMMISSIONER

One of the most iconic buildings of Ancient Greece, the Parthenon temple on Acropolis was commissioned by Pericles, as were many of the surrounding buildings of the site. It symbolises the height of Athenian power as well as that of the great leader who championed its construction.

02 He secured Athenian democracy

Pericles is remembered as a great orator and is famed for his speeches espousing the value of democracy. In an address during the Peloponnesian War he declared: "[The Athenian] constitution favours the many instead of the few; this is why it is called a democracy."

03 Early theatre patron

From early on in his career, Pericles patronised the theatre, including the tragedian Aeschylus. Later, in his attempts to promote Athenian culture, Pericles used state funds so poorer citizens could attend the theatre, subsidising their entry fee. He was also a friend of the playwright Sophocles.

04 He created an Athenian empire

During Pericles' rule, Athens became the foremost member of the Delian League, a group of hundreds of Greek city-states formed to oppose Persia's invading forces. This became an Athenian empire, establishing colonies in Italy and expanding into the Mediterranean.

05 He ruled almost unchallenged

Pericles' popularity with the citizens made it easy for him to remove political opponents, many of which, such as his predecessor Cimon, were exiled by popular vote or ostracism. Though he suffered accusations of corruption and tyranny himself, his political influence was such that he was only deposed once, briefly, during his entire rule.

DEATH OF THE SAMURAI

How Japan's warrior class was defeated

As the Sun crept over the mountains, only 40 samurai rebels felt its warmth touch them - the rest of their group had been killed over the previous months in a series of battles. Saigo Takamori, the leader of the rogue group of samurai, and formally a highly respected field marshal in the Imperial army, had been wounded in his leg and stomach during the fighting and so beseeched his friend, Beppu Shinsuke, to carry him to a quiet spot. Once there he committed seppuku - a form of suicide by disembowelment practiced by the samurai, which was considered an honourable way to die. With their leader dead and a force of around 30,000 Imperial forces commanded by General Yamagata and his technologically advanced weaponry close by, there seemed little hope for the warriors that for centuries had played a prominent role in Japanese society. Rather than suffer the shame of surrender, Beppu Shinsuke gathered the remaining samurai and led them - brandishing their swords fiercely - on a suicidal charge against the Imperial forces. The Gatling guns barked in the early morning air and cut the doomed men charging straight at them to pieces. The era of the samurai had thereby ended in a brutal yet emphatically memorable fashion.

For much of the previous 1,000 years it would have been unthinkable that the samurai would cease to exist as they had played such an important and vital role in Japanese society and seemed ingrained in the fabric of the country. However, the world in which the samurai lived was changing. Advances in technology aligned with Japan ending its isolationist ways and opening trade routes - and with it an exchange of knowledge and culture - signalled the beginning of the end for a proud warrior caste that did not want to, or see why it should, change its ways. In a world in which immense firepower from Gatling guns existed, pumping out an almost continuous stream of murderous bullets, and ships that could fire artillery on a town from a safe distance, were the samurai really such a valuable commodity anymore?

Although samurai developed a complex code of honour, rituals and ethics (Bushido) that meant being a samurai was a whole way of life, they originally came into existence and then prominence through their fighting skills. In 646CE the Taika reforms in Japan led to the country being dominated by a handful of large landowners and created a feudal system similar to that of medieval Europe. These large landowners needed their land to be protected from those who would take their crops or land. In this lied the origins of the samurai, as the men hired to provide protection slowly began to develop a code. After a succession of weak emperors, the Heian Dynasty began to lose control of the country and the warriors began to move into the power gap created. By 1100CE they held significant military and political power over the land.

This ushered in a golden period for the samurai and throughout the next centuries until the end of the Edo period (1603-1868CE) this warrior class was at the heart of Japanese life, as rival clans battled each other for control of the country and dominance. The Edo period saw greater peace and stability that meant many samurai were not needed for combat and so became teachers and members of government. Despite the decline in use of the samurai, they were still revered in society and were the only class allowed to carry swords, which was a mark of their rank. This period of peace may have reduced the key role of samurai in Japanese society, but it was nothing compared to what was to come. The world was experiencing political and social revolutions and against it a bow and arrow or a sword would be unable to hold back the tide of change that was washing in.

For Japan, this change began when in 1853 Commodore Matthew Perry of the United States entered Edo Bay (Tokyo Bay) to seek trade links. Japan had previously adopted an isolationist position, but some of the country's political elite began to realise that their country was lagging behind other nations in terms of technology - Japan had not industrialised - and modernisation was key

"In a world in which immense firepower from Gatling guns existed... were the samurai really such a valuable commodity anymore?"

THREE LEGENDARY SAMURAI

A fantastical illustration of Miyamoto Musashi slaying a giant creature

A 19th-century, Edo-period, woodblock print depicting Minamoto Tametomo

Saigo Takamori was the leader of what is held to be the last stand of the samurai

Miyamoto Musashi

It is believed that Musashi fought over 60 duels without loss and is credited with creating the two-sword fighting technique Nitoryu, where both a standard large sword and a smaller one are used. He began formal sword training very young and one of the books he wrote declares that he fought his first duel aged 13. Musashi was a skilled writer and painter and his text, *The Book of Five Rings*, covering martial arts and kenjutsu is still read to this day.

Minamoto Tametomo

Samurai weren't just deadly swordsmen - many were also highly skilled with a bow and arrow and Tametomo was one of the best proponents of this. Supposedly he was born with a left arm six inches longer than his right, meaning he could generate greater power on his shots by drawing the bowstring further back. The great bowman committed seppuku in 1170CE after he was captured during battle and the tendons in his left arm were severed, thus rendering him useless as an archer.

Saigo Takamori

Although he is famous for leading the revolt against the Imperial army, Takamori actually had a part in establishing the new government as in 1867CE his troops supported the Emperor in the Meiji restoration and he was Imperial advisor to the new government. He became disillusioned with what he saw as the country's Westernisation, failure to invade Korea and the dismissing of samurai importance, so he eventually led a doomed revolt against the Imperial forces.

BUSHIDO – THE WARRIOR CODE

Loyalty

忠義

Samurai developed in feudal Japan where they were employed by large landowners to protect their territory. Samurai were famously loyal to their masters and were expected to show complete obedience to them.

Integrity

義

One of the most important elements in the code – many samurai believed that without this the rest of the code would fall apart. Integrity is doing what the samurai believes is right without wavering, no mater what.

Courage

勇

Samurai were expected to show courage at all times and to commit seppuku to avoid capture. If they were in a position on the battlefield where they could not help their side, they were also expected to take their own life.

Mercy

仁

Samurai had the power of life and death in their hands –w if they felt that a peasant had offended their honour, even if they hadn't, they had the right to kill them. With such power mercy is an important part of the warrior code.

Respect

礼

Politeness and courtesy were a large part of samurai life and they were expected to show both to fellow samurai, as well as to their masters and superiors. Failure to adhere to this tenet was a risky and often lethal business.

Honour

名誉

Fear of disgrace hung over the head of all samurai. Any loss of honour often resulted in long and deadly blood feuds between rival factions. In many cases, committing ritual seppuku was the only honourable option left.

Honesty

真

It was held that true samurai disdained money and that having wealth led to luxury, which was seen as a menace to manhood. The Confucian philosophy of the samurai dictated that simplicity was the only way of the warrior.

in order to compete with other world powers. At this point Japan was still, in practice, ruled by an emperor, but the real power resided with the shogun. Understanding that the country needed drastic change, two daimyos (powerful territorial lords) formed an alliance against the ruling shogun and aimed to give the Emperor genuine power. The ruling shogun, Tokugawa Yoshinobu resigned from his position but had no intention of giving up real power and when Emperor Meiji issued an Imperial decree dissolving his house, he sent his samurai army to the Imperial city of Kyoto with the aim of deposing the emperor.

As swords from the two opposing factions clashed and clinked in battle, the fate of the country hung in the balance. The battle of Toba-Fushimi on January 27 1868CE ended in defeat for the shogun and lit the touch paper for the Boshin war that lasted until May 1869CE. The war followed the same path as the battle and the Emperor, with more-modern weaponry and tactics, prevailed. With victory secured, the young Emperor – allegedly influenced by his advisors – began the process of reshaping Japan. Social reforms such as universal elementary education for children were introduced, as was investment in heavy machinery to breathe new life into their manufacturing industry. There was also a focus on Westernisation, with an edict issued in 1871CE encouraging the adoption of Western-style clothing and food. Arguably the biggest change that affected the samurai though was the forming of a modern conscript army, which meant that their role as the primary fighting men in the country was disappearing and that they were not the only strata of society allowed to bear weapons. These new weapons – guns and rifles – required much less skill to operate than those of the samurai and meant that a peasant with a gun could now conceivably defeat a samurai in combat.

If the implementation of a conscript army indicated that the days of the samurai were slipping away, then the next decree by the Emperor in 1876CE left no one in any doubt; samurai were banned from wearing swords. Their position as a special class had ended. Even though their position of prestige had been in

> "As word spread of the rebellion, samurai and peasants from across Japan flocked to join the cause"

Samurai during the Boshin war period

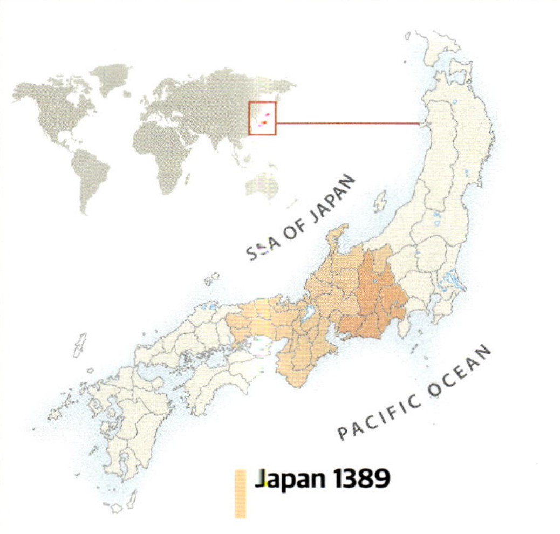

SAMURAI

Samurai were warriors that emerged in Japan with the appearance of the shogunate in the 12th century. Trained in the art of war, they cultivated a philosophy of life called Bushido

Social structure of feudal Japan

Japanese society was organised into clans or families who disputed over farmland

Emperor
Of divine origin, the emperor did not care much about politics or the economy.

Shogun
Shogun were military leaders with political and economic power.

Daimyo
Powerful court nobles who held large domains and collected ichimangoku (salaries).

Samurai
In service to a daimyo, samurai owed him absolute obedience and loyalty.

Craftsmen, villagers, merchants
Under the protection of a daimyo.

Ronin
Wandering, masterless samurai who were often dishonoured and outcast from society.

Kabuto
Crash helmet of iron.

Mempo
Protective masks painted with fierce faces were used to frighten the enemy.

Yodare-kake
Throat protection.

Sode
Shoulder protector.

Do
Breastplate which allowed large and free movements.

Kote
Arm protector.

Tekko
Hand protector.

Kusari
Kusari protected the upper thigh and was made from lacquered iron plates connected together with several silk cords.

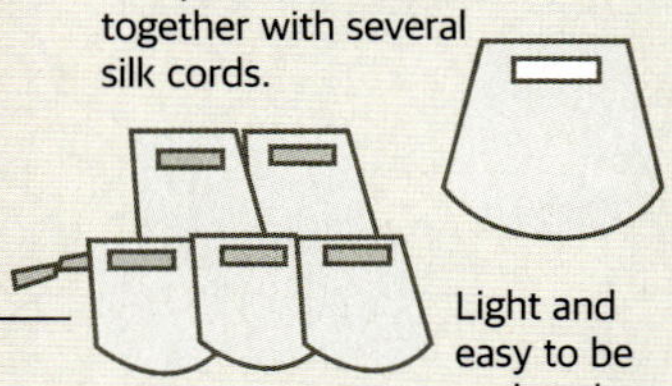

Light and easy to be replaced

Haidate
Haidate protected the lower part of the thigh and was worn under the kusazuri.

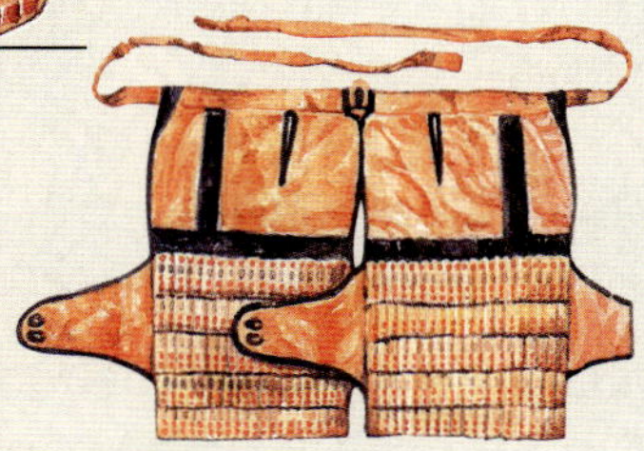

Suneate
Made from leather and cloth, suneate were tied with cords around the calves to protect them.

Sandals

The warrior

His aim was to achieve an heroic death in battle.

Weapons

Each warrior wore two swords as a symbol of distinction of their samurai caste.

Swords were initially straight. Later the curved shape was preferred, in the search for an even stronger edge.

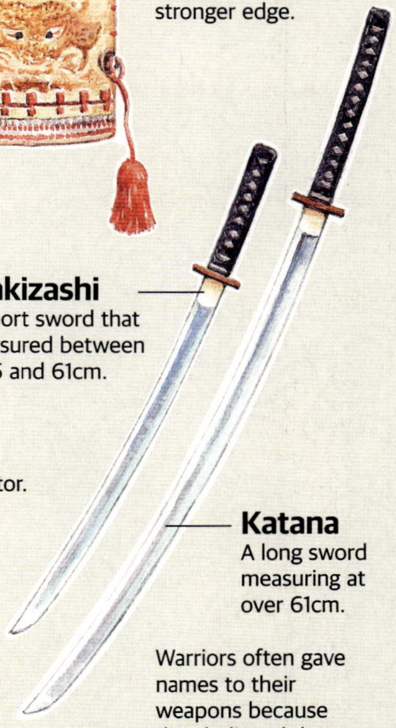

Wakizashi
A short sword that measured between 30.5 and 61cm.

Katana
A long sword measuring at over 61cm.

Warriors often gave names to their weapons because they believed they were the soul of their fighting capacity.

Bushido code

Bushido means 'way of the warrior-knight' and required an almost religious dedication to military life. This code set moral standards and behavioural patterns.

Seppuku

Only samurai carried out this ritual suicide in preference to a dishonorable death.

Samurai cut their own stomach and then a trusted friend cut off their heads.

steadily decline, for many samurai this was the final insult. The Japanese leaders felt they needed to modernise to avoid being left behind and the samurai were simply one of the casualties of war; the government believed that in their current form they belonged to a different era and had no relevance in this new Japan they were forging.

There were some samurai that adapted to this modernisation process and, for the good of the country, abandoned their old beliefs and tried to put themselves at the forefront of this new Japan. The government instigated a programme to rehabilitate samurai, help them find employment and try to place them at the head of enterprises, as they were more educated than the majority of the population. However, a group of samurai decided that the country was changing too fast and losing its culture and traditions. They were led by Saigo Takamori and decided to take a stand.

Saigo Takamori was a great bear of a man who stood nearly six-feet tall with a stout and sturdy frame. Born the son of a low-ranking samurai he had previously fallen into disgrace following the death of his lord and had been banned to a

> "Being unable to fight, Takamori did what honour dictated, as did the remaining samurai who charged into the bullets"

Imperial officers in their Western-style uniforms accept the surrender of un-uniformed rebels

marched on the well-fortified Kumamoto Castle and, with their samurai and peasant army armed with guns, surrounded the castle. For two bloody nights the army threw itself at the walls in a ferocious attempt to scale them, but the attacks were repelled time and again by gunfire and had no co-ordinated plan for how to breach the fortifications.

When a government relief force arrived and engaged with the rebels, several sharp clashes ensued before both sides retreated. The rebellion went on to last for six months and while both sides gained victories, the government army could replenish any lost forces much easier than the rebels, who were gradually ground down by superior technological firepower, such as warships. It is estimated that the Imperial forces lost more than 6,000 troops and had 10,000 wounded, while the much smaller samurai army had 7,000 casualties and 11,000 wounded. Following a series of engagements, the depleted rebel force sneaked into Kagoshima and took possession of a castle mountain in Shiroyma. It took the government troops several days to locate them but when they did, there was no doubt what the eventual outcome would be. Takamori organised a sake party for his closest friends, an impressive display of bloody-mindedness, as he must have known what was coming.

It was to be his last night alive, as at 3.00am Imperial forces stormed the mountain castle. By the time they were repelled, only 40 of the rebels were still alive and Takamori was badly injured. Being rendered unable to fight, Takamori did what honour dictated, as did the remaining samurai who charged into the bullets of the waiting Imperial army. The age of the samurai may have been extinguished that day, but it was done in such a way as to display perfectly all of the central ideals that had made this warrior class so legendary - honour, courage and loyalty.

Ancient Maya

MAYAN CIVILISATION
MESOAMERICA 1800BCE-900CE

Who were they?
The Maya were one of the most prominent ancient civilisations of the cultural Americas. Like the Aztecs who later dominated the area in the 14th century, the Mayan race left behind vast and elaborate stone cities and documented evidence of their existence.

Class and society
Society was split into rigidly defined class structures and professions: the nobility, priesthood, common people and slaves. They were ruled by kings, or 'kuhul ajaw' (holy gods), who were viewed as semi-deity figures and representatives of the gods.

Where were they?
The Mayan civilisation spanned the breadth of ancient Mesoamerica, the name of the area that encompassed the Yucatán Peninsula and modern-day Guatemala, as well as parts of Belize, Honduras, El Salvador and a few of the states of Mexico.

They loved sport

The Maya even had their own ball game, which involved bouncing a rubber ball through hoops located alongside a massive stone court. The games had enormous cultural significance, and are believed to have involved human sacrifices as part of the occasion.

Sacrifice and torture

There is also a darker side to Mayan civilisation. There were frequent bloody civil wars between rival Mayan city states, and torture, self-mutilation and human sacrifice were vital components of their religious festivals, with bloodshed being believed to be necessary to sate the Gods.

Huge monolithic Mayan stone calendar carvings such as this have been discovered throughout the centuries

How advanced were they?

Evidence suggests the Maya were more advanced than other American civilisations of the time, notably in the fields of astronomy and mathematics, creating a 365-day calendar and using the number zero. They also wrote in hieroglyphics and made paper from bark.

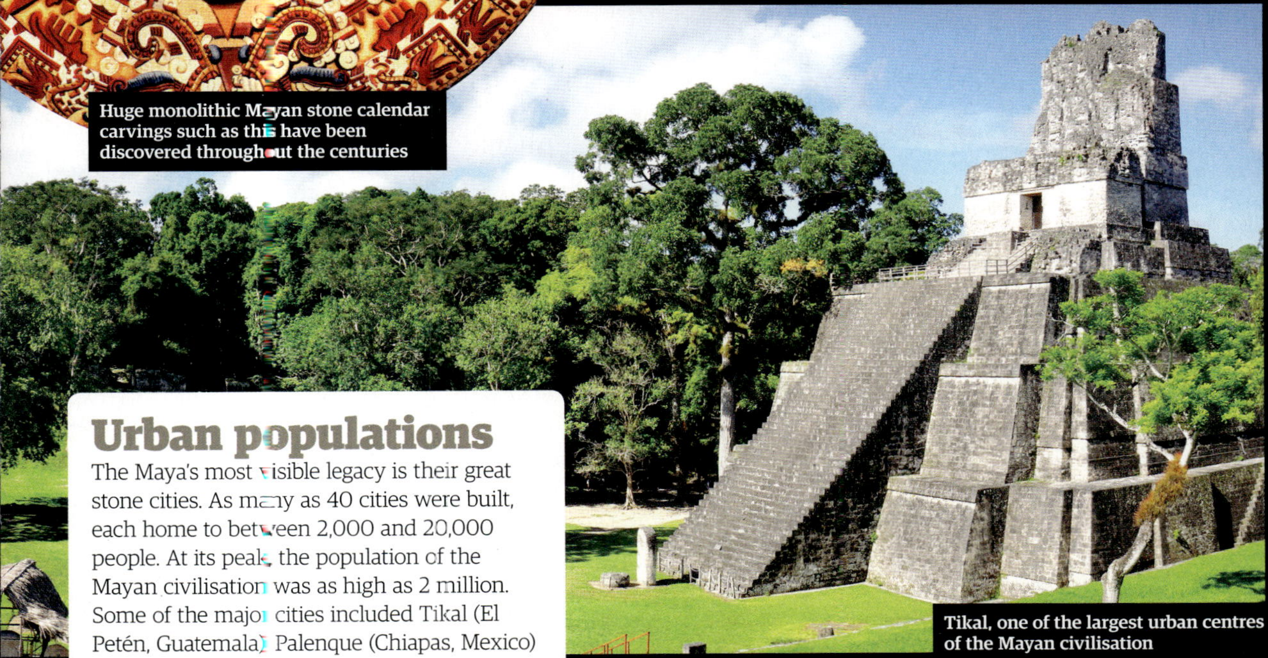

Tikal, one of the largest urban centres of the Mayan civilisation

Urban populations

The Maya's most visible legacy is their great stone cities. As many as 40 cities were built, each home to between 2,000 and 20,000 people. At its peak, the population of the Mayan civilisation was as high as 2 million. Some of the major cities included Tikal (El Petén, Guatemala), Palenque (Chiapas, Mexico) and Quiriguá (Izabal, Guatemala).

Trade and commerce

Much of the Mayan civilisation was based on using local resources, like the rainforests, to their advantage, participating in long-distance trading with other Mesoamerican races. Routes were established stretching from the Gulf of Mexico to Colombia, in addition to sea routes to the Caribbean islands.

The unexplained apocalypse

Between 800 and 900 CE, the Maya fell into decline. Cities were abandoned until the civilisation had all but vanished. The reason for this remains inconclusive, but while some blame overpopulation and war, recent theories suggest it was a weather phenomenon such as drought.

Key figures

Pakal the Great
603-683 CE

This Mayan emperor ruled for 80 years. He was behind some of Maya's finest architecture.

K'inich Kan B'alam II
635-702 CE

K'inich Kan B'alam II was the son of Pakal. He was responsible for building the famous three-temple complex in Palenque.

Jasaw Chan K'awiil I
682-734 CE

The ruler of Tikal (one of the biggest Mayan cities) who cemented strength with victory against rival city Calakmul.

Yik'in Chan K'awiil
734-766 CE

Yik'in is the son of Jasaw. He consolidated his father's reign by greatly expanding the great city of Tikal.

Itzamná
N/A

The Mayan god of agriculture, creation, writing and healing was Itzamná, which roughly translates as 'iguana house'.

Major events

Mayan alphabet
700 BCE

The first developed system of written language is introduced among Mayans in the pre-Columbian Americas.

Hierarchical system
300 BCE

The hierarchical system of ruling with kings and nobles is adopted by the Mayans.

Teotihuacán built
100 BCE

This was the largest and most significant of the Mayan cities. It was the trading centre of Mesoamerica.

Destruction of Teotihuacán
750 CE

An unknown event – possibly a fire during a civil war – destroys the city, marking the beginning of the decline.

End of the Mayans
900 CE

The ancient city of Tikal is abandoned, which indicates the end of the Classic Mayan civilisation.

ALEXANDER THE GREAT

At the head of the world's most feared fighting force, Alexander the Great took for himself a vast empire through the sword, and has been called a hero, tyrant and a god

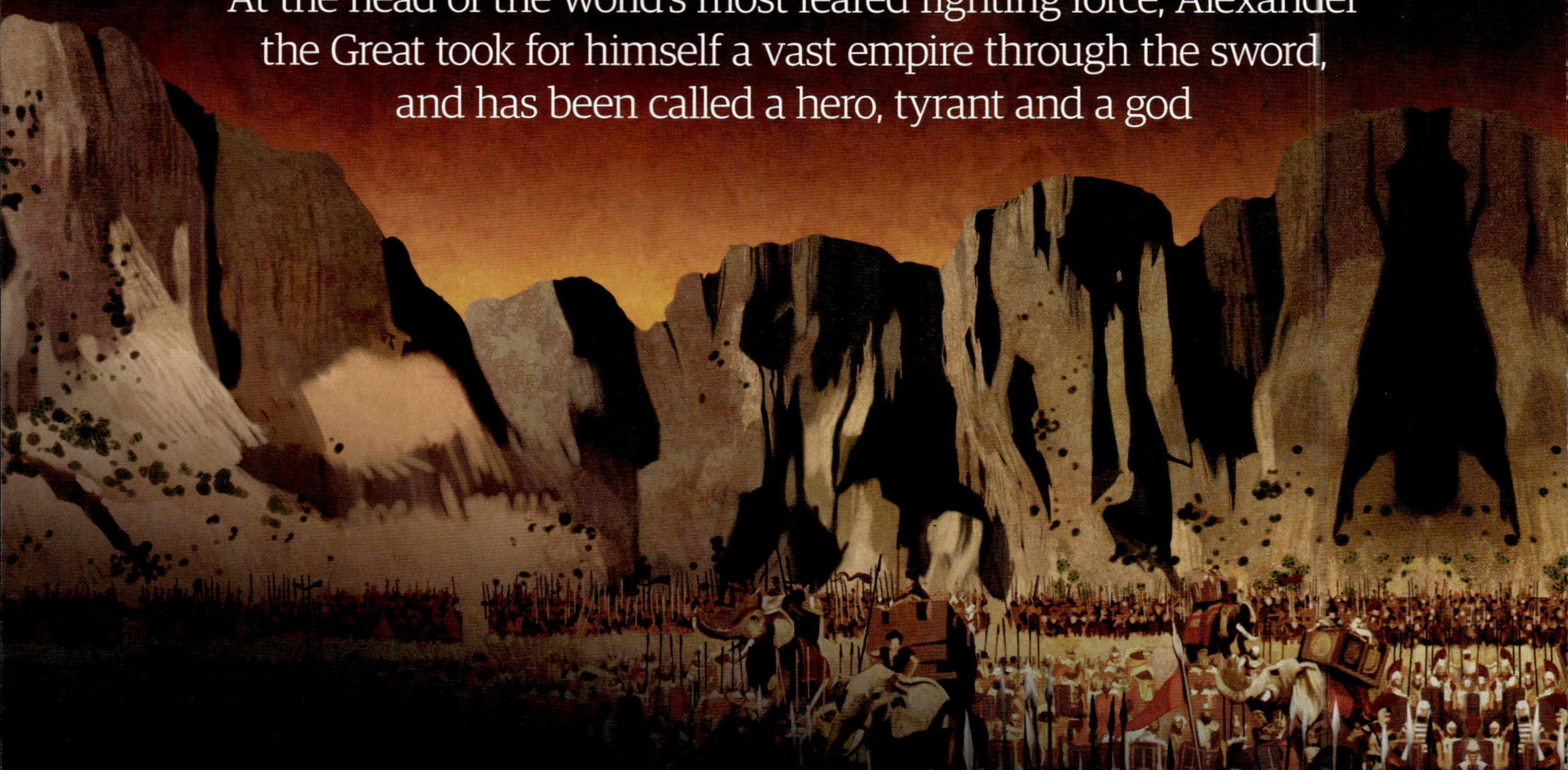

The king died quickly, his white robes soaked red. The laughter and rejoicing of a royal marriage - the wedding of his daughter - had quickly turned to screams and wails of lament as Pausanias, a member of the king's personal guard, turned on his master, driving a dagger between his ribs. Tripping on a vine as he fled the scene for his getaway horse, the assassin was brutally stabbed to death by the furious spears of pursuing guards. Philip II died as he had lived: awash with blood and surrounded by intrigue. His legacy would leave bloody footprints across the whole of Central Asia and the Middle East.

Over a 23-year reign from 359 to 336 BCE, the king of Macedon - a mountainous land overlapping modern northern Greece, Albania, Bulgaria and Macedonia - had gone from ruler of a barbarous backwater of tribal highlanders to the overlord of the fractious Greek kingdoms and city-states. Bringing his rival monarchs in line through war, military alliance and marriage, Philip II had reformed the Macedonian army into one of the most feared fighting forces in the ancient world, with a view to bloodying their most hated foes, the Achaemenid Empire of Persia, which had humbled and humiliated the Greeks in the Greco-Persian Wars a century earlier. Aged just 20, Alexander III of Macedon - soon to be remembered as Alexander the Great - took the throne as the head of a military machine on the brink of war and legendary status, and gleefully drove it full throttle over the edge.

Alexander had been groomed for greatness from birth, but he was no pampered prince. Tutored by the austere Leonidas, who forbade all luxury, the general Lysimachus and the philosopher Aristotle, Alexander was proficient with weapons, horse riding and playing the lyre, and an expert in ethics, philosophy and the skills of debate. He trained daily in pankration, an Ancient Greek martial art, which focused on savage grapples, punches, kicks and choke holds. A Renaissance man before the Renaissance, he was schooled in the skills to conquer and the knowledge to rule. At 16 he had governed Macedon as regent while his father warred far from home, the young heir putting down rebellious tribes in Thrace and founding a whole new city, Alexandropolis - the first of many that would bear his name.

Like so many civilisations before and after them, the Ancient Greeks loved to gossip. Philip's death, they said, was an act of revenge from his scorned lover Pausanias, but two other people immediately benefited: Olympias, mother of Alexander and once-favoured wife of Philip, had been in danger of losing her status to a younger

ALEXANDER THE GREAT

Greek, 356-323 BCE

Brief Bio

Becoming king of Macedon after his father's murder, Alexander led the Greeks into war against the powerful Persian Empire. With charisma and cunning, he led from the frontline to create an empire that stretched from Libya to India, creating a new golden age for Hellenic culture.

A picture showing Alexander the Great suppressing a rebellion in Greece

bride; and Alexander himself, who promptly executed all other contenders for the crown and crushed rebellions across Greece. Olympias, too, set about consolidating her power, having Cleopatra Eurydice, her replacement as consort to the dead king, and her baby daughter burned alive.

The dubious heroes of myth were Alexander's own blueprint for greatness. With legendary figures on both sides of the family tree, it was hard not to be convinced of his own special destiny. His father's bloodline claimed descent from Hercules - the son of Zeus and bull-wrestling demigod of Twelve Labours fame - while his mother's family looked up to Achilles, the all-but-invulnerable champion of the fabled Siege of Troy. Omens and portents prefigured every decision, but as much as this ambitious new king gave every appearance of being a slave to destiny - looking for meaning in flights of birds and consulting oracles at every turn - he steered destiny himself, consciously building a legend that would lift his accomplishments well beyond those of his father and into the same world of the legendary journeys and heroic battles that had once inspired him. In just shy of a decade, he crushed the life out of the once-mighty Persian state and expanded the borders of his domain from Libya to India to create a mighty empire.

Fittingly, this conquest began with some mythical brand management. Picking up where Philip II's army of invasion had been poised, Alexander crossed the Dardanelles - the narrow channel connecting the Black Sea to the Mediterranean, and Europe from Asia Minor - in early 334 BCE with 47,000 soldiers and mercenaries from across Macedon and the Greek kingdoms. Leaping from his warship in full ceremonial armour, vast plumed helmet and golden breastplate, the emperor-to-be sent a spear whistling through the air to crash into the undefended soil of Asia Minor. It was the first blow in a war that would claim for Alexander over 200,000 square miles of land and leave between 75,000 and 200,000 dead.

> "He trained in pankration - an Ancient Greek martial art, which focused on savage grapples, punches and kicks"

The coastline of what is now Turkey was littered with Greek cities ruled by the Persian invaders, and of them Troy had particular significance for Alexander. The alleged site of his maternal ancestor Achilles' most celebrated victory and tragic death, Alexander carried with him on his journey the story of the Trojan War, Homer's epic *Iliad* (a gift from his tutor Aristotle), and quoted from it often. First, he had the tomb of Achilles opened so he could pay tribute, then riding to a nearby temple of Athena, the Greek goddess of wisdom, the Macedon king was shown what they claimed were the weapons of Achilles. There, he took down a shield, replacing it with his own. Alexander wasn't merely content sharing a fanciful familial association with Achilles; he wanted to rival him, visiting this site of bloodshed and heroism, and taking the mantle of one of Ancient Greece's greatest heroes.

Was it a propaganda stunt that spurred on his army, or did he believe it? His fierce pragmatism and ambition would suggest both - a dangerous and unpredictable combination that made him one of the battlefield's most iconic generals.

First meeting the Persians in battle in 334 BCE, Alexander quickly established a formula for swift and decisive victory at the Battle of the Granicus, just outside of his beloved Troy. Leading from the front ranks, a feint drew the stronger Persian units and their battle-hardened Greek mercenaries out, spreading their line thin and allowing Alexander's cavalry to hammer through their scattered ranks. He was welcomed as a liberator by the Greek subjects of Asia Minor, and endeavoured to win over the local population too. Claiming to distrust tyrants, he appointed local rulers and allowed them relative independence, but with a new centralised tax system he ensured their autonomy was reliant upon his handouts.

With Persia's control of the vast expanse of Asia Minor resting on its superior navy, Alexander opted to scatter his own vessels rather than fight a sea war he couldn't win, and marched down the coast to take the enemy's largest naval port, Halicarnassus - now Bodrum in Turkey - by land, forcing his way through the walls until the Persians

BATTLE OF THE GRANICUS (334 BCE)

Alexander's first victory against the Persian Empire

The first real clash between Persian troops and Alexander's newly minted invasion force remains the best example of his signature battle tactic.

Using heavy cavalry to prise apart the weakest part of the enemy line while his finely drilled infantry kept the bulk of the enemy tangled up on their spears, it relied upon the professionalism of Macedon's army, as well as the unique talents of its core units.

It showed that Alexander knew how best to use the forces that his father had amassed.

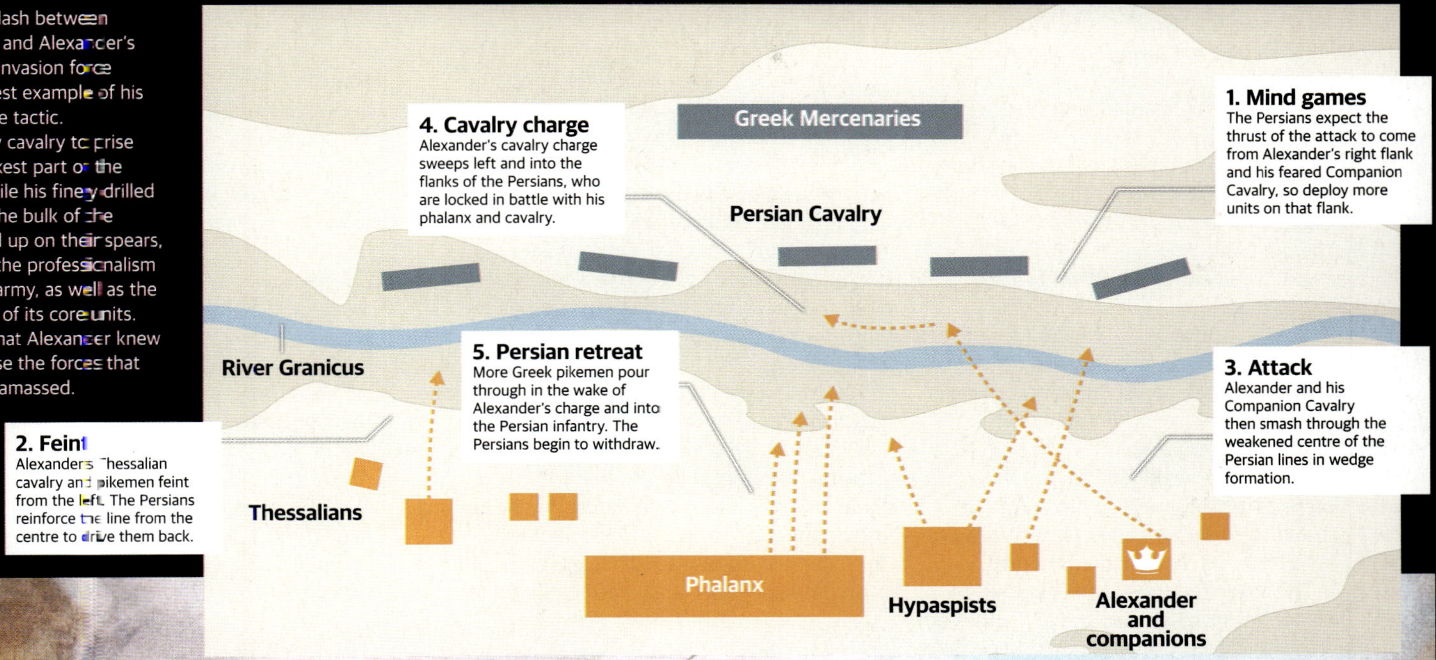

The Battle of the River Granicus, in which Alexander secured his first victory over the Persian Empire

had to abandon their own city. After passing through Cappadocia with scarcely any resistance thanks to incompetent local governors in 333 BCE, Darius III, the Persian Shahanshah - king of kings - could stomach this embarrassment no longer, and with an army that outnumbered the Greeks by two to one, confronted Alexander at the Battle of Issus. Were the king to fail here then Darius' army would be able to link up with his powerful navy and Alexander's whole campaign, resting as it did on his thin line of victories down the coast, would be wiped out and all dreams of Greek civilisation free from the menaces of its aggressive Eastern neighbour would spill out into the dust like so much wasted Macedonian blood. At Issus, like many battles before and after, Alexander rode up and down his ranks of assembled men to deliver an address worthy of heroes, playing on old glories and grudges.

"He excited the Illyrians and Thracians by describing the enemy's wealth and treasures, and the Greeks by putting them in mind of their wars of old, and their deadly hatred towards the Persians," wrote the historian Justin in the 3rd century CE. "He reminded the Macedonians at one time of their conquests in Europe, and at another of their desire to subdue Asia, boasting that no troops in the world had been found a match for them, and assuring them that this battle would put an end to their labours and crown their glory."

With shock etched upon his face, Darius fled the battlefield as the Greek charge cut through his ranks like a scythe, with Alexander at its head, crashing straight through the Persian flanks and then into their rearguard. With their king gone they began a chaotic and humiliating retreat. With only one Persian port left - Tyre, in what is now Lebanon - and the hill fort of Gaza in modern Palestine both falling in 332 BCE, the thinly stretched Achaemenid defences west of Babylon quickly crumbled or withdrew before the relentless march of Alexander.

Unexpectedly, he then turned his attention not east toward the enemy's exposed heart, but west in the direction of Egypt and Libya. They, like the Greek colonies of Asia Minor, would welcome him as a saviour. With no standing army and whole swathes of the country in the hands of Egyptian rebels, the Persian governor handed over control of the province outright. The last set of invaders had disrespected their gods, so perhaps the Egyptians were keen to take advantage of Alexander's vanity and safeguard their faith by placing this new warlord right at the heart of it. Maybe, too, Alexander had seen how illusionary Persian authority was in Egypt, and wanted to try a different tack. He may have been one of the world's greatest generals, but he knew the sword was not the only path to acquiring new territory.

Riding out to the famous Oracle of Amun - the Egyptian answer to Zeus - at the Siwa oasis, Alexander was welcomed into the inner sanctum of this ancient temple, an honour usually afforded only to the ordained priests of Amun, while his entourage was forced to wait in the courtyard. The exact details of Alexander's exchange with the Oracle remain a mystery, but the end result was unambiguous. Alexander was now more than merely a hero of legend. Even the myth of Achilles reborn could scarcely contain his ambition, and he declared himself the son of Zeus. His worship spread across Egypt, where he was raised to the rank of Pharaoh. This didn't sit well with Alexander's countrymen, but here at least, the king didn't push it.

"[Alexander] bore himself haughtily towards the barbarians," recalled the army's official historian Plutarch, "and like one fully persuaded of his divine birth and parentage, but with the Greeks it was within limits and somewhat rarely that he assumed his own divinity." Despite his 'haughtiness', Alexander had been raised on tales of the Egyptian gods from his mother, and Greeks - the philosopher Plato among them - had long journeyed to this ancient land to study in what they regarded as the birthplace of civilisation. Standing amid the great pyramids and temples, the 25-year-old Alexander either saw around him an ancient power to be held in great respect or feats of long-dead god-kings that he had to better.

The result was the city of Alexandria, planned in detail by the king, from wide boulevards and great temples to defences and plumbing. Construction began in 331 BCE, and it remains the second-largest city and largest seaport in Egypt, linking the king's new world to his old one, both by trade across the Mediterranean and by culture. In making Alexandria the crossroads between two great civilisations, a great centre of learning where Greek and Egyptian religion, medicine, art, mathematics and philosophy could be bound together was created, and the city came to symbolise the

> "The power-drunk Alexander burnt the palace to the ground in, it is believed, retaliation for the sack of Athens"

A LAND SOAKED IN BLOOD

How Alexander's mighty empire grew year-by-year and some of the cities founded in his wake...

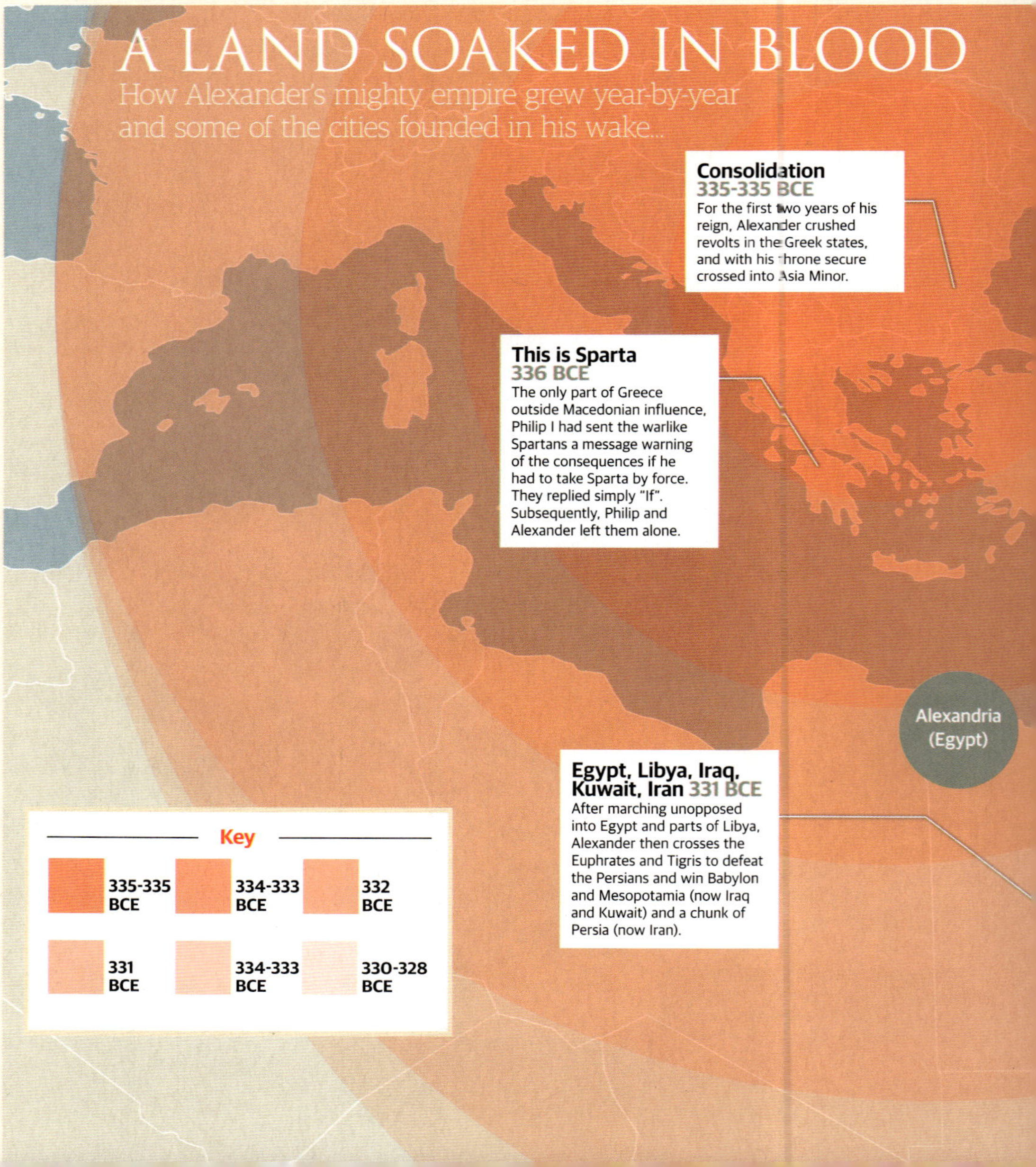

Consolidation
335-335 BCE
For the first two years of his reign, Alexander crushed revolts in the Greek states, and with his throne secure crossed into Asia Minor.

This is Sparta
336 BCE
The only part of Greece outside Macedonian influence, Philip I had sent the warlike Spartans a message warning of the consequences if he had to take Sparta by force. They replied simply "If". Subsequently, Philip and Alexander left them alone.

Egypt, Libya, Iraq, Kuwait, Iran 331 BCE
After marching unopposed into Egypt and parts of Libya, Alexander then crosses the Euphrates and Tigris to defeat the Persians and win Babylon and Mesopotamia (now Iraq and Kuwait) and a chunk of Persia (now Iran).

better aspects of Alexander's nature, his desire for education and learning and his patronage. Darker days, though, lay ahead.

Like an angel of death, Alexander turned from his 'liberation' of the Achaemenid Empire's downtrodden subjects and drove east with a vengeance. Now in the belly of the beast, Alexander's less heroic qualities were beginning to show themselves with greater regularity - an arrogance, cruelty and obsessive drive that had he failed in his conquest, would have been remembered as the madness of a tyrant rather than the drive of a king.

Breaking out of a pincer movement to defeat Darius again at the Battle of Gaugamela in 331 BCE, Alexander seized Babylonia. Provincial rulers loyal to the humiliated king of kings promptly surrendered. With his authority crumbling, Darius was stabbed by one of his generals, Bessus, and left by the roadside, where pursuing Greek scouts found him in 330 BCE. Overcome with pity - and perhaps respect for this foe they had chased across mountains and deserts - they offered the dying king of kings water from a nearby spring. In declaring himself Shahanshah, Bessus's throne was

A picture depicting Alexander founding Alexandria, which would become the ancient world's most prosperous city

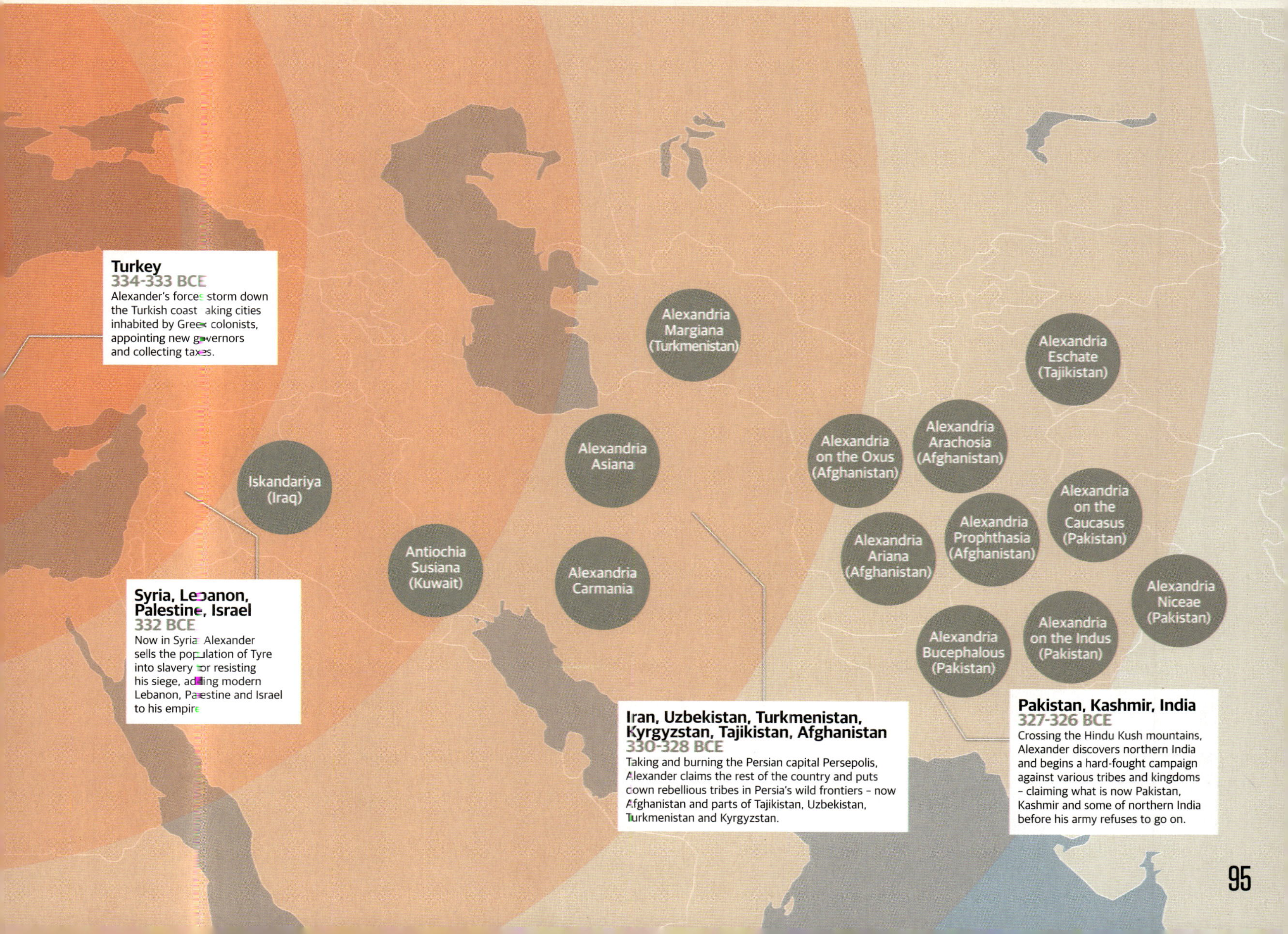

ALEXANDER'S ARMY

How the Ancient Greeks fought and conquered

1. Companion cavalry

Strengths

Well trained, wedge formation made turning easier, heavy bronze armour.

Weaknesses

Vulnerable to tightly packed infantry.

How did Alexander deploy them?

Led by Alexander personally, the Companion Cavalry were the unstoppable knights of Macedonia. Usually stationed on the right flank, they would punch through the enemy lines with their xyston lances and then wheel round to charge the rear.

2. Thessalian Cavalry

Strengths

Well trained, diamond formation for manoeuvrability, variety of weapons.

Weaknesses

Lighter armour than most heavy cavalry.

How did Alexander deploy them?

Similar to the Companion Cavalry, the Thessalian Cavalry's lighter armour and shorter spears and javelins made them an effective defensive unit. Stationed on the left flank, they could go where they were needed to see off any attackers.

3. Hoplites

Hoplites were the basic foot soldier of the Greek states.

Strengths

Versatile and adaptable.

Weaknesses

Low training, light armour.

How did Alexander deploy them?

Hoplites were the citizen men-at-arms of the other Greek states and one of the army's main cornerstones. Versatile but not necessarily as well-trained or heavily armoured as other units, Hoplites were placed behind the phalanx to prevent the army being encircled.

4. Phalanx

Strengths

The phalanx formation is devastating against cavalry, well trained and fast moving.

Weaknesses

Vulnerable in the flanks and rear, lightly equipped.

How did Alexander deploy them?

Created by Alexander's father the well-drilled and fast-moving pikemen fought in the dreaded Macedonian phalanx with their 18-foot sarissa lance. Deployed in the centre of the battle line, the phalanx could rush forward to tie down enemy cavalry or infantry.

5. Hypaspists

The Hypaspists were Alexander's close-quarter shock troops.

Strengths

Versatile close combat specialists, well-trained veterans.

Weaknesses

Vulnerable to cavalry and massed infantry.

How did Alexander deploy them?

Macedonia's elite commandos, the Hypaspists carried large round shields, thrusting spears and swords, and were placed on the flank of the Foot Companions for their protection. Devastating in closed spaces.

BATTLE OF THE PERSIAN GATE (331 BCE)

Alexander turns defeat into victory to take the Persian capital

Failure could have left Alexander's Persia divided between the Macedonian king and usurper Bessus, vulnerable to revolt and invasion from central Asia.

Despite a rare crushing defeat in the bloody bottleneck of the Persian ambush, Alexander was able to make use of local knowledge, as well as his hardy skirmishers and turn the wild terrain in his favour, ambushing the Persians in turn and decimating them with his two forces. Historians have called this victory 'complete' and 'decisive' and it left him able to take the ancient capital of Persepolis unopposed and claim its massive wealth for himself. On leaving the city he burnt it to the ground.

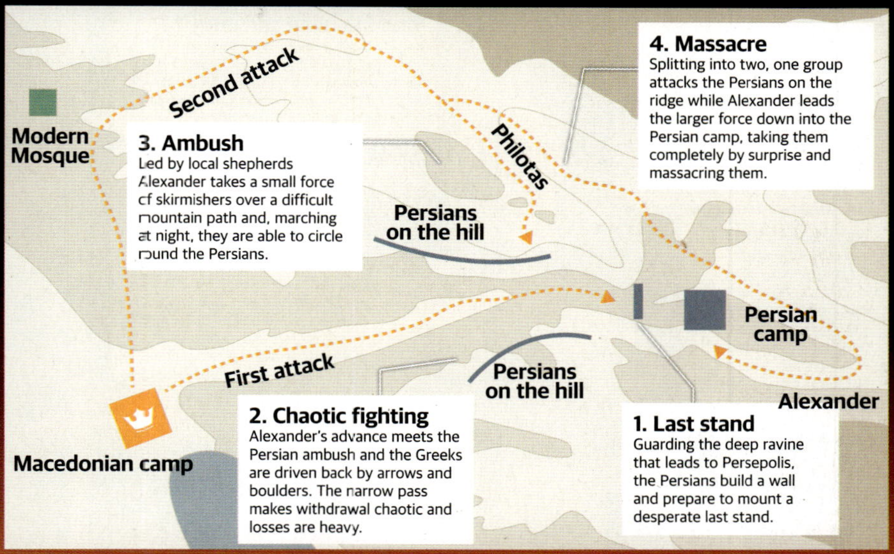

Left **A painting showing Alexander the Great and his forces battling an Indian army**

a fiction, and only a handful of frontier provinces remained in the usurper's blood-slick hands. The once glorious Persian Empire, for 220 years the largest in the ancient world, had died by the roadside, humiliated and betrayed.

Taking the capital Persepolis after a last-ditch attempt to hold back the Greeks at a narrow pass called the Persian Gates, the power-drunk Alexander burnt the great palace to the ground in, it is believed, retaliation for the Persian sack of Athens in 480 BCE. Casting the first torch into the building himself, looting and burning spread across the city. Priests were murdered and Persian women forced to marry his soldiers. Zoroastrian prophecy had foretold "demons with dishevelled hair, of the race of wrath" and now, Persia's holy men realised, the demons were here.

As his predecessor Darius had been, Bessus was chased down by the ferocious and dogmatic Alexander into what is now Uzbekistan and Afghanistan. Across deserts with little supplies, Alexander rode along his lines, picking up men who fell and lifting their spirits. A charismatic leader even against the backdrop of the bloodiest of campaigns, he had the power to inspire his weary soldiers. Eventually, Bessus' support collapsed. With no army worth a damn, he had been forced to burn crops and stores before the Greek advance in a last-ditch attempt to slow Alexander's terrible pursuit. Fittingly for the betrayer of the last Shahanshah, his own men handed him over to the Greeks. His nose and ears were cut off at Alexander's command, and he was sent back to Persia in chains to be impaled, the Persian punishment for traitors.

This rampage across Persia and her furthest fringes wasn't the first time Alexander's determination had taken on a more murderous hue. In 334 BCE, he had marched his men into the sea up to their chins rather than turn back along the beach, only surviving because the tide began to change direction with the wind, and in 332 BCE this sheer bloody-mindedness joined forces with his ruthlessness at Tyre - the first of many appalling massacres. Refusing to surrender and believing their island fortress was impregnable from land, Alexander laid siege, blockaded the port from the Persian navy and over seven months built a causeway from the mainland to the city - an incredible feat of engineering that allowed his catapults to come within range of the city. Tyre was soon breached, and Alexander's fury fell upon the city's population. Of the 40,000 inhabitants of Tyre, 2,000 were crucified on the beach, 4,000 were killed in the fighting, a handful were pardoned, and over 30,000 sold into slavery.

This act of impossible engineering and bloody vengeance was later repeated in northern India at the Battle of Aornos in 327 BCE, where the crossing of a mountain ravine by improvised wooden bridge - built over seven days and seven nights - was followed by the massacre of the tribal Aśvakas. Welcoming Alexander with open arms, the Greek-speaking Branchidae were set upon when it became known their ancestors had collaborated with the Achaemenids, while other defenders were murdered because they surrendered too late, or been promised safe passage to lure them from behind their walls and into the spears of the Macedonian phalanx.

Like arterial spray on armour, growing accounts of sackings, burnings, enslavement and murder pepper the record of Alexander in gore. It seemed like the further he got from home, the darker his deeds became.

While the rewards of conquest - plunder, wives, riches and glory - had been great, the Greeks were

6. Light cavalry

Strengths

Easily replaced, some horse archers.

Weaknesses

Variable equipment and training, light armour of leather or linen.

How did Alexander deploy them?

A combination of lighter armed and armoured cavalry from the other Greek states and local horsemen conscripted in Asia. Deployed dependant on weapons and training, Alexander came to rely on them as the traditional Greek heavy cavalry dwindled.

ALEXANDER'S INJURIES

The warrior king spent his reign at war and certainly suffered for it...

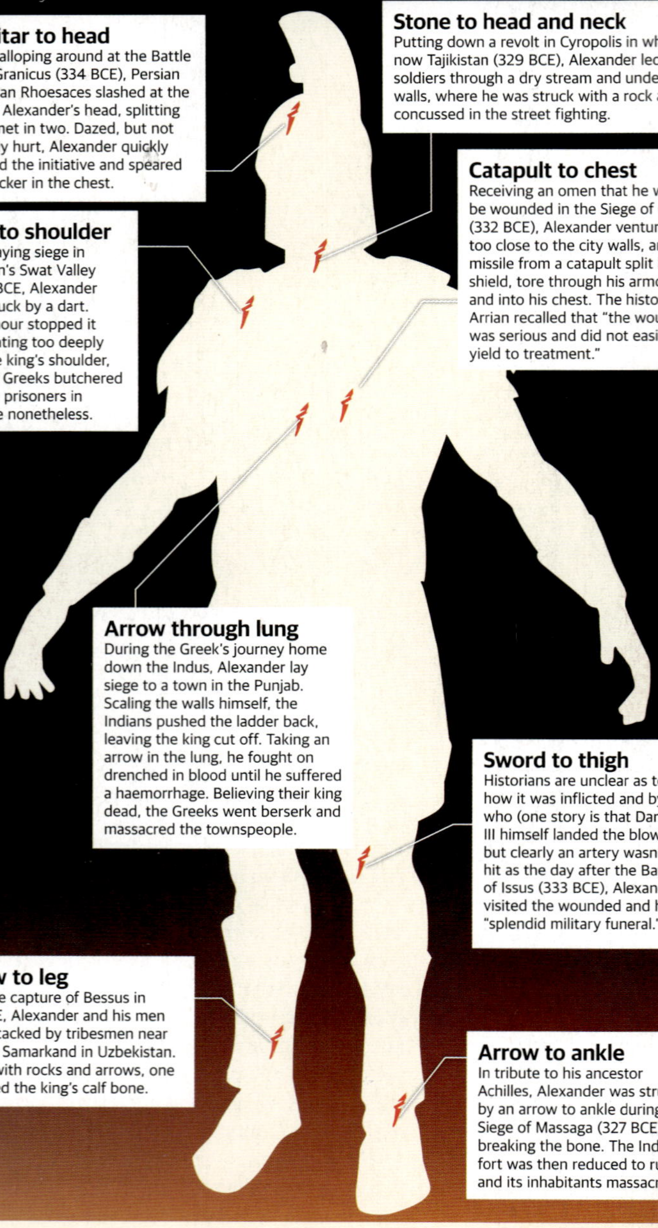

Scimitar to head
While galloping around at the Battle of the Granicus (334 BCE), Persian nobleman Rhoesaces slashed at the back of Alexander's head, splitting his helmet in two. Dazed, but not seriously hurt, Alexander quickly regained the initiative and speared his attacker in the chest.

Stone to head and neck
Putting down a revolt in Cyropolis in what is now Tajikistan (329 BCE), Alexander led his soldiers through a dry stream and under the walls, where he was struck with a rock and concussed in the street fighting.

Dart to shoulder
While laying siege in Pakistan's Swat Valley in 327 BCE, Alexander was struck by a dart. His armour stopped it penetrating too deeply into the king's shoulder, but the Greeks butchered all their prisoners in revenge nonetheless.

Catapult to chest
Receiving an omen that he would be wounded in the Siege of Gaza (332 BCE), Alexander ventured too close to the city walls, and a missile from a catapult split his shield, tore through his armour and into his chest. The historian Arrian recalled that "the wound was serious and did not easily yield to treatment."

Arrow through lung
During the Greek's journey home down the Indus, Alexander lay siege to a town in the Punjab. Scaling the walls himself, the Indians pushed the ladder back, leaving the king cut off. Taking an arrow in the lung, he fought on drenched in blood until he suffered a haemorrhage. Believing their king dead, the Greeks went berserk and massacred the townspeople.

Sword to thigh
Historians are unclear as to how it was inflicted and by who (one story is that Darius III himself landed the blow), but clearly an artery wasn't hit as the day after the Battle of Issus (333 BCE), Alexander visited the wounded and held a "splendid military funeral."

Arrow to leg
After the capture of Bessus in 329 BCE, Alexander and his men were attacked by tribesmen near modern Samarkand in Uzbekistan. Pelted with rocks and arrows, one shattered the king's calf bone.

Arrow to ankle
In tribute to his ancestor Achilles, Alexander was struck by an arrow to ankle during the Siege of Massaga (327 BCE), breaking the bone. The Indian fort was then reduced to rubble and its inhabitants massacred.

Above Alexander the Great's army defeat the Greek city state of Thebes, 335 BCE

beginning to tire not just of this endless war that had taken them further and further from home, but Alexander's increasing pretensions. This monarch from Greece's barbarian hinterland had begun to dress in Persian robes, train Persians for the army and insist on courtiers throwing themselves to the ground in the manner of subjects before the Persian king of kings - an affront to the dignity of the Greeks, who took pride in never bowing to their monarchs. On top of that, he now wished to be worshipped as a god.

After one drunken celebration in 328 BCE, this discontent found voice when Cleitus the Black, an old Macedonian general who had served under Philip II and saved Alexander's life in battle, decided he'd had his fill. The general bristled, turned to Alexander, and told him that he would be nothing without the accomplishments of Philip, and all that he now possessed was earned by the blood and sacrifice of Macedonians. Alexander, more petulant than entirely regal in his fury, threw an apple at the general's head, called for his guards and then for a dagger or spear, but wary of escalation, those present quickly began bustling Cleitus from the room and tried to calm their monarch. Either Cleitus wasn't fully removed or then returned, but having clearly passed the point of no return, continued to vent his spleen, until Alexander, finally grabbing hold of a javelin, threw it clean through the old warhorse's heart.

Cleitus was one of the first to challenge the king, but he wasn't the last. In 327 BCE, a plot against him was betrayed, and the conspirators - his own royal pages - stoned to death. Then, later that year he struck another body blow against his traditional supporters. Callisthenes, grand-nephew of Alexander's tutor Aristotle and one of the many historians in Alexander's retinue, had become increasingly critical of his delusions of grandeur, and taunted him with a line from his beloved *Iliad*: "A better man than you by far was Patroclus, and still death did not escape him." In short - you're no god, and you'll die just like the rest of us. Alexander accused Callisthenes of collusion in the pages' conspiracy, and had him put to death.

It was the beginning of the end. Convinced he was a god, it would be the needs of men that would bring the conquests of Alexander to heel. Adamant that they were at the edge of the world and expecting to see the great sea that the Ancient Greeks believed ringed their continent from which they could return home, Alexander pushed his increasingly mutinous army into India. Confronted with valley after valley of new lands to conquer and battles to wage, they drove on - winning a costly victory against 200 war elephants fielded by King Porus on the banks of the Indus River. Battered and broken after 22,000 kilometres and eight years, monsoon season arrived and drenched the army in water and disease. Rumours also reached the camp that India was a bigger than they had previously heard, and contained armies even greater than that of Porus.

Alexander's generals, mindful of the fate that had befallen other critics of their king, approached cautiously and appealed to his nobility. Coenus - one of Alexander's most trusted commanders - implored him to let them return home to their families, saying so eloquently, "We have achieved

BATTLE OF THE HYDASPES (326 BCE)

Alexander's battle for the Punjab opens up India to the Greeks

Despite leaving him with 1,000 Greek dead, Alexander was eventually able to overcome the numerically superior force and deadly war elephants of King Porus. He managed to do this by using a classic pincer movement and refusal to bow down to nature - in this case, the fast-moving waters of the Hydaspes River.

Porus' defeat left the Punjab region of northern India open to the Greek invaders, but the death toll would add to rumblings of mutiny in Alexander's ranks.

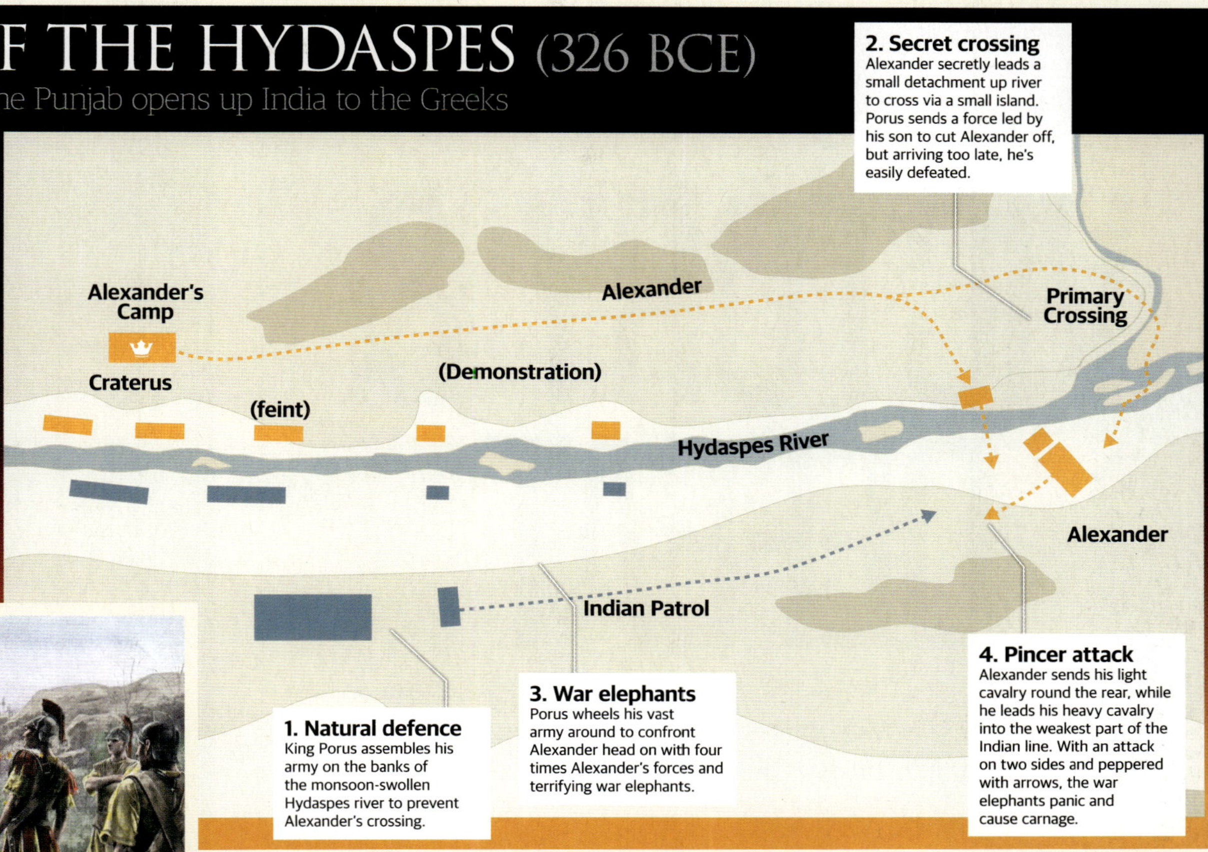

King Porus of India surrenders to Alexander the Great after the Battle of Hydaspes in 326 BCE

"Even with his dreams of ceaseless conquest doused like campfires before battle, Alexander fought fiercely"

so many marvellous successes, but isn't it time to set some limit? Surely you can see yourself how few are left of the original army that began this enterprise... Sire," he concluded, "the sign of a great man is knowing when to stop."

Reluctantly, the warrior king agreed. Building a temple to Dionysus on the riverbank and leaving the inscription 'Alexander stopped here', they built a fleet of flat-bottom ships and began a long voyage home. Alexander the Great's conquest began with Homer's *Iliad* as its guide - a tale of triumph and conquest - and ended with the *Odyssey* - a desperate voyage home.

There were more battles, tragedies and triumphs to come, and many would never see home thanks to the long-running battles with the Indian kingdoms they passed through on their way down the Indus River toward the Arabian Sea, from where they could sail to Persia's southern coast. One battle in early 325 BCE against the Malhi people of Punjab nearly cost Alexander his life as a siege ladder collapsed behind him, leaving him stranded on enemy ramparts, with his bodyguard panicking below. Even with his dreams of ceaseless conquest doused like campfires before battle, Alexander fought fiercely until an arrow pierced his lung, his chroniclers describing air escaping with the blood. Even with all Alexander had subjected them to, his army remained devoted to their monarch - believing him dead, they rampaged through the city, looting, killing and burning in retaliation. Patched up by his doctor, gaunt and unsteady, Alexander had to be sailed past his army while lined up on the riverbank before they would accept he was still alive.

With one force exploring the Persian Gulf, Alexander led the remnants of his army through what is now the Balochistan province of Iran - a sparsely populated landscape of arid mountains and desert. His men died in their hundreds, gasping for water, stumbling through the baking sands in their tattered sandals and blinking into the brilliant sun. By 324 BCE they had reached the Persian city of Susa, but back in the heart of the empire he had stolen, his trials continued - his childhood friend, stalwart general and, some historians have implied, lover Hephaestion died, and then in August the Macedonians in his army mutinied. The Macedonians he placated, but the grief he felt at the loss of "the friend I value with my own life" could not be so easily put right.

While his father died with dreams of a Persian conquest upon his lips, Alexander succumbed to a fever in 323 BCE with greater dreams still. Before his eyes poured the spears of the phalanx south into Arabia and west into Carthage and Rome. "Who shall lead us?" his followers whispered to their dying king. "The strongest," he replied, and with his passing the great empire splintered.

In his tactical genius, charismatic leadership, enduring legacy and fanatical drive, Alexander was far removed from those around him. Perhaps in his view, 'elevated' above those around him, he was so far removed as to be incomparable. He was never defeated in battle, partly because of his tactical skill, leadership and army, but also because he was prepared to pay a toll in human lives.

Tales of the Greek gods endure not just because they present an ideal of heroism and greatness, but because they were flawed beings - a soap opera on a cosmic scale. Like the squabbling deities of Mount Olympus, Alexander the Great was violent, vain, petty and cynical, and like them he overcame impossible odds and accomplished breathtaking feats through ingenuity, charisma, martial prowess and force of will. His example were venerated by emperors, tactics studied by leaders for over 2,000 years, and in the Middle East, tales of 'Alexander the Cursed's' savagery are still told in the lands he wronged. For good and ill, the shadow he casts is still the stuff of legend.

VICTORY & DEFEAT

The political powerhouses and iconic battles that changed the course of history forever

LIONHEART

Born to royalty but educated in the charnel gutter of war, King Richard brought the religious fanaticism of the Christian West on the Muslim East in a quest to claim the fabled Holy Land

For almost a year the mighty city of Acre held firm. Despite wave after wave of Christian knights pouring all their religious fervour and military might into its ancient walls, it had held back the tide and somehow halted the progress of the foreign hordes that now threatened to overrun the entire Near East.

More and more men came, though – the attacks were relentless. When the first army had been held at bay, the city's inhabitants thought they were safe, that the invasion was defeated. However, then yet another army landed and the city's main artery, its port, which provided passage in and out of its walls, was taken. The city's defences were tested once more, with an even more ferocious attack battering at the doors and calling for blood. Luckily for those within, once more the city held off the mass of warriors, its infidel leaders repelled.

Then, with the new year's sailing season, another invader arrived by sea with a fresh bloodthirsty army. He was followed in May by yet another, with tens of thousands of soldiers joining the infidels' camp outside the walls, swelling their numbers to terrifying proportions. They attacked again and the losses on both sides were massive. The lack of food and supplies in the city, and the spread of disease within the invaders' camp drove both sets of warriors to extremes, stoking the fires of faith that lay within their hearts to pursue bolder and bolder acts of violence.

Today is the eighth day of June 1191 and, as Acre slowly suffocates in the oppressive heat of the Levant's summer months, yet another fleet is landing in the city's once-prosperous port, this time with one of the biggest forces the city has ever seen. If the ruler of Acre, the noble and great Saladin, doesn't send meaningful reinforcements soon, then the city will fall and the gates to the Holy Land will be brutally wrenched open to the Christian hordes.

They call this one, this man-mountain stepping off his ship onto the dusty dry shore, the Lionheart, and he is here to kill them all in the name of his god and glory. The passage had been long and painful, featuring storms, shipwrecks and a mad despot who threatened to derail the Third Crusade before it had even begun. No matter, King Richard the Lionheart and his army had survived the trip across the Mediterranean Sea and reached the Holy Land. After months of pursuit and planning, they were primed to fulfil their mission, Richard's mission, God's mission, to take the Holy Land by storm and cut a direct path to the holiest of all cities, Jerusalem.

"To the disgrace of all of Christendom, Jesus's city had fallen to the Saracens"

Richard the Lionheart

English, 1157-1199

Brief Bio

King of England from the 6 July 1189 until his death, Richard I was the third of five sons of King Henry II of England and Eleanor of Aquitaine. At 16, Richard took control of his own army and thanks to a series of victories over rebels threatening his father's throne, developed a reputation as a great military leader. Following his father's death and his own coronation he launched the Third Crusade.

BATTLE OF ARSUF

A major battle in the Third Crusade, Arsuf saw Richard and Saladin face off

CRUSADERS

NUMBER OF TROOPS: 20,000

LEADER

RICHARD THE LIONHEART

Excellent on the battlefield, Richard the Lionheart was a brutal killer and a gifted tactical thinker, leading an army of religious fanatics with ruthless efficiency.

Strength Amazing warrior and powerful military leader.

Weakness Politically and economically reckless as king.

KEY UNIT

TEMPLAR KNIGHT

The most skilled Christian fighting unit to take part in the Third Crusade, the Knights Templar were wealthy, well-trained and fanatical fighters, driven by a holy purpose.

Strength Well-equipped and trained in hand-to-hand combat.

Weakness Few in number and fanatically religious, leading to recklessness.

KEY WEAPON

BROADSWORD

The most popular hand-to-hand weapon of all Christian knight orders, including the Knights Templar and Knights Hospitaller, the broadsword was a well-balanced and deadly weapon capable of stabbing and cleaving.

Strength Great all-round weapon that also allowed shield use.

Weakness Could be out-ranged with two-handed swords and spears.

01 The Wood of Arsuf

After taking Acre, Richard set out for his next target, Arsuf. To get there, he had to move south along the coast of the Mediterranean Sea and then traverse the Wood of Arsuf, one of the few forested regions in all of the Levant. Saladin knew this and after tracking and harassing Richard's slow-moving baggage train and infantry, decided the woods would be the ideal position to strike.

02 A narrow plain

Richard, wary of an assault on his convoy, proceeded slowly through the Wood of Arsuf, making the first 10km (6mi) without incident. Saladin had already identified a striking point however – a narrow clear plain in the forest approximately 9km (5.5mi) from Arsuf. Saladin intended to engage in skirmishes along the length of the convoy and then hit its rear with a decisive attack.

03 Scouts at dawn

Moving out of their camp at dawn on 7 September 1191, Richard's scouts reported Saladin's scouts could be seen. Richard realised that this meant Saladin's full army was nearby and started to arrange his army. Men were deployed at the fore and rear of the convoy column, with the van – the foremost division – made up of the Knights Templar under the command of their 11th grand master, Robert de Sable.

04 Saladin attacks

As soon as Richard's convoy reached the plain Saladin's forces attacked. At the front, Saladin sent a dense swarm of skirmishers, while behind them streamed squadrons of heavy cavalry and foot and horse archers, splitting so that the army attacked from the centre, left and right.

05 Crusader flanks hold

Saladin's chief tactic was to break the flanks of the crusader column and ordered incursions of javelin throwers and mounted archers to perform lightning strikes along their flanks and retreating before crusader crossbowmen could retaliate. The flanks held, though.

To the disgrace of all of Christendom, Jesus's city had fallen four years previous to the Saracen Ayyubid hordes, which was now not only ruled by Christianity's arch-nemesis Saladin, but also defiled by their very presence within its hallowed walls. The city, which had been safely held in Christian hands for almost 100 years since the First Crusade had established the Kingdom of Jerusalem in 1099, had been ordered to be retaken by none other than the Pope in Rome. Richard, a devout and deeply religious king, had heeded the call. Here he now stood, ready to do his duty to the one true god. Conquering Acre was merely the first step in wrestling Jerusalem from Saladin's grip.

Counter seal (1195) of Richard I of England

So far the city's capture and wider crusade had been in the hands of a number of other leaders. These included Guy of Lusignan – a proud Poitevin knight and the supposed rightful king of Jerusalem through his marriage to Sibylla of Jerusalem – and King Philip II of France, who had helped raise the 'Saladin tithe' to pay for the crusade. The Duke of Austria, Leopold V, had overall command of the imperial forces. There had been yet more leaders at the

10 Ayyubid army scatters
Its right wing smashed, the Ayyubid army soon routed, scattering back into the hills and forests south of Arsuf. Richard, realising the pursuing knights could be ambushed in a surprise counterattack, drew the warriors back into an orderly formation at Arsuf and ordered them to pitch camp at the now-secure fortress. Saladin was forced to retreat with his reputation as an invincible leader tarnished.

09 Templars let loose
Freed from the tactical order to defend and maintain discipline, the crusader knights took the fight to the Saracens, unleashing their hatred and combat prowess in one brutal wave of death. The right wing of Saladin's army couldn't sustain the assault and collapsed almost immediately, with Richard himself weighing into the heart of the fighting. As a bloody revenge for the day's attacks was complete, the Knights Templar set off in pursuit of the fleeing Saracens.

08 Counterattack slams home
Garnier de Nablus disobeyed orders in counterattacking, but with the Hospitaller charging, Richard knew they needed support and ordered his army to engage with them. The full weight of the crusader army therefore suddenly switched emphasis from defence to attack, ramming into the Ayyubid army with immense ferocity.

06 Hospitallers come under attack
Saladin shifted the focus point of his army to the rear of column, engaging the Knights Hospitaller. Saladin joined the assault along with his brother to inspire his men to make a breakthrough. Richard held the convoy together despite some losses and edged them toward Arsuf.

07 Knights break rank
Richard reached Arsuf in the middle of the afternoon, with the besieged Hospitaller vanguard retreating into the fortress city. Line discipline was finally lost and a melee began. Seeing his men in trouble, the grand master of the Knights Hospitaller, Garnier de Nablus, broke ranks and charged the Saracens.

siege's instigation the summer previous but illness and disease had claimed many over the winter months, with Frederick of Swabia and even the holy Patriarch Heraclius of Jerusalem all passing from this mortal world into the next.

The siege itself had stalled, so every passing week threatened to allow Saladin to outmanoeuvre the crusaders. Richard, being the honed and experienced military leader that he was, realised this and after meeting with the other leaders, gave orders for vast siege engines to be built, ones that could bring down the city's walls. These engines, these machines of death, once completed, towered over the Christian knights and, when unleashed, brought the siege into a deadly endgame. Colossal boulders rained down upon Acre's walls, smashing against them with thunderous brutality. Corpses of animals and Muslim soldiers littered the city's streets, spreading disease and sapping the morale of the terrified residents. Most fearsome of all though, flaming balls and arrows set ablaze anything that wasn't made out of stone, causing panic to quickly spread among Acre's populace.

The surviving Muslim soldiers defended bravely, but the sheer carnage and chaos the machines and men of war now levied on the city was too much and, after a month of death and destruction, the remaining Muslim garrison within the city surrendered, which was a direct violation of

MUSLIMS

NUMBER OF TROOPS: 25,000

LEADER
SALADIN
He attained his exalted position as leader of the Ayyubid army and founder of the Ayyubid dynasty and was a wise and experienced military commander.
Strength Respected tactical thinker and powerful politician.
Weakness Hands-off leader with little personal combat prowess.

KEY UNIT
MOUNTED ARCHER
The light cavalry of Saladin was feared throughout the world due to its ability to strike quickly and at range, with skilled marksmen riding the world's fastest horses.
Strength Fast units that excelled in ambush and hit-and-run attacks.
Weakness Easily cut down by knights in hand-to-hand combat.

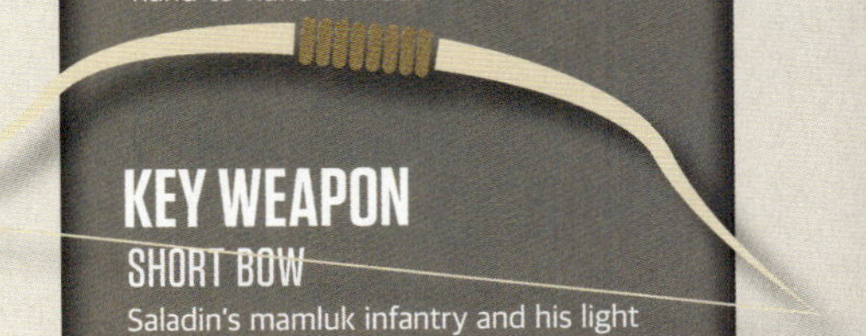

KEY WEAPON
SHORT BOW
Saladin's mamluk infantry and his light cavalry units excelled in bowmanship, with their short bows used to swarm arrows on crusader forces at every opportunity.
Strengths Fast to fire and reload with good stopping power.
Weakness Could be outranged by the longbow and all-but-useless in hand-to-hand combat.

Due to its position of strategic importance Acre was often the scene of violence

LIONHEART'S CRUSADE

The Third Crusade faced challenges even before reaching the Holy Land

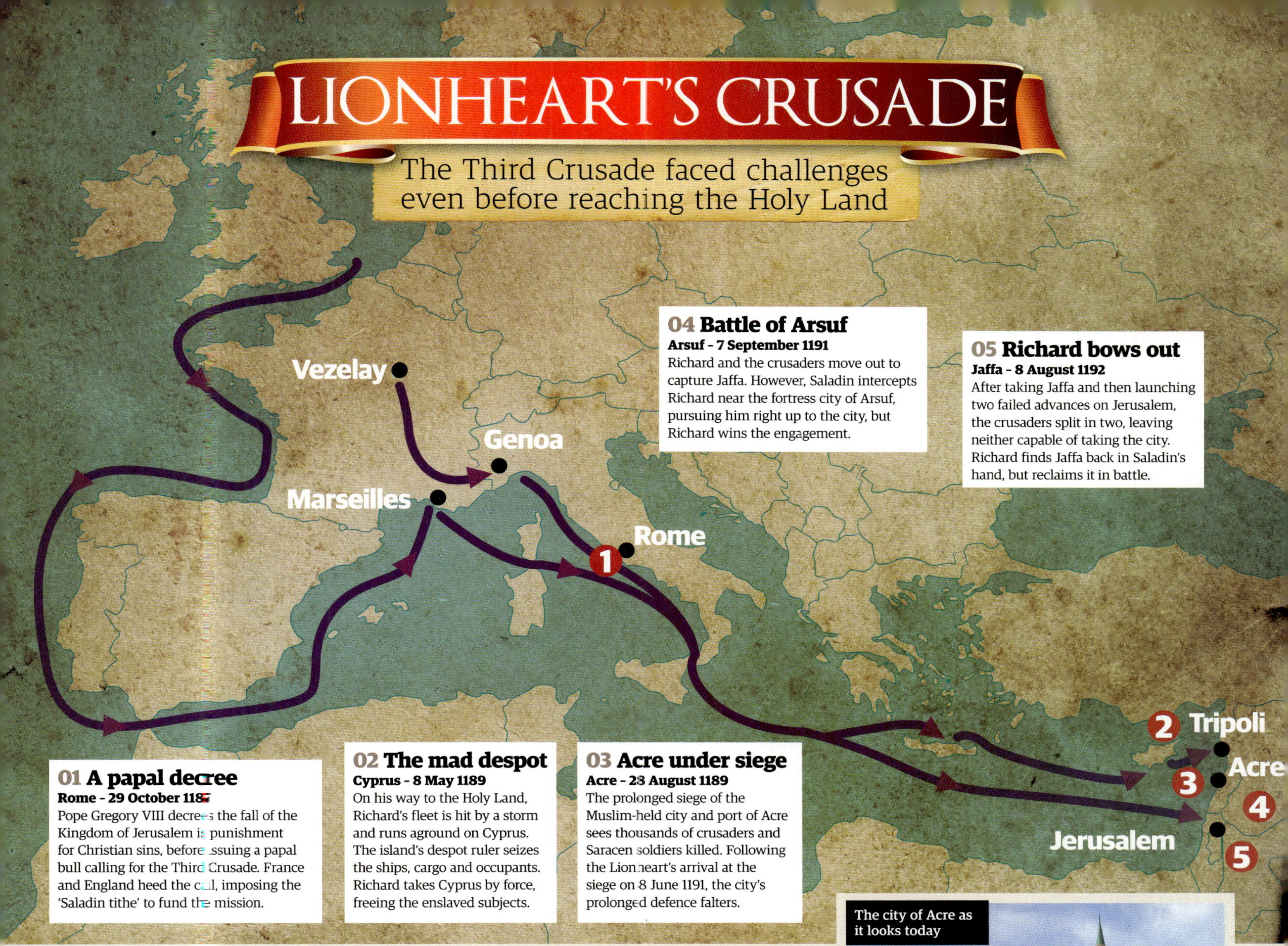

01 A papal decree
Rome - 29 October 1187
Pope Gregory VIII decrees the fall of the Kingdom of Jerusalem is punishment for Christian sins, before issuing a papal bull calling for the Third Crusade. France and England heed the call, imposing the 'Saladin tithe' to fund the mission.

02 The mad despot
Cyprus - 8 May 1189
On his way to the Holy Land, Richard's fleet is hit by a storm and runs aground on Cyprus. The island's despot ruler seizes the ships, cargo and occupants. Richard takes Cyprus by force, freeing the enslaved subjects.

03 Acre under siege
Acre - 28 August 1189
The prolonged siege of the Muslim-held city and port of Acre sees thousands of crusaders and Saracen soldiers killed. Following the Lionheart's arrival at the siege on 8 June 1191, the city's prolonged defence falters.

04 Battle of Arsuf
Arsuf - 7 September 1191
Richard and the crusaders move out to capture Jaffa. However, Saladin intercepts Richard near the fortress city of Arsuf, pursuing him right up to the city, but Richard wins the engagement.

05 Richard bows out
Jaffa - 8 August 1192
After taking Jaffa and then launching two failed advances on Jerusalem, the crusaders split in two, leaving neither capable of taking the city. Richard finds Jaffa back in Saladin's hand, but reclaims it in battle.

The city of Acre as it looks today

"THEY CALL THIS ONE THE LIONHEART AND HE IS HERE TO KILL THEM ALL IN THE NAME OF HIS GOD AND GLORY"

Saladin's orders. On receiving the news of Acre's fall, Saladin immediately set out for the city. On his way he received news that Richard had taken the surrendering Muslim garrison of 2,400 men captive and was offering their return for a ransom. Saladin, known for his loyalty to his men and his wisdom, agreed to the ransom, which not only included monetary compensation but also the release of all of his Christian prisoners.

In Acre the banners of the Kingdom of Jerusalem, France, England and the Duchy of Austria fluttered in the light breeze. With Acre down, Richard knew that only the city of Jaffa to the south stood in their way of making a direct assault on Jerusalem, so he began making preparations for the continued crusade, as well as for the reparation of the sacked city. These preparations were swiftly interrupted by an argument that developed between the conquering leaders as to how the city should be divided up and to how the spoils of their victory should be apportioned. This quarrelling led Richard to strike down the Austrian standard from above the city's walls, slighting Leopold, as the king of England sided with Guy of Lusignan rather than Philip and Leopold over who should become king of Jerusalem when the city was taken. Philip and Leopold preferred fellow crusader and Italian nobleman Conrad of Montferrat, with Phillip so angry he threatened to return to Europe.

This cauldron of scheming and disagreement was tipped over the edge when Saladin delayed in paying the garrison's ransom. An already irate and disgruntled Richard deemed the lateness a massive slight and ordered every single one of the garrison to be executed. Saladin reached the city just as the decision was made, but could only watch as man after man was publicly executed, their heads lopped from their shoulders atop the city walls. Thousands died. The enraged Saladin replied like-for-like, executing the 1,000 Christian prisoners in his custody.

£70,000
Amount raised by the 'Saladin tithe' to fund the Third Crusade

Whatever deal could conceivably have been reached between the rival leaders now lay in ruins, seemingly as dead as the unfortunate prisoners.

Angered and frustrated with Richard and Guy, Philip and Leopold finally decided that their participation in the Third Crusade was at an end, leaving in late August for their European homes.

ANATOMY OF A TEMPLAR KNIGHT

The key kit and weapons carried by the most elite of Christian warriors

Helmet

Decapitation resistance

The great helm was the mainstay of the Templar Order and offered excellent protection against blows, as did the sugarloaf helmet. Due to narrow viewing corridors and high temperatures experienced in the Holy Land, many opted for more lightweight alternatives with open faces.

Jerkin

A guaranteed chafe-free experience

Unseen, however often critical in keeping a Knight Templar breathing, was the haubergeon, a padded jerkin that sat against his skin. The jerkin extended over much of the upper body and was the last line of defence from enemy blows. In colder climates, it also helped keep the warrior warm – not an issue in the Holy Land.

Broadsword

Designed to hack and slash

As standard for western knights, the typical Knight Templar was armed with a broadsword, however when fighting on horseback spears were also used. Sometimes, two-handed broadswords were opted for while fighting on foot, but while they granted extra reach and cleaving power, they left the knight shieldless.

Surcoat

It ain't half hot in the Holy Land

Above the knight's chainmail sat the visible surcoat. This white garment not only kept the Sun off their metal armour, also displayed the symbols of the Order.

Chainmail

Thy enemy's blade shall not pass

The primary form of defence against enemy strikes, the hauberk, a long-sleeved shirt of chainmail fitted with chain covers for the hands and a chain coif hood for the head, was a knight's armour. The chainmail would be partnered with iron chausses to protect their legs.

Shield

The first and best line of defence

Adorned with the Christian cross of their order, the Templar shield was large and long, with a teardrop design protecting their entire torso and upper legs. It was constructed from wood and had a metal rim, the latter helping to protect against it splitting under the weight of sword blows. It had a leather handgrip at the rear.

For Richard, though, such betrayal of faith was unimaginable, and after calling on the Philip to do right in the eyes of god, managed to persuade him to leave behind 10,000 French crusaders along with the necessary funds to pay for their upkeep. The Lionheart was now the central remaining commander of over 20,000 crusaders, knights and soldiers alike and, burning with glorious purpose, ordered the continuation of the crusade, with the bulk of the crusading army marching out of Acre in August's final days. This was no doubt who was now leading this holy crusade.

The next city on the crusaders' relentless march to Jerusalem was Jaffa, an important port that provided passage into the southern Mediterranean Sea. As long as Jaffa remained untaken Saladin had a natural avenue to pour more of his troops into the region from his impregnable stronghold of Egypt, but if it fell to the crusaders Saladin would be forced to move men over land, a far less effective and more time-consuming proposition. The city also lay a mere 65 kilometres (40 miles) from Jerusalem, making it the ideal coastal base for crusaders. Before it could be taken, though, the crusaders needed to get there in one piece. Richard knew Saladin was somewhere in the nearby area and, aware of his enemy's skill in arranging ambushes, ordered his troops to march down the Mediterranean coastline, with the baggage train protected by being nearest to the coast. This tactic prevented Saladin from attacking on one flank, as Richard also got his fleet to sail down the coast in parallel with them, shutting off the sea as an avenue of possible attack.

8,000 English knights and soldiers who journeyed to the Holy Land

However, to the north of Jaffa lay the Wood of Arsuf, one of the only forested areas in all of the Levant. The woods ran parallel to the coastline for over 20 kilometres (12 miles) and had to be traversed by Richard's army if they were to reach Jaffa. After harassing Richard's troops with small hit-and-run attacks within the woods, Saladin sanctioned a full-scale assault on the crusaders, which led to the largest pitched battle of the Third Crusade. Saladin knew the battle would be decisive, but couldn't possibly have foreseen how disastrous for him it would be. As the Sun went down on 7 September 1191 the Saracen army had

"SALADIN COULD ONLY WATCH AS MAN AFTER MAN WAS PUBLICLY EXECUTED, THEIR HEADS LOPPED FROM THEIR SHOULDERS ATOP THE CITY WALLS"

been routed in a decisive counterattack led by Richard's Knights Hospitaller. Saladin retreated from Arsuf to regroup what was left of his battered army and lick his wounds.

The crusaders made a beeline for Jaffa, swiftly besieging and taking it. Despite some disagreement with the other crusader leaders, Richard – with Jerusalem almost in sight – decided to open negotiations with his enemy. Saladin, who was being questioned by some of his subjects following the defeat at Arsuf, agreed to the negotiations and sent his brother, Al-Adil to Jaffa to lead the talks. Despite headway being made – at one time Richard's sister Joan was being talked about as a potential bride for Al-Adil with Jerusalem as a wedding gift – the talks ultimately broke down.

2,700 Muslim prisoners Richard had executed in the city of Acre

The breakdown of the talks caused unrest in the crusader ranks, with arguments arising about the best way to proceed toward their goal. Richard, growing tired of the constant in-fighting, acted decisively and ordered the army to move on Jerusalem in November, first moving through Ascalon and then Latrun. The Christian army was soon at Beit Nuba, a mere 20 kilometres (12 miles) from Jerusalem. The news quickly spread of the crusaders' progress and the morale in the Muslim garrisons within the city crumbled. Saladin's forces had been crushed, Acre, Arsuf and Jaffa taken and Jerusalem looked set to be next. Victory for the Third Crusade seemed inevitable.

At this vital point hesitation crept into the crusader ranks, though. Saladin had proven himself a worthy and tricky foe and, not knowing the extent to which his forces had been depleted, Richard feared that a retaliation attack, most likely another large-scale ambush, was very near. In addition, the weather in the winter months had taken a marked turn for the worse, with heavy rain and hail leading to poor conditions under

KNOW THY ENEMY: SALADIN

The main features and kit of the most respected Muslim warrior of all

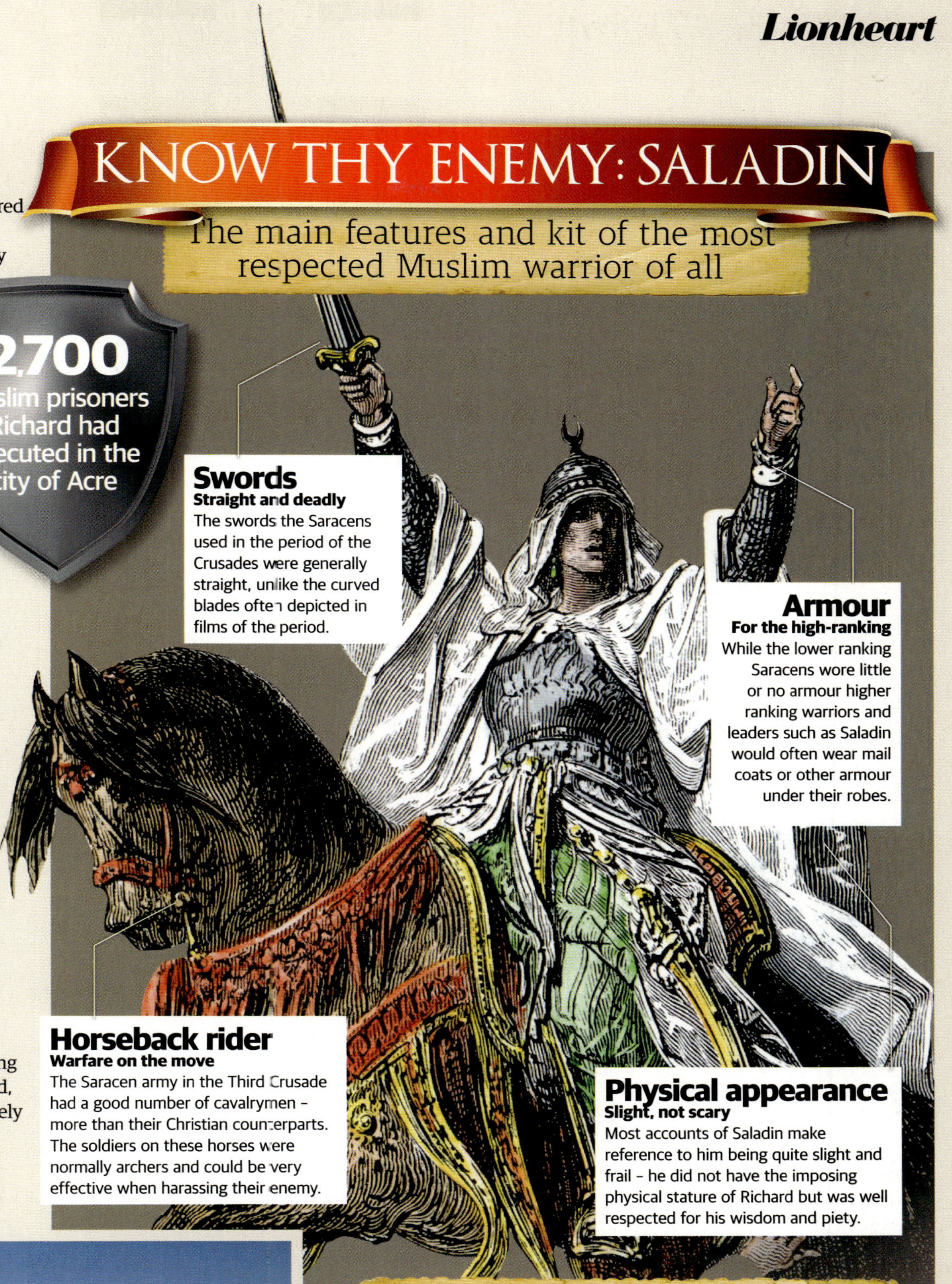

Swords
Straight and deadly

The swords the Saracens used in the period of the Crusades were generally straight, unlike the curved blades often depicted in films of the period.

Armour
For the high-ranking

While the lower ranking Saracens wore little or no armour higher ranking warriors and leaders such as Saladin would often wear mail coats or other armour under their robes.

Horseback rider
Warfare on the move

The Saracen army in the Third Crusade had a good number of cavalrymen – more than their Christian counterparts. The soldiers on these horses were normally archers and could be very effective when harassing their enemy.

Physical appearance
Slight, not scary

Most accounts of Saladin make reference to him being quite slight and frail – he did not have the imposing physical stature of Richard but was well respected for his wisdom and piety.

Salāh ad-Dīn Yūsuf ibn Ayyūb (Saladin) was the first sultan of Egypt and Syria and the founder of the Ayyubid dynasty. He was elevated to this lofty position through a series of military victories, first under the Fatimid government and then his own leadership, with him overseeing the decisive Battle of Hattin in 1187. It was due to Saladin himself that the Third Crusade was instigated, with the fallout from the Battle of Hattin and the fall of Jerusalem leading to the famous 'Saladin tithe', a tax levied in England and some parts of France to finance an army that was capable of reclaiming the holy territory.

Despite Saladin and Richard's armies clashing multiple times during the Third Crusade, the two men famously shared a more complicated relationship than would have been expected, with great respect reported on both sides. After the Battle of Arsuf – a battle in which Saladin's army was soundly beaten – Saladin sent Richard two excellent horses as Richard had lost his own in the battle. The two men never met in person, though, and Saladin died a year after the Third Crusade, struck down by a fever while staying in Damascus.

The modern day city of Jerusalem

foot. These factors caused Richard to pause for thought rather than make straight for the holy city and he consulted his fellow crusaders. It was agreed that if they started besieging Jerusalem and were hit with a relieving force from Saladin, the general poor conditions would lead to a massacre. As such, Richard ordered a retreat back to the coast. The attack would have to wait.

2,000
Christian soldiers fought in the Third Crusade's last battle at Jaffa

The invading army spent the rest of the winter months in Ascalon before continuing hostilities in the spring of 1192. Saladin, who had been forced by his emirs (commanders) to disband much of what was left of his army - the emirs favouring consolidation rather than open hostilities - launched no major attack. However, bands of Saracen troops constantly plagued the crusaders, with a series of small fights and skirmishes slowly eroding the crusader army's numbers and morale. This came to a head on 22 May when the fortified town of Darum fell to the crusader forces after five days of bloody fighting. The crusaders had won great battles in the Holy Land but no more armies were journeying across the Mediterranean to bolster their forces; those men who fell in battle weren't going to be replaced. Richard's crusade was faltering, its primary purpose slipping away like sand in an hourglass.

The crusading king of England managed to marshal his remaining forces together for one last advance on Jerusalem, marching inland in June of that year. This time, far from being checked at Beit Nuba, the crusaders actually came within sight of the hallowed city. The time, it appeared, had finally come. Richard was to return Jesus's city to its rightful owners and reinstate Christianity as the dominant religious and military power in the Holy Land. However, as the tired, dusty and bronzed warriors stood there watching the distant city from afar, once more the poison of dissent started to seep among its leaders.

Despite standing before the city, months of resentment over the course the Crusade had taken boiled over among the military commanders, with debate over the best military course of action descending into personal attacks and squabbles. The majority of the leaders, including Richard, believed the best way to take Jerusalem was not besiege it but to attack Saladin directly in Egypt, thereby forcing him to relinquish it of his own free will as a bargaining chip to prevent his own fall. However, the leader of the surviving French crusaders, the Duke of Burgundy Hugh III, believed the only course of action was an immediate and direct assault on the city. News of the split in the leaders' plans filtered down to the crusaders themselves, with the knights and soldiers now breaking previous allegiances and siding with one side or the other, splitting the crusader army in two. Neither of the two forces were now powerful enough to assault a city, let alone Jerusalem, and as such Richard was forced to order a retreat.

While progressing back toward the coast, angry with the French, Richard decided to return to England. However, just as he was approaching Jaffa, news arrived via a scout that the city had fallen to Saladin, who had personally overseen the assault. Furthermore, the scout reported that the lives of all the people there were under a very real threat as the Muslim ruler had lost control of his army, the thousands of Muslim soldiers driven berserk due to the massacre at Acre. With the lives of the surviving crusaders in his hands (after all, it had been Richard who ordered the Acre executions) a return to England would have to wait. With a band of 2,000 surviving knights and soldiers, Richard launched one final assault on Saladin, approaching Jaffa by sea in a surprise attack. The Ayyubid soldiers who had only just taken the city were completely unprepared for the attack and were soon overrun, with a combination of knights and crusader crossbowmen decisively breaking their resistance. The attack was so brutally effective that Saladin was forced to flee from Jaffa to the south.

This would be the final battle of the Crusade for Saladin and Richard. Following Jaffa's second fall, the region entered a limbo-like stasis, with

CRUSADING KING OR BLOODY MURDERER?

Historian Douglas Boyd gives his verdict on the Lionheart

Despite Richard's leading role in the Third Crusade, the opinion of Victorian historian Bishop William Stubbs was that this king was "a bad ruler, whose love of war effectively disqualified him from being a peaceful one; his utter want of political common sense from being a prudent one." Stubbs called him "a man of blood, whose crimes were those of one whom long use of warfare had made too familiar with slaughter, and a vicious man."

Respected historian of the crusades Sir Steven Runciman balanced the two sides of Richard's character: "He was a bad son, a bad husband and a bad king, but a gallant and splendid soldier." While Richard consistently displayed supreme physical courage, gallant and splendid are not adjectives one would use today of the man who slaughtered 3,000 prisoners at the siege of Acre and nearly bankrupted the kingdom twice in his ten-year reign. The enduring legend of Richard as a heroic Christian warrior is due to the brilliant public-relations campaign of his mother, Eleanor of Aquitaine, to raise the ransom when he was taken hostage returning to England after the events of the Third Crusade.

Douglas Boyd is the author of *Lionheart: The True Story Of England's Crusading King*, published by The History Press.

"RICHARD BELIEVED THE BEST WAY TO TAKE JERUSALEM WAS NOT BESIEGE IT BUT TO ATTACK SALADIN DIRECTLY IN EGYPT"

Richard the Lionheart's forces on the march toward Jerusalem

WHY WAS JERUSALEM SO SOUGHT AFTER?

The geographical region of Palestine, between the River Jordan and the Mediterranean Sea, was referred to as the Holy Land by Christians and Muslims alike. Both religions claimed ownership due to an association with their faith, with the city of Jerusalem held in particular esteem. Both Islam and Christianity were Abrahamic monotheistic religions and as such, both sides considered the other to be unbelievers in the one true god and considered their presence heretical.

By the Third Crusade, Jerusalem and large parts of Palestine and the Levant region had changed hands again and again, with conflicts destabilising the region. Richard, coming from the Christian West, therefore perceived the fall of Jerusalem to Saladin's forces in 1187 as a direct attack on his faith. From Saladain's point of view he was merely taking back the spiritual heartland of his own faith; one that had previously rested in the hands of infidels.

the Christian crusaders and Muslim Ayyubids sapped of any further willpower for bloodshed. The fighting had gone on for three years and large parts of the historic area lay in ruins. Tens of thousands of men, women and children had lost their lives and, despite some areas of the Levant changing hands, nothing had really changed.

Jerusalem remained under Muslim control, Saladin was ruler of the Ayyubid Empire and Richard the Lionheart was still the fierce warrior king with a renowned reputation in Europe without a firm foothold in the Holy Land. What had changed, though, was Saladin and Richard's desire for more war and bloodshed, and so a treaty soon followed. Jerusalem would remain under Muslim control but from now on, Christian pilgrims and traders would be permitted to visit the city, with their rights protected by law. For Richard, the treaty was to be his last act in the Holy Land and the final curtain for the Third Crusade, with the king setting out on his return to England immediately after. His return journey, though, would not be as straightforward as the one over, with a series of events leading to his own capture, temporary imprisonment and yet more battles.

17
Months Richard the Lionheart remained in the Holy Land

However, the war he would go down in history for was his quest for the Holy Land – a journey full of bloodshed, plunder and religious fanaticism, but little territorial success. It ensured his legacy would forever be debated between those who see him as a crusading Christian king and others who view him as an amoral, cold-blooded killer, a debate that still rages on today.

BATTLE OF WATERLOO

WATERLOO, BELGIUM 18 JUNE 1815

The bloody culmination of the Waterloo Campaign, the Battle of Waterloo was one of the most explosive of the 19th century, with a British-led allied army under the command of Arthur Wellesley, the Duke of Wellington, defeating a French army under the command of Napoleon Bonaparte and ending the latter's 100-day reign as emperor of France.

The war had begun after Napoleon I returned from exile on Elba (an island off Tuscany) to Paris on 20 March 1815. This set into motion a chain of events that would see Napoleon reclaim his position as emperor, the Congress of Vienna declare him an outlaw and the Seventh Coalition pledge to field a large army to bring his rule to an end.

With hundreds of thousands of soldiers drafted to take Napoleon down, it was only a matter of time before blood was spilt - something that occurred two days prior to Waterloo when Napoleon struck at the Prussian army before it could join up with Wellington's on 16 June.

The French ruler did this by splitting his army into three groups, with two dedicated to the Prussians. The following exchange was the Battle of Ligny and saw Napoleon defeat the Prussians by causing their centre to collapse under repeated French assaults. While the Prussians lost men, they were not routed however and - as we shall see - were disastrously left to retreat uninterrupted, with only a cursory French force giving chase.

On the same day as the Battle of Ligny, Napoleon's army's remaining left flank had been engaged with some of Wellington's forces at Quatre Bras, where they had attempted unsuccessfully to overrun the Prince of Orange's position. With the Prussians apparently defeated, Napoleon turned his attention on Quatre Bras, reaching the area the following day. By this point, however, Quatre Bras had been abandoned by both sides; Wellington could not hold it without the Prussians. After catching up with his left flank commander, Marshal Michel Ney, who was pursuing a retreating Wellington towards Waterloo, Napoleon ordered his right flank commander, Marshal Emmanuel de Grouchy, to see off the Prussians more definitively.

By this time, with Napoleon issuing the order late on the afternoon of 17 June, the Prussians had already made significant ground and regrouped at the town of Wavre - a position from which they could easily rejoin Wellington at Waterloo - and Marshal Grouchy was unsuccessful in catching them. Despite eventually defeating a solitary Prussian Corps at Wavre on 18 June, by this time the Battle of Waterloo was in full swing and Grouchy was unable to take part.

After Napoleon had issued the order to Marshal Grouchy he continued to hunt down Wellington with his remaining forces before making camp south-west of Wellington's position at Waterloo. The scene was now set for the Battle of Waterloo the next day (18 June), which, as we all know, resulted in a famous victory for the Duke of Wellington and a final defeat for Emperor Napoleon.

As a consequence of Napoleon's loss at Waterloo, the French monarchy was restored, with King Louis XVIII regaining the throne on 8 July 1815, while the emperor himself was banished to the volcanic island of Saint Helena in the Atlantic Ocean. Napoleon would live on Saint Helena for a further six years, before passing away in May 1821.

NAPOLEON'S BODYGUARD

Protecting Napoleon during the battle were his Old Guard - elite veterans of the Imperial Guard that he handpicked based on their combat experience. One of the most common traits was above average height, meaning that they towered over many other units on the battlefield.

SCOTS GREYS

The charge of the Royal Scots Greys at Waterloo became symbolic of the courage demonstrated by Coalition forces in the face of the might of Napoleon's army. Their charge famously repelled a key French advance, caused the complete destruction of a large French infantry column and led to the capture of Napoleon's 45th Regiment of the Line's eagle standard.

SEVENTH COALITION

While the primary antagonists of the Battle of Waterloo were the UK and France, a host of other nations played a part, joining with the British to form a coalition against the new emperor of France. These included the Netherlands, Hanover, Nassau, Bavaria and Prussia – the latter contributing most significantly.

HEAVY LOSSES

While Waterloo was not a medieval meat-grinder of a battle, with tactics very firmly on display, it still had a huge casualty list. Of Napoleon's 72,000 troops, around 25,000 were killed outright or wounded, 8,000 were taken prisoner and 15,000 went missing. The total for Wellington and his allies' soldiers killed, wounded or missing came to around 24,000.

Seventh Coalition

TROOPS 118,000
CAVALRY 11,000
CANNONS 150

DUKE OF WELLINGTON

LEADER

Rising to prominence in the Napoleonic Wars, Arthur Wellesley remained commander-in-chief of the British Army until his death in 1852.
Strengths Very confident and energetic leader
Weakness Not the most tactically astute of generals

INFANTRY

IMPORTANT UNIT

Among the best on the planet, the infantry dug in deep at Waterloo to deny many French cavalry charges.
Strength Versatile troops that could fight at close to medium range
Weaknesses Easily outflanked by cavalry and vulnerable to cannons

CANNON

KEY WEAPON

Very destructive, the Coalition's artillery helped slow the French forces and break up their lines.
Strengths Cannons had excellent range and could do a lot of damage
Weaknesses Needed supporting troops for protection as fairly fragile under fire and few in number

01 First foray

Between 10 and 11.30am on 18 June the Battle of Waterloo began with a French attack on a Coalition position at Hougoumont, a large farmhouse that served as a tactical outpost. This fighting was low key at first with few troops from each side engaged, but by the early afternoon it had become a bloody epicentre for much of the fighting, with the Coalition forces holding out against numerous French assaults.

02 GRANDE BATTERIE

Around midday Napoleon ordered his grande batterie of 80 cannons to open fire upon Wellington's position. The cannons caused many casualties in Wellington's cavalry, opening a potential weak point in the defending lines.

10 French army retreats

With the French left, right and centre now disintegrating, the only cohesive force left available to Napoleon were two battalions of his Old Guard. Despite hoping to rally his remaining troops behind them, the strength of the Coalition's forces left this untenable, and all Napoleon could do was order a retreat. His exit was covered by the Old Guard, many of whom died holding back the Coalition's advance.

03 French infantry attack

After the Coalition's lines had been weakened, Napoleon began his attack proper, with numerous infantry corps advancing. The initial fighting went the way of the French, with the left's infantry pressing Wellington's forces back. However, just when it looked like Napoleon would make a decisive break, he was informed that Prussian troops were fast approaching. He tried to send word to Marshal Grouchy to engage with them, but his commander was in Wavre.

04 British heavy cavalry attack

Seeing their infantry was about to buckle, Wellington's First and Second Brigade of heavy cavalry charged and smashed into the French infantry. By the time they reached the bottom of the hill, they had completely halted the infantry's advance. In doing so, however, they had left themselves exposed and without backup.

09 PLANCENOIT RECAPTURED

The Prussian army retook Plancenoit and targeted Napoleon's right flank, giving Wellington the upper hand. The Old Guard who had been supporting the French position at Plancenoit beat a hasty retreat.

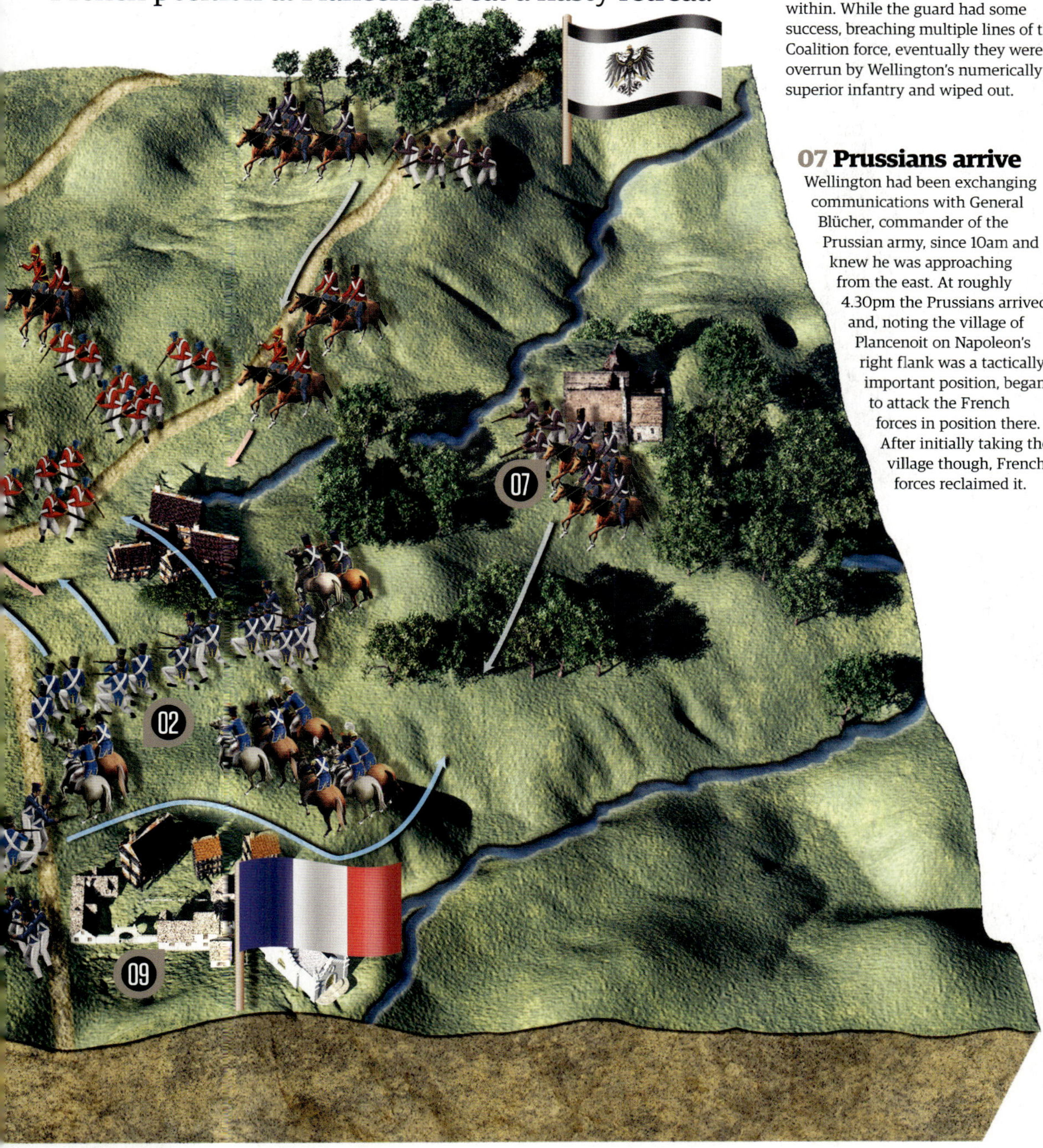

08 Imperial Guard attacks Wellington

With his forces temporarily holding off the Prussians at Plancenoit, Napoleon went on one last major offensive. He sent the supposedly undefeatable Imperial Guard into Wellington's army's centre in an attempt to break through and attack his flanks from within. While the guard had some success, breaching multiple lines of the Coalition force, eventually they were overrun by Wellington's numerically superior infantry and wiped out.

07 Prussians arrive

Wellington had been exchanging communications with General Blücher, commander of the Prussian army, since 10am and knew he was approaching from the east. At roughly 4.30pm the Prussians arrived and, noting the village of Plancenoit on Napoleon's right flank was a tactically important position, began to attack the French forces in position there. After initially taking the village though, French forces reclaimed it.

05 Napoleon counters

With the Coalition's heavy cavalry now facing squares of French infantry to the front and with no support, Napoleon ordered a counterattack, dispatching his cuirassier and lancer regiments from his own cavalry division. A massive central battle ensued, with cavalry, infantry and artillery all involved. While Napoleon's cavalry regiments took out much of the Coalition's heavy cavalry, they could not wipe them out. Napoleon also dispatched troops to intercept the Prussians.

06 Stalemate

At the heart of the battle, Coalition and French squares then undertook a series of back-and-forth exchanges. All the while cannon and musket fire continued to rain down from all sides and, aside from one more combined arms assault by the French on the centre-right of Wellington's lines, a general mêlée ensued, with each side seeing their numbers steadily chipped away.

France

TROOPS 72,000

CAVALRY 14,000

CANNONS 250

NAPOLEON BONAPARTE

LEADER

Emperor Bonaparte became famous for his tactical genius, enabling him to take over much of central Europe.

Strengths A savvy strategist with plenty of battle experience

Weaknesses Erratic; he took a detached approach to fighting

CAVALRY

IMPORTANT UNIT

French light cavalry was considered the best of its kind in the world and played a large part in holding off the Coalition's heavy cavalry charges.

Strength Fast, agile units capable of easily outflanking the enemy

Weakness Direct cavalry charges rely on surprise to be most effective

MUSKET

KEY WEAPON

The musket was wielded by Napoleon's Old Guard with deadly accuracy, picking off large numbers of Coalition soldiers at Waterloo.

Strength Excellent medium-range stopping power

Weaknesses Slow to reload and also poor in hand-to-hand combat

Hitler at War

To what extent did the Führer's military leadership style affect the outcome of World War II? Discover the expert verdict on Adolf Hitler's tactical prowess

Since the fall of the Third Reich in 1945, our verdict on Hitler's leadership has mostly come from the pens and mouths of his generals. Many of these men had grown to resent their former leader, and with the fall of Germany they seized the opportunity to criticise and embarrass the Führer at every opportunity. But beneath the façade of slander and betrayal, was Hitler's military leadership style truly so unpopular - and to what extent did his decisions determine the outcome of World War II?

"So much of what we thought we knew about Hitler for many years came from his generals, and they have a lot of reasons to either consciously or unconsciously falsify what happened," says Dr Geoffrey Megargee. "They more or less accused him of starting the war against their advice and then of losing it through his meddling, but that doesn't really give us an accurate picture."

When Germany declared war on Poland on 1 September 1939, they had not expected to encounter such fierce opposition from Britain and France. After both countries declared war on the Third Reich in response, the German population were distraught; World War I was still fresh in the nation's memory, and the country had only just started to thrive again from the harsh penalties imposed after their defeat in 1918 and later the Great Depression of the 1930s.

Now the leader of the Nazi party was dragging them into another war against familiar foes. Despite his popularity, Hitler was not immune to criticism and the start of World War II saw a significant drop in morale in Germany.

But that all changed when France fell in just a matter of weeks to Germany's Blitzkrieg tactics. According to Dr Megargee, "Once France was knocked out of the war, I suspect at that point Hitler probably reached about the high point of his popularity with the German population because Germany had just managed to defeat in a matter of weeks this enemy that had defeated them over four years of combat in World War I. That was quite a coup."

Riding on this success, Hitler quickly involved himself in all aspects of the operations of the German army - much more so than the respective leaders of other countries. He was known for an attention to detail that was interfering at best, and detrimental at worst. "Hitler was in charge of strategy from the start, figuring out against whom Germany was going to fight, and his decisions were not nearly so unpopular as [his generals] tried to say later on.

"They were all in favour of starting a war against Poland, they were all in favour of starting a war against the Soviet Union - these were not unpopular decisions on Hitler's part.

"But when we get down to the next level of warfare - operations, ie planning and conducting campaigns - here Hitler was on weaker ground. He had some good insights, and some of his decisions turned out well, but he didn't have any systematic training in this kind of warfare and that showed."

The popular picture of Hitler is of a man that heeded no advice - a leader that would rather listen to his own gut instinct than to the rational arguments of his generals. This was true to an extent; Hitler was distrustful of some of his senior officers, who in turn criticised him for his inexperience in warfare, and he certainly grew more distrustful and erratic as the war progressed.

That being said it was largely the officers themselves that have swayed our view of Hitler's leadership, as they resented his involvement in their military, as Dr Megargee points out. "General [Franz] Halder, for example - who was chief of the general staff from October 1938 to September 1942 - maintained a sort of passive-aggressive relationship with Hitler. He would agree openly with what Hitler had to say, but would then try to work around the decisions that Hitler made." However, for the first few years of the war at least, Hitler relied upon his generals greatly and would seek their advice on both strategy and tactics, albeit some more so than others.

The Führer, though, was not blithely ignorant; he was well aware of the hatred some of his officers felt towards him, and he used this to his advantage at every available opportunity. "He tended to play off commanders against each other. They would throw in their opinions at briefings and he would go with whoever he agreed with, so it was sort of a divide-and-conquer kind of approach to leadership. And once he made up his mind on something he could be extremely stubborn about it."

As mentioned the Führer had an uncanny attention to detail and thus involved himself in the smallest of minutiae about particular units, and many of his generals would be caught short if they could not supply him with precise information - such as, for instance, the number of tanks in a particular division. By 1943 Hitler had started bringing two stenographers (court recorders) to each of his meetings, and although many records were burned at the end of the war, those that survived reveal Hitler's meetings to be intricate to the point that they were discussing the movements of very small units on the front and their equipment.

Hitler's level of involvement was beginning to pose a problem. "You could argue that Hitler was too detailed. When you start talking about how many trucks a particular unit has at its disposal, that's just ridiculous for a head of state to try to interpret as a military commander. There's no way that he can understand the situation well enough to an extent that it's going to make a positive difference on the battlefield." Such was the extent of his attention for detail that by the end of the war almost no major unit was allowed to move without Hitler's permission - especially one on the retreat.

The Invasion of Poland

1-27 September 1939

On 1 September 1939, Nazi Germany invaded Poland, and just two days later both Britain and France declared war on Germany. World War II had begun.

The campaign in Poland was devised by General Franz Halder, chief of the general staff, but it was ultimately Hitler who gave the order to invade. Germany employed Blitzkrieg (which translates as 'lightning war') tactics, denting Poland's front lines with Panzer tanks and aircraft before troops moved through gaps this created. The approach was hugely successful, although it was not one that Hitler came up with. On 27 September 1939 Poland surrendered, albeit with a Soviet invasion from the east dividing the country.

The effects of this campaign were felt across the globe and signalled the start of World War II. Hitler would go on to employ the same tactics in other countries, including France in 1940.

The expert's view

"If Germany was going to have a war, then September 1939 was probably the best time to attack," says Dr Megargee. "The Allies were getting stronger, so the timing was working against Germany at that point and I think Hitler even said that. But, of course, he was counting on Britain and France to stay out of it. He figured they would let Poland go; he underestimated them on that point."

Verdict: Success

"The whole idea of starting the war was a poor strategic decision, but if Hitler was going to start one this was probably the best he could do."

General Franz Halder (left) with General Von Brauchitsch

Hitler watches on as German troops march towards Poland

"When you start talking about how many trucks a particular unit has at its disposal, that's just ridiculous for a head of state to try to interpret"

General Halder (at Hitler's left), discussing plans with General Jodl (at Hitler's right) and others over a large map

The Fall of France

10 May – 22 June 1940

Resigned to the fact that both Britain and France had declared war, Hitler knew that he needed to nullify France to have any chance of fending off the Allies. So, on 10 May 1940, Germany invaded its Gallic neighbour.

The campaign consisted of two operations. The first was Case Yellow (Fall Gelb), where German forces advanced into the Ardennes region and pushed the Allied forces in Belgium back to the sea. This ultimately resulted in the mass evacuation of the British Expeditionary Force at Dunkirk between 26 May and 4 June.

A second operation known as Case Red (Fall Rot) began on 5 June, with Germany's air superiority and armoured units overcoming the depleted French forces. German forces pushed into Paris on 14 June, and by 22 June they had signed an armistice with the French that would see Germany occupy the north and the west of the country until 1944.

The two major operations were not Hitler's doing. However, it was Hitler that ultimately convinced the German High Command to accept the plan, which undoubtedly was a significant factor in defeating France. The campaign prevented the stalemate that had occurred in World War I, and enabled Germany to begin focusing its attention on other foes.

The expert's view

"Hitler – especially at this stage of the war – was extremely nervous about how it was going to all work out. He was very worried about the left flank of that attack going through the Ardennes to the coast of the English Channel, and he was worried that the French might counterattack. He was [pivotal] in getting the German High Command to accept [Erich von] Manstein's plan to go through the Ardennes."

Verdict: Success

"Hitler had a good instinct to go with what Manstein proposed. Hitler was on the right side of that decision."

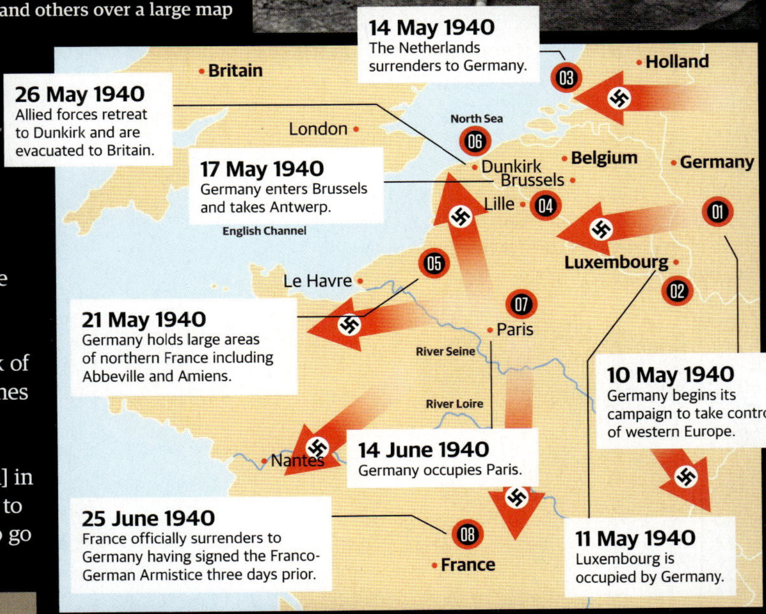

Who was Erich von Manstein?

Born in Berlin on 24 November 1887, and after seeing service during World War I, Manstein was the chief of staff to Germany's Army Group South at the start of World War II. He was one of the main instigators of an offensive through the Ardennes (known as Case Yellow or Fall Gelb) during the invasion of France in 1940, which ensured Germany a swift victory in Europe. He later attained the rank of general, but his constant criticism of Hitler's strategies coupled with his failure to turn the tide at the Battle of Stalingrad in 1942 saw him ousted from the German army in March 1944. He was captured and imprisoned by the British in August 1945, and died almost 30 years later on 9 June 1973.

Hitler in Paris following the fall of France

Aside from Hitler's over-reliance on details, as the war dragged on he began to rely more and more upon his instincts, and "there were times that served him well, but a lot of times that didn't," Dr Megargee continues. "By [1944] he was sort of living in a fantasy land, frankly; he thought he was going to burst through the Allied lines and separate the British from the Americans and the whole Allied Western coalition would fall apart and he could go back to fighting the Russians [in the east]. By then his instinct had become delusional." At this point in the war Hitler's generals were doing their best to convince him of employing different tactics, such as initiating smaller offensives instead of large ones, but Hitler was having none of it.

For all his shortcomings, though, Hitler did at times make some smart decisions, but embarking on a war at all was a poor one. "The whole war was badly conceived to begin with. The idea that Germany could take on the British Empire, the Soviet Union and then the US at the same time was at the very least problematic. I've had people ask me when do I consider the war to have been lost, and I semi-jokingly say, '1 September 1939'."

With the hand Hitler had been dealt - or rather the hand he had dealt himself - he managed to conduct himself, and the army, in a reasonable manner at the start of the conflict.

The Battle of the Atlantic

3 September 1939 - 8 May 1945

For all his inexperience in ground warfare, Hitler was even more of a novice when it came to the sea. He didn't have any considerable knowledge of navies, and thus for the most part he left naval operations in the hands of generals he trusted including Erich Raeder and Karl Dönitz, who both served as commander-in-chief of the Kriegsmarine during the war.

The Battle of the Atlantic was the longest military campaign of World War II, running continuously from the outbreak of war on 3 September 1939 to 8 May 1945. The majority of the campaign was fought between the Kriegsmarine and the combined Allied navies of Britain and Canada, and later in 1941 the US. The Germans relied considerably on their U-boat submarines, with only a handful of warships available.

The campaign revolved largely around the Allied blockade of Germany and a subsequent counter-blockade by the Kriegsmarine. German U-boats attempted to attack convoy ships travelling across the Atlantic, but the strength of the Allied navies, combined with Hitler's decision to pull many U-boats away for other campaigns, would see the Allies gain control of the Atlantic and the Channel by 1944.

The expert's view

"Hitler was involved in some key decisions, especially to take U-boats away from the Atlantic and send them to Norway and the Mediterranean. One probably can't argue that those decisions weakened the Atlantic campaign fatally, but they certainly didn't help it."

Verdict: Failure

"Hitler's on-again, off-again decisions regarding resources for the construction of U-boats did hurt the [campaign] considerably."

The British Royal Navy battleship HMS Barham explodes as her 38cm (15in) magazine ignites

Officers on a destroyer, escorting a large convoy of ships, keep a lookout for enemy submarines in 1941

Key moments in World War II

1939

Outbreak of WWII
Hitler invades Poland and, two days later, Britain and France declare war on Germany, heralding the start of World War II.
1 September 1939

Atlantic warfare
For almost six years the longest military campaign of WWII sees the Allied and Axis powers fight for control of the Atlantic.
3 September 1939

Blitzkrieg strikes
Germany takes control of large portions of western Europe, including Belgium, culminating in the surrender of France.
25 June 1940

Luftwaffe air raids
The German Luftwaffe begins an air campaign against the UK, but the Royal Air Force (RAF) stands strong and is victorious almost four months later.
10 July 1940

The Battle of Britain

10 July - 31 October 1940

With France defeated with surprising swiftness, Hitler was unsure what to do next. The German High Command had been especially unconvinced that France would fall in such a short amount of time, and thus they set about deciding what Germany's next course of action should be.

Hitler was all too aware that Britain posed a significant threat and, with little chance of a diplomatic resolution, he would have to attack. The prospects of a potential invasion of Britain (known as Operation Sealion), however, were incredibly slim. The Royal Navy was far superior to the German Navy (Kriegsmarine), while the Royal Air Force posed a formidable threat in the skies. If an invasion were to happen, the German army wanted to get as many troops ashore as possible, while the Kriegsmarine was adamant that such an operation would be impossible.

With numerous options available, Hitler eventually opted to test out the defensive capabilities of Britain with an attack from the air. If the German Luftwaffe could manage to gain air superiority over the Royal Air Force, it could then keep the British Royal Navy at bay while Germany mounted an all-out ground invasion.

Britain, however, proved a much more stubborn opponent than Germany had ever anticipated, and ultimately the RAF was never in too much danger of succumbing to defeat. One of the key factors that affected the outcome was the decision for the Luftwaffe to switch from bombing British military targets and airfields to bombing cities such as London as a terror tactic.

With the Luftwaffe unable to gain air superiority, Hitler postponed Operation Sealion indefinitely in October 1940.

"The Battle of France is over. The Battle of Britain is about to begin"

Winston Churchill, 18 June 1940

About 6,000 Heinkel He 111s were built, but for the most part they were outperformed by British Hurricanes and Spitfires

However, the bombing of civilian Britain continued in what was to become known as the Blitz.

The expert's view

"The popular image is that the RAF was sort of on the ropes when the Germans made the switch [from bombing airfields to cities], and that in effect took the pressure off [Britain]. On the other hand, while the RAF was having a hard time all they really had to do was withdraw a little farther back into the country and husband their resources and they still could have stopped an invasion quite effectively. I don't get the impression the Luftwaffe ever really had a good chance of knocking out the RAF."

Verdict: Failure

"Hitler may have been involved in the decision to go from attacking British airfields and radar stations to bombing London, but this certainly did not help the campaign."

USSR invasion
Germany invades the Soviet Union, reneging on the Non-Aggression Pact that the two countries had signed in 1939.
22 June 1941

Pearl Harbor attack
Japanese fighter planes attack the American base at Pearl Harbor, killing over 2,000 people. Four days later, the USA enters the war.
7 December 1941

D-Day landings
An Allied campaign of over 300,000 soldiers begins landings in Normandy in northern France in order to break Germany's stranglehold on Europe.
6 June 1944

Hitler dies
Hitler commits suicide in his Führerbunker as Germany faces defeat in the Battle of Berlin with the Soviet Union. Germany surrenders six days later.
1 May 1945

1945

Nuclear attack
The US drops atomic bombs on Hiroshima and Nagasaki in Japan, killing tens of thousands in an instant. On 2 September Japan surrenders and WWII ends.
6 and 9 August 1945

The invasion of the USSR

22 June 1941 – 24 July 1944

The height of Hitler's involvement with his army came in 1941 when he decided to invade the USSR. Germany's battle with the Red Army began with the five-month-long Operation Barbarossa on 22 June 1941, and culminated in the Soviets liberating Minsk (Belarus) and Majdanek (Poland) in July 1944.

Hitler and his generals believed that the Soviet Union would fall if Germany mounted a sustained attack. They presumed, somewhat naively, that the Red Army would collapse and the Soviet people would surrender after a short military campaign, allowing Germany to occupy large portions of the USSR while focusing their efforts on Britain in the west. This, of course, was anything but what really happened, and Hitler's underestimation of the Soviet Union was a major failing of the entire campaign.

Hitler held a great number of debates in Barbarossa itself regarding the direction of the main attack: whether it should go to Moscow or into the Ukraine and up through Leningrad. Hitler ultimately made the choice to focus on the economic resources of the Soviet Union rather than the capital. Hitler had good instincts in this regard, but the overall decision to attack the Soviet Union was a poor one.

The Soviets refused to 'roll over' the way the Germans had expected them to, and while Hitler's direction of the campaign in the summer of 1941 was adequate, his refusal to heed the advice of his generals as the invasion dragged on was a major flaw on his part.

Germany's Blitzkrieg tactics that had been so successful earlier in the war were nullified by the Red Army's tactic of holding back before launching counteroffensives. In December 1941 Germany was at the gates of Moscow, but the Soviets kept attacking and wore the Germans down. With winter approaching, many of Hitler's generals suggested the German army should retreat and consolidate before attacking again in spring 1942. Hitler, though, was adamant the army should hold everywhere to ensure they didn't lose any of their heavy equipment, which he came under much criticism for. His decision was arguably the right one at first, but later in the war he became too enamoured with the technique.

With their first attempt at defeating the Soviet Union unsuccessful, Germany would try again before the war was out. Hitler and his generals were convinced the Red Army was on the ropes, and sustained attacks would wear them out. But the Russians stood strong and, after successfully defending key cities including Moscow in 1942, Hitler was left with few options but retreat.

The expert's view

"The genocide of the Jews and the general abuse and destruction of the Soviet population really made it impossible to come to any kind of arrangement with the Soviet people. There's an argument to be made that if the Germans had gone in with a different attitude they could have [tempted] Ukraine and the Baltic states, and perhaps other portions of the Soviet Union, away. But Hitler assumed they were going to have a quick military victory and saw no reason to compromise. He convinced himself that the Red Army must be on the ropes, and they kept pushing in the winter, still trying to take Moscow and still trying to advance in the south, and they ran out of steam. As a result, Germany found itself in the middle of winter without the proper equipment, with no place to go, and vulnerable to the Soviet counteroffensive."

Verdict: Failure

"If you ignore the bad decision of attacking the USSR to begin with, on an operational level Hitler did fairly well [at first, but he lost his way]."

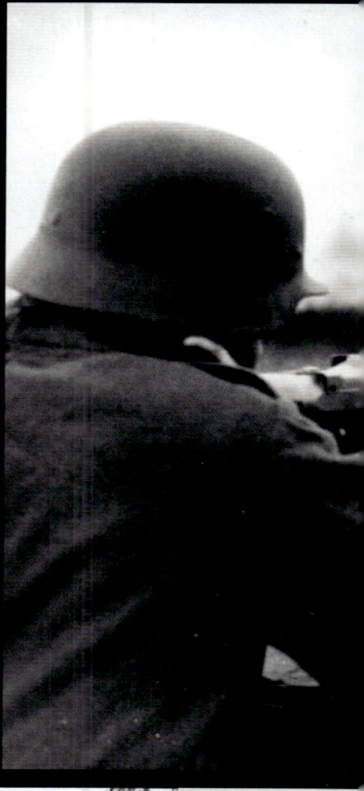

SS Division Panzer Totenkopf (ie 'skull') awaiting orders in 1941

German troops moving into Russian territory in armoured vehicles in June 1941

Hitler poses with his senior officers and generals in June 1940

A soldier defending the German line with an MG 34 machine gun

To start with Germany made good progress into Russia, but the tide began to turn as winter set in

"By 1945 Hitler was all but dictating to his generals exactly what to do, and he had little trust left in any of them"

The invasion of Poland was arguably his only course of action once the wheels of war had been set in motion, and the manner in which Germany conquered not only Poland but other nations, such as France, was commendable; they had swiftly and effectively seized control of a large chunk of Europe, thanks to Hitler's belief that France could be beaten. What he didn't count on, however, was the steadfast refusal of Britain to enter into any sort of diplomatic negotiations.

"With Britain not giving up his options were becoming extremely limited. He was in an economic bind; he was not going to be able to continue this war over the long run against the British because, sooner or later, Germany was going to run out of strength for that - even with the tentative support of the Soviet Union.

"So he made the decision for strategic and economic and ideological reasons to attack the Soviet Union - something he was more or less intending to do all along anyway. That decision was based on the assumption - which his generals shared and backed - that the USSR would collapse - that there would be one short military campaign which would destroy the Red Army. Obviously that didn't work out very well."

Indeed, the war came to a point in 1941 where defeat for Germany seemed all but inevitable and Hitler's strategic choices became ever-more limited. By 1942, after a second attempt at defeating the Soviet Union had failed, Dr Megargee suggests that, for Hitler, it became "just a matter of holding out as best he could in the hope that the Allied coalition would break up. And it became more based on delusion than anything else."

By 1945 Hitler was all but dictating to his generals exactly what to do, and he had very little trust left in any of them. But by then, and possibly even much earlier, for all the strategic knowledge in the world, Hitler had no hope of leading the Third Reich to an eventual victory. "I think quite honestly his biggest strategic mistake was starting the war.

"Beyond that you get into details, and there are arguments to be made for each of the strategic decisions he made after that - declaring war on the Soviet Union and the United States, for example - but that's all within the context of a war in which Germany was, I won't say fated to lose, but certainly was not going to win easily."

Hitler's deterioration from sanity to irrationality, therefore, was not the deciding factor in the war, however there can be little doubt that his leadership style did little to help what was already a difficult cause for Germany.

Perhaps even with the greatest generals in the world the Third Reich would have been defeated; of that we cannot be certain. What we do know, however, was that Hitler was not the great military leader he himself thought he was. For his handful of victories there was a huge truckload of defeats, and his refusal to listen to reason ultimately accelerated Nazi Germany down the path to an unavoidable defeat.

American Civil War

USA 12 APRIL 1861 – 10 MAY 1865

What was it?

The American Civil War was a conflict between the 11 Confederate states who sought independence from the remaining Northern and other loyal states. The key issues causing division between the North and South were state rights, the economy and - tied up in both of these - the abolition of slavery.

How did it start?

Tensions between the largely industrial North and agricultural South had been rising, but the election of Abraham Lincoln as president on a platform of keeping slavery out of the new territories tipped the balance. Before he even took office in March 1861, seven Southern states had seceded from the Union.

Where did they fight?

Some of the biggest battles were fought in Pennsylvania, Georgia, Virginia, Maryland and Tennessee, although conflict reached many corners of the USA. It didn't quite reach the north-east heartland of the Union though.

The Battle of Gettysburg

Also known for Lincoln's Gettysburg Address, this small borough of Pennsylvania was the ground for one of the bloodiest confrontations of the Civil War. Casualties from Gettysburg are estimated to have been around 51,000 - that accounts for around eight per cent of all casualties during the four-year conflict.

The first industrial war

The American Civil War is considered to be the template for many subsequent industrial wars that would follow. It became characterised by large-scale conscription of the civilian population, use of railroads and other fast transportation for troop deployment, and communication by telegraph and wireless devices.

The end of slavery
The Emancipation Proclamation was an executive order issued by President Lincoln on 1 January 1863, freeing slaves in the Confederate states. It paved the way for the 13th Amendment, which was passed by the Senate in April 1864 and ratified in December the following year, abolishing slavery nationwide.

The signing of the Emancipation Proclamation at the start of 1863

An illustration of the first day of fighting at the Battle of Gettysburg

Union vs Confederacy
The Union, ie Northern States, was made up of 20 free states and five border slave states and stood against 11 Southern slave states, making up the Confederacy. It has been estimated that the forces on each side numbered around 2.13 million Union troops against 1.08 million Confederate troops.

Death by disease
More troops were killed in the Civil War than in any other conflict in which the USA has been involved before or since. Even so, more men died of disease during the war than from combat. Of the estimated 620,000 casualties, almost two-thirds are believed to have perished to disease.

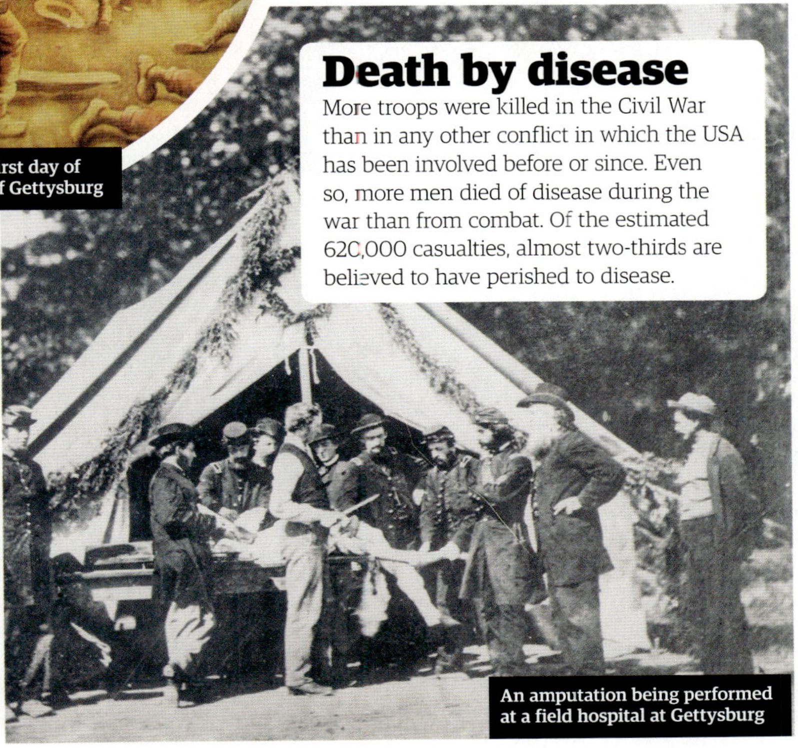

An amputation being performed at a field hospital at Gettysburg

Lincoln's assassination
On 14 April 1865, as the Union celebrated victory, President Lincoln was shot and killed by actor John Wilkes Booth while attending Ford's Theatre, Washington DC. Lincoln was pronounced dead at a nearby guesthouse at 7.22am on 15 April.

Key figures

Abraham Lincoln
1809-1865
A Kentucky-born congressman for Illinois, Lincoln was a lawyer before running for president.

Robert E Lee
1807-1870
General and commander of the Confederate army, he was actually offered command of Union forces first.

Ulysses S Grant
1822-1885
Lieutenant general during the Civil War, Grant was later elected president, holding office from 1869 to 1877.

Jefferson Davis
1808-1889
Confederate president during the Civil War, he was captured but freed after two years without facing treason charges.

John Wilkes Booth
1838-1865
The assassin who killed Lincoln at Ford's Theatre had originally plotted only kidnap before changing the plan to murder.

Major events

Lincoln elected
6 November 1860
Abraham Lincoln wins a very divisive election despite receiving no support from a single Southern state.

Confederacy formed
8 February 1861
The Confederate States of America is formed by six of the seven secession states.

Fort Sumter attacked
12-14 April 1861
The Battle of Fort Sumter near Charleston, South Carolina, and its surrender mark the first engagement of the Civil War.

Emancipation Proclamation
22 September 1862
Lincoln announces a preliminary proclamation stating his aim to free Southern slaves, making abolition the focus of the war.

Gettysburg
1-3 July 1863
Described as the turning point of the war, the Battle of Gettysburg is also the bloodiest confrontation of the conflict.

THE NIGHT

While total war brought women into factories and farms in the US and Britain, in Soviet Russia they took to the skies to defend their motherland

Nadezhda 'Nadia' Popova was just shy of her 20th birthday when her brother was killed, and the Gestapo ejected her family from their home near Donetsk in Ukraine, smashed the windows and chopped down the cherry trees. A member of one of the Soviet Union's numerous flying clubs – aviation was one of the many symbols of modernity and dynamism that gripped the imagination of communist society – since she was 15 years-old (she hadn't told her parents), Nadia had completed her first solo flight and her first parachute jump aged 16. As soon as war was declared she abandoned the dress she was ironing and rushed to the airfield to enlist, but it would only be October 1941 – four months of heartbreak later – that her offer would be accepted.

She would become part of a unit – a squadron leader, no less – that flew up to 30,000 missions and dropped an estimated 23,000 tons of bombs, outfoxed the growling Messerschmitt fighters of the Luftwaffe with the most primitive of planes and struck fear into the hearts of the most feared fighting force of the 20th Century. She lost 30 comrades in action, and would be one of the 23 women of her regiment awarded the nation's highest honour – the gold star and red ribbon of the Hero of the Soviet Union, along with the Order of Lenin and three Orders of the Patriotic War. By 1945, this incredible young woman from the coal fields of eastern Ukraine would write her name in pencil on the wall of Reichstag in Berlin, the red flag of the Union of Soviet Socialist Republics fluttering victoriously through the smoke and booming artillery as Hitler's empire finally died.

Nadezhda Popova was a Night Witch, and institutionalised disdain was as implacable an opponent as the Nazi aggressors she lined up in her sights.

In June 1941 the Wehrmacht ground a murderous trail across the vast unprepared expanse of the Soviet Union; Operation Barbarossa was well underway. Hitler's plan to seize vast swathes of fertile Belorusian farmland, Ukrainian oil fields and Russian industrial centres had taken Soviet despot Joseph Stalin by surprise. Stalin had absolute faith in 1939's Molotov-Ribbentrop Pact which defined the spheres of influence between the obviously incompatible superpowers.

WITCHES

Germany's Nazi regime nursed a pathological hatred of communists, Jews and Eastern Europe's Slavic peoples which they believed to be racially inferior to Germanic 'Aryans', and millions of Slavs were to be murdered or deported to make way for German settlers. More than a war of conquest, this was, in the Fuhrer's own words, a "war of annihilation" that transformed Europe's eastern fringe into a great and terrible charnel house. Steeling the will of his commanders, Hitler reminded them in a secret briefing, "This struggle is one of ideologies and racial differences and will have to be conducted with unprecedented, unmerciful, and unrelenting harshness."

The unprepared Red Army was overrun, and by October 1941 the swastika was flying over Estonia, Lithuania, Latvia, Belarus, and Ukraine.

"Lenin left us a great estate and we made s**t out of it," Stalin reflected later in the war.

Despite the number of women prepared to fight or fly to defend their homeland and avenge their loved ones, and the supposed egalitarianism of communist society, women were refused combat roles. One young woman, eager to serve, recalled a recruiting officer telling her, "Things may be bad but we're not so desperate that we're going to put little girls like you up in the skies. Go home and help your mother."

It would take a personal plea to Stalin from Marina Raskova - "Russia's Amelia Earhart," according to the international press - for the situation to change. Raskova, who was 29 when war broke out, was one of the Soviet Union's most famous aviators. In 1933 she became the first female navigator in the Soviet Air Force, became the first woman to teach at Zhukovsky Air Academy in 1934 - instructing male navigators who were initially sceptical of her abilities - and achieved celebrity status in 1938 when the 26 year-old Raskova, along with two other women, broke the record for a women's straight-line flight, travelling non-stop for over 5,900 kilometers (3660 miles) for Moscow to Komsomolsk in the Soviet Far East - bailing out with her parachute when they couldn't find the landing strip, Raskova spent ten days lost in the dense swampy taiga with no food, survival equipment or water. Unsurprisingly, they were proclaimed Heroes of the Soviet Union on their return and toasted by Stalin who declared that "Today these three women have avenged the heavy centuries of oppression of women."

How could he resist her after that?

"She said to Stalin, 'You know, they are running away to the front all the same,'" recalled one of her future comrades-in-arms, Yevgeniya Zhigulenko after the war. "It will be worse, you understand, if they steal airplanes to go...'"

With Stalin's blessing Raskova formed and trained the 586th Fighter Aviation Regiment, flying Yakovlev Yak-1, Yak-7B and Yak-9 fighters, Raskova's own 125th Guards Bomber Aviation Regiment which flew state-of-the-art Petlyakov Pe-2 dive bombers, much to the envy of male bomber regiments, and arguably the most famous of the lot - the 588th Night Bomber Regiment. Later renamed 46th 'Taman' Guards Night Bomber Aviation Regiment, it would become better known by the name given to it by its German enemies - die Nachthexen, or the Night Witches, as they would idle the engines and drop through the clouds at a glide to bomb German units in near-silence, with only a broomstick-like rustling of the canvas body to give them away. Specialists in precision bombing of supply depots and command

Marina Raskova (first right) and her co-pilots in 1938, right before their record breaking flight to Kosomolsk

Lydia Litvyak (left) plots her route with her colleagues on the tail of one of their regiment's Yak-1 fighters in 1942

Polikarpov Po-2 biplanes being flown before the war

Clad in her Air Force dress uniform, Nadezhda Popova (second right) and her comrades pour over a magazine in 1945

centres, and 'harassment bombing', in which the Night Witches' role was to keep the enemy on edge, unable to sleep or rest without fear of death from the skies at any time.

"We flew in sequence," recalled Nadia Popova in a 2009 interview for PRI's 'The World'. "One after another, and during the night we never let them rest so they called us 'Night Witches.' And the Germans made up stories. They spread the rumour that we had been injected with some unknown chemicals that enabled us to see so clearly at night."

"They would have to run out into the night in their underwear, and they were probably saying, 'Oh, those night witches!'" said Galina Brok-Beltsova, who flew with the Night Witches' sister regiment the 125th, in a 1996 issue of *FAA Aviation News*. "Or maybe they called us something worse. We, of course, would have preferred to have been called 'night beauties,' but, whichever, we did our job."

So unnerved were the enemy that many refused to smoke at night, lest the glow of their cigarettes reveal their positions, and an Iron Cross - the highest military honour awarded to German soldiers - would be issued to anyone who brought down a Night Witch.

They used wood-frame Polikarpov Po-2 biplanes - mockingly referred to as 'sewing machines' - that first saw service in 1928 and had since been relegated to crop-dusting and training. The Po-2's open cockpit exposed the pilot and navigator to frostbite, the small carrying capacity meant their two bombs were at the expense of even a radio and often a light machine gun, and so to keep up constant pressure on the Nazis were forced to fly over and over again - Popova's record was 18 gruelling sorties in one night. With an all-female ground crew as well as pilots, they moved from airbases behind Soviet lines to temporary airfields closer to the front and, as night fell, they deployed on their seemingly neverending missions from Popova's native Donetsk Basin to the besieged Crimea, to Belarus and Poland, and eventually even Germany itself, with planes landing and taking off three minutes apart. Always on the move and always in action, each Night Witch would fly around 1,000 missions by the end of the war when the average for a British bomber crew was 30. All this discomfort was nothing compared to the incredible dangers posed by their

THE WITCHES' BROOM

Close up on the Night Witches' infamous Polikarpov Po-2 'sewing machine' dive bomber

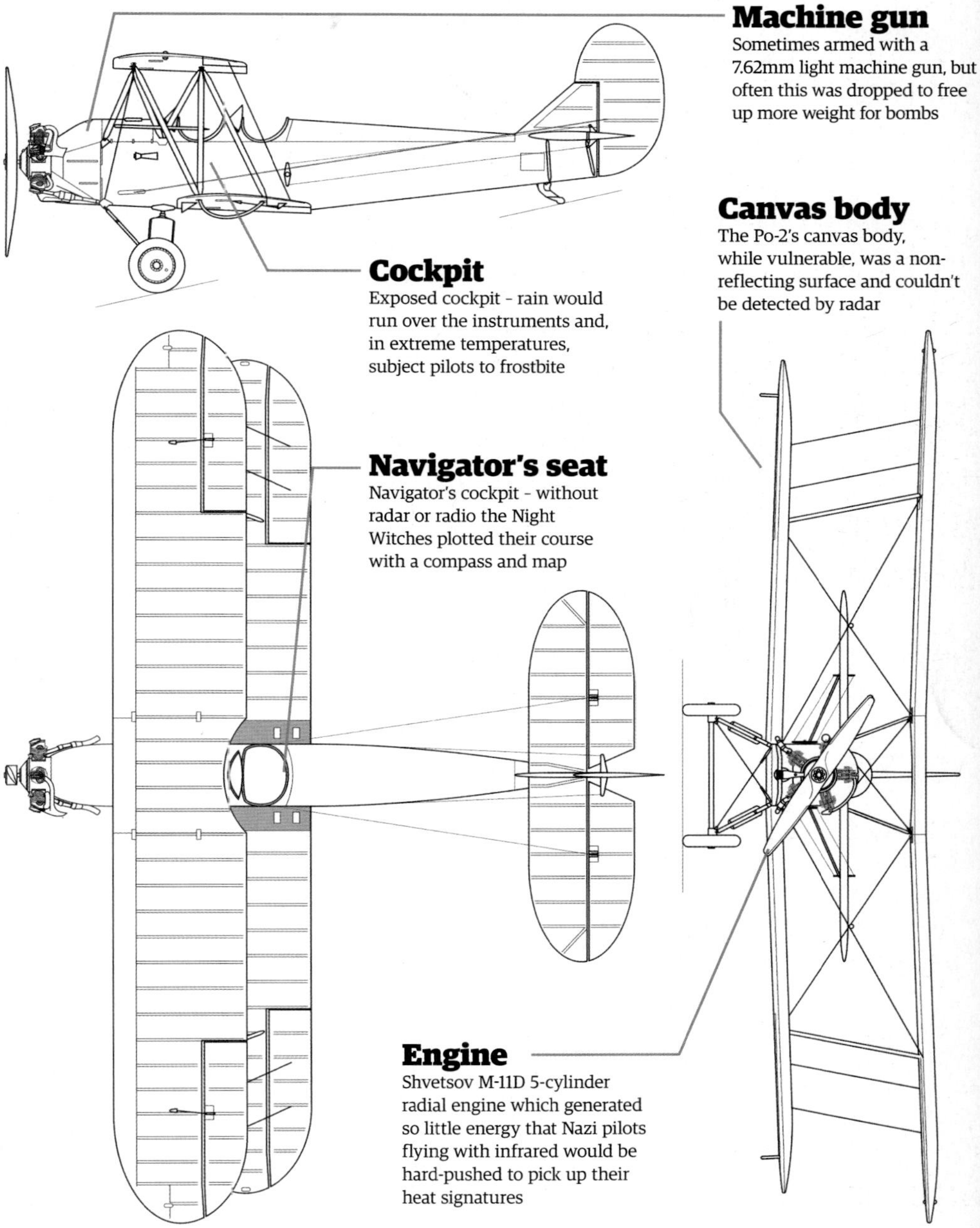

Machine gun
Sometimes armed with a 7.62mm light machine gun, but often this was dropped to free up more weight for bombs

Canvas body
The Po-2's canvas body, while vulnerable, was a non-reflecting surface and couldn't be detected by radar

Cockpit
Exposed cockpit - rain would run over the instruments and, in extreme temperatures, subject pilots to frostbite

Navigator's seat
Navigator's cockpit - without radar or radio the Night Witches plotted their course with a compass and map

Engine
Shvetsov M-11D 5-cylinder radial engine which generated so little energy that Nazi pilots flying with infrared would be hard-pushed to pick up their heat signatures

THE LUFTWAFFE

Model - Focke-Wulf 190

Entered combat - 1941

Max speed - 426 mph

Max altitude - 40,000 feet

Weapons -
2X 13 mm machine guns
2X 20 mm cannons

"I became a concentration of nerves and tension. My whole body was swept by fear of being killed"

The Night Witches receiving their orders on the Belorusian Front in 1944

obsolete biplanes which flew too low to bail out of, and would burst into to flames with sickening ease when hit by tracer shells from the 'circus of flak' – the rings of wicked 37mm anti-aircraft guns pointed skyward, guided by searchlights whose touch often meant death.

To combat the searchlights the Night Witches developed a strategy that tested their already beleaguered nerves, flying in groups of three, the first two planes would deliberately probe the circus until they had the attention of the searchlights and their accompanying symphony of gunfire, allowing the third plane to dip in and deliver its payload.

"We were flying without parachutes," said Popova. "We were not able to bail out. The whole crew which was shot during the night flight was burning alive, and it was awful. It was an absolutely unbearable sight. This was the most tragic part."

"You shouldn't misinterpret my words and think we faced death openly and bravely – it is not true," said Mariya Smirnova, one of the unit's most decorated pilots. "We never became accustomed to fear. Before each mission and as we approached the target, I became a concentration of nerves and tension. My whole body was swept by fear of being killed."

With a top speed of around 151 kilometres per hour (94 miles per hour) when fully loaded, this was well below the speed at which the engines of the Luftwaffe's infamous Messerschmitt Bf 109 and Focke-Wulf Fw 190 fighters would stall, making the Polikarpov Po-2 too slow and nimbly manoeuvrable to effectively engage in air combat – often dropping out of sight in the darkness by the time the German fighters had turned back around. Eventually the Germans were forced to start deploying their own mothballed biplanes to counter them. As advantages go, having a plane too clunky to dogfight was scarcely a fair trade for their vulnerability or the punishing frequency of their deployment, nor to the standard by which they were held by male airmen when they first deployed. Though the Night Witches were eventually awarded the coveted 'Guards Regiment' status, along with the variety of battle honours and medals they had rightfully earned, the prejudices that kept women out of combat until Operation Barbarossa reached its height weren't easily dispelled.

Clad in poorly fitting second-hand uniforms cast aside by male pilots, oversized boots stuffed with newspaper and given two years' training in only six months, Comrade Stalin may have held Marina Raskova in some regard, but to many male airmen and officers, these 20-somethings were nothing more than the 'skirt regiment.' Some male pilots refused to let their planes be maintained by female ground crews, and officers made disparaging reports of airwomen colouring in their lips with navigation pencil used to mark routes on maps, dancing on the airfield and keeping kittens in their barrack.

"What an exceptional case!" read one official report. "A regiment composed solely of girls! And what's more, these girls were eager to fight! But, after all, they were bound to become scared and cry! Besides – the crux of the matter was – could they fight?"

They could and they did, and amazingly the Soviet Union's female flyers managed this without sacrificing their femininity. While well aware that they were being held to the same – if not higher – standards of male pilots, the motto of the 588th was "You are a woman, and you should be proud of that."

Nobody exemplifies this better than the 'White Rose of Stalingrad', Lydia Litvyak, a pilot with one of the Night Witches' sister regiments. The world's first female fighter ace – a title awarded for a certain number of enemy kills, usually around five – she was reported to have painted a white rose on the nose of her Yak-1 fighter and kept bouquets

MAGNIFICENT FEMALE FLYING ACES

The other female flyers that took to the war-torn skies of the Thirties and Forties

THE WOMEN OF THE ATA (UK)

Originally set up to fly mail and medical supplies in 1940, with the demand for pilots flying military duties the Air Transport Auxiliary began to ferry planes from factories to airfields. Over 160 women from Britain and the Commonwealth (plus volunteers from other nations) would fly everything from the Spitfire to the B-25 Mitchell, and by 1943 their pay would be placed in line with their male counterparts. Credited with a vital role in the Battle Of Britain, 15 would be killed in service, including pioneering aviatrix Amy Johnson – the first woman to fly from England to Australia – who crashed into the Thames Estuary.

THE WASPS (USA)

With male pilots needed at the front the Women Airforce Service Pilots was formed in 1942 and, like the two earlier organisations it replaced, ferried planes around the US, but also transported cargo, towed targets in live fire exercises and a few even tested the new generation of rocket and jet-powered fighters for the US Air Force. Rather wonderfully WASP's winged munchkin mascot, the gremlin Fifinella, was invented by children's author Roald Dahl and drawn by founding father of feature-length animation Walt Disney. 1,074 women would serve in total and, although they never saw combat, 38 died in accidents.

SABIHA GÖKÇEN (TURKEY)

Lydia Litvyak may have been the first female fighter ace in history, but in 1936 Sabiha Gökçen became the world's first female fighter pilot. Adopted by Turkish leader Mustafa Kemal Atatürk when she was 12 years old, Sabiha became captivated by an airshow ten years later. Upon telling her adopted father that she wanted to become a pilot, Atatürk enrolled her as the Turkish Airforce's first female trainee. Though combat missions were rare (32 hours in all), she nonetheless flew 22 different types of aircraft and racked up a notable 8,000 hours in the air during her career.

of wildflowers in the cockpit, dyed her hair with peroxide obtained from the nearest hospital and would make scarves out of parachute material.

Nadia Popova similarly never forgot the motto of the 588th – despite the rigours of war, she would fluff up her hair – pressed flat by the leather flying cap – in a tortoiseshell mirror after each flight, and would eventually meet her future husband – pilot Semyon Kharlamov – in a convoy, after being shot down and separated from her unit. When Popova ended the war in the ruins of the Reichstag, Semyon was by her side, and they wrote their names together on the crumbling walls.

Like so many of Popova's contemporaries, Marina Raskova and Lydia Litvyak died in combat – Raskova in 1943, crashing into the banks of the Volga river in a violent snow-storm, and Litvyak later the same year, ambushed by Messerschmitts while she attacked a German bomber. She was only 21.

Popova survived, married, and returned to her home town a hero, greeted by crowds throwing flowers and a marching band – a more triumphant and provincial echo of Marina Raskova's state funeral in Moscow; the first the Soviet Union had given in wartime and a tribute to her status.

A Polikarpov Po-2, similar to that used by the Night Witches, being flown by partisans in

Despite the glory and the tragedy, the 588th and its sister regiments would be sadly disbanded and, much like in Britain and America, the role of women who had served their country every bit as faithfully and bravely as their husbands, fathers and brothers was expected to return to its pre-war setting. While many of them were forced to return home and become housewives – their deeds largely unremarked upon until the Eighties when the old authoritarian Russian regime began to crumble and the Europe bequeathed by Joseph Stalin was finally dismantled – Nadia Popova continued to work as a flight instructor, and when she died on 8 July 2013, aged 91, her death was mourned not just in her native Russia, but around the world.

History provides few enough examples of women being able to endure the same terrible hardships and perform the same incredible feats as men, and fewer still exist where they were allowed to accomplish these things on their own terms – as women. These 20-something girls from collective farms and steel towns defied society once when they became pilots, and then defied it again when they abandoned their ironing and took to the skies in war, and their example in an era when the idea of women in combat roles is still contested defies it once more. Throughout it all they never forgot, "You are a woman, and you should be proud of that."

"At night sometimes," Popova recalled. "I look up into the dark sky, close my eyes and picture myself as a girl at the controls of my bomber and I think, 'Nadia, how on earth did you do it?'"

EXPLORATION & DISCOVERY

Discover the incredible advances in human endeavour that helped create the world as we know it today

U.S

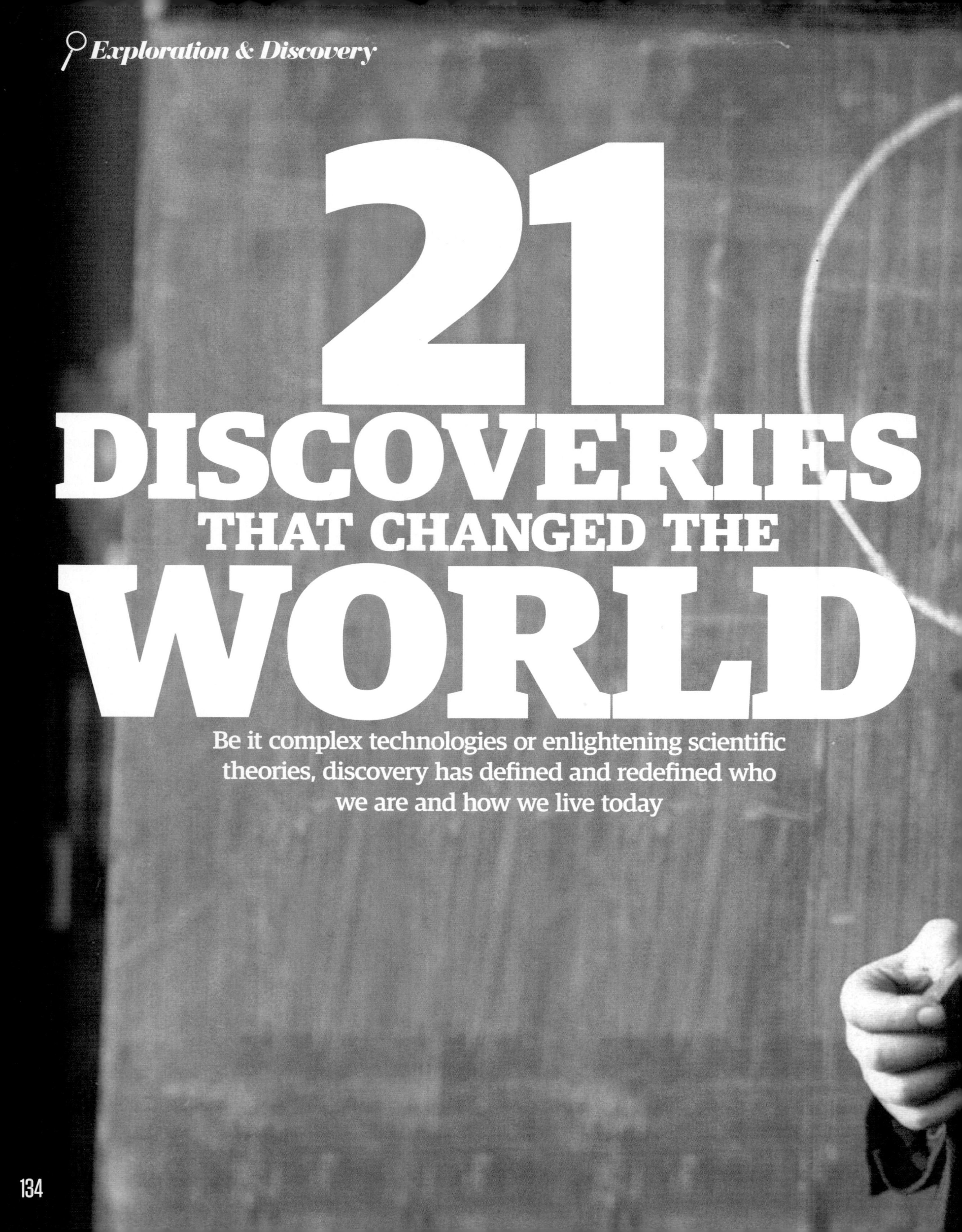

21 DISCOVERIES THAT CHANGED THE WORLD

Be it complex technologies or enlightening scientific theories, discovery has defined and redefined who we are and how we live today

E=MC²: THE EQUATION THAT REWROTE PHYSICS 1905

Easily Albert Einstein's most famous discovery, this deceptively simple equation states that mass and energy are related, and can work out how much energy is generated from mass being converted. After its conception it became a central tenet of all physics and remains so to this day.

While it's myth the apple fell on Isaac Newton's head, the apple inspiring him is thought to be true

NEWTON'S LAWS OF GRAVITY 1687

Prior to Isaac Newton's revelation of the force of gravity the question of why objects were bound to the Earth was limited to quasi-mystical explanations. However, when Newton introduced his law of universal gravitation in *Principia Mathematica* in 1687, he helped lay down a coherent explanation of how the physical world worked that would dominate science for centuries. The theory of gravitation was, according to Newton himself - who liked to repeat the story to colleagues - first formulated as he sat in Cambridge's Trinity College (though alternative locations have been claimed) and witnessed an apple fall from a tree. While it is myth that the apple fell on Newton's head, texts from the time - such as William Stukeley's *Memoirs Of Sir Isaac Newton's Life* - confirm the incident, with Newton being inspired to determine why that apple should always descend perpendicularly to the ground.

"Newton helped lay down a coherent explanation of how the world worked"

Calculus - the science of change 1687

Today, calculus has innumerable uses in the spheres of science, economics and education. The precursor to modern calculus was discovered in the 17th century, when English mathematician Isaac Newton and German mathematician Gottfried Leibniz both created their own systems. Newton's was based on the idea that change was a variable over time, while Leibniz's was based on the difference ranging over a sequence of infinitely close values.

UNRAVELLING THE TRUE NATURE OF DNA 1953

The tale of the discovery of DNA (deoxyribonucleic acid) begins with a Swiss physician and biologist named Johannes Friedrich Miescher. Originally training to become a doctor, after suffering a severe bout of typhoid fever that damaged his hearing, he was forced to abandon that vocation and instead turned to physiological chemistry. He thought at first he would study lymphocytes (one type of white blood cell), but was subsequently pointed in the direction of leukocytes (all white blood cells) by German biochemist Felix Hoppe-Seyler. As far as the world of science is concerned, it was very fortunate he did!

After filtering cell samples, Miescher attempted to isolate the nuclei from the cytoplasm, which he achieved by subjecting the nuclei to an alkaline extraction and then acidification. The result? Something that Miescher called nuclein, which today we know as DNA.

Interestingly, while Miescher and his fellow researchers continued to study nucleic acids for several years, they didn't realise DNA's significance at the time, with its double helix structure and true nature only hit on later by American James Watson and Englishman Francis Crick in 1953. Today, of course, DNA has been studied extensively and revealed to be responsible for the encoding of genetic instructions in the functioning of every living organism on the planet.

"After a bout of typhoid he was forced to abandon training to become a doctor"

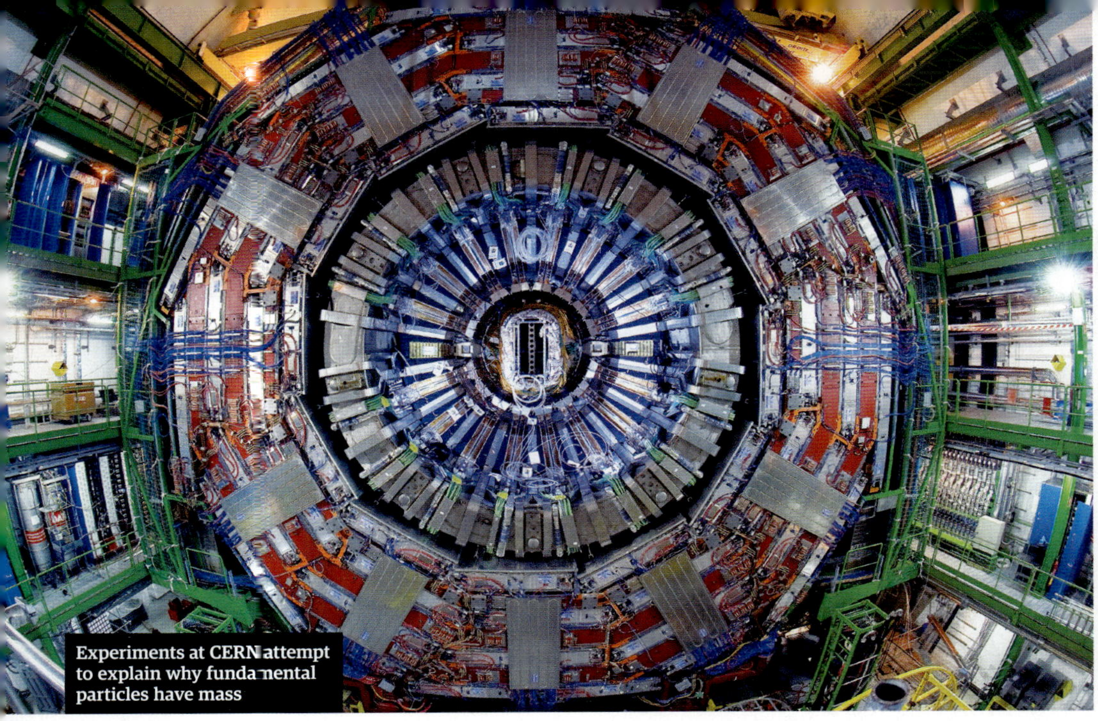

Experiments at CERN attempt to explain why fundamental particles have mass

SEARCH FOR THE GOD PARTICLE 2012

The Large Hadron Collider provided the final piece in the physics puzzle

The Higgs boson's tentative confirmation on 14 March 2013 ended an almost 50-year search for the elementary particle. Originally theorised to exist in 1964 by Peter Higgs and five others, the boson's discovery in July 2012 is a milestone, as it is considered the pivotal missing element in the Standard Model of physics. It explains why fundamental particles have mass – a key building block for the construction of the universe.

Interestingly, despite its discovery being considered monumental, at this present juncture there is no immediate benefit that the Higgs boson brings. Scientifically, if it were conclusively proven to exist, then it could answer many currently unexplained questions such as how particles gain mass, how cosmic inflation occurs and even what might happen to the universe in the far future. However, finding the Higgs boson in the Large Hadron Collider at CERN is purely academic. Whether or not it will have an impact on society later – much like quantum mechanics from the early-20th century – remains to be seen.

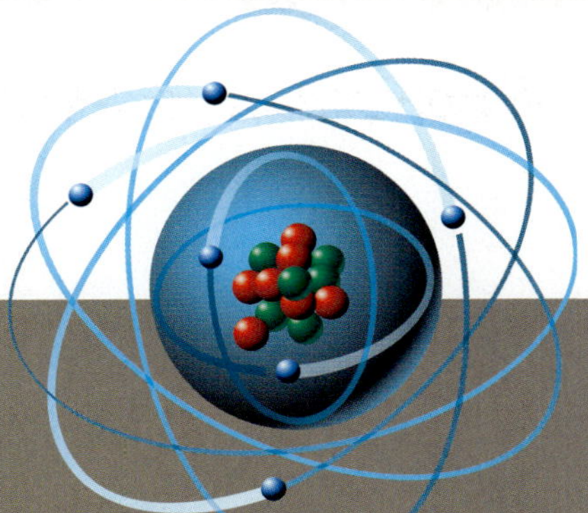

THE MIGHTY ATOM 1808

Nothing can come from nothing – so modern physics tells us. And this is the exact thinking pioneered by Ancient Greek philosopher Democritus in the fifth century BCE. He eventually concluded that everything in the cosmos was constructed from tiny, invisible particles called 'atamos' (meaning 'indivisible'). This was the birth of atomic theory and a crude notion of atoms that would remain largely unchallenged until the 19th century. Indeed, nothing really changed until English scientist John Dalton produced his own atomic theory, published in *A New System Of Chemical Philosophy* in 1808. This is considered the birth of modern atomic theory, as it eloquently describes how elements are made from extremely small particles called atoms and that atoms of different elements combine to form compounds. Of course, one thing Dalton didn't realise was that atoms could be split – something that would be achieved just over a century later by New Zealand-born scientist Ernest Rutherford.

THE ALL-SEEING RAY 1895

Wilhelm Röntgen's discovery of the X-ray let us see inside the body for the first time

The first X-ray produced was of the hand of Röntgen's wife (inset)

German physicist Wilhelm Röntgen first found the electromagnetic radiation X-rays in 1895. He not only discovered them but was the first to call them 'X-rays'; they were originally referred to by the establishment as 'Röntgen rays'. His breakthrough was the result of studying Crookes tubes – experimental discharge tubes invented by scientists investigating cathode rays and tubes in the 1870s. They were the precursor to the cathode-ray tubes used in computer monitors and televisions.

These discharge tubes generated free electrons that were accelerated out of the devices at such high speed that, when they hit the glass walls of the cylinder, they produced X-rays. Röntgen studied this phenomenon extensively, creating numerous X-ray images – the first of which was of his wife's hand. From this point on, the potential of X-rays became ever-more evident, with numerous applications emerging from precise, full-body medical X-rays through to the X-ray microscope and the high-powered X-ray-producing synchrotron devices capable of imaging cells and soft tissues in unprecedented detail today.

ORIGIN OF THE UNIVERSE 1931

Georges Lemaître publishes his Hypothesis Of The Primeval Atom, becoming the first to accurately describe the Big Bang

If you are looking for discoveries that broadened humanity's horizons then look no further than the Big Bang theory. For thousands of years the origins of the Earth and the universe had been held captive by a mixture of ignorance and religious scripture. Of course, while the Big Bang theory still remains a theory, it provides a plausible model for its formation and continued activity - one that is increasingly being backed up by scientific evidence.

The origin of the Big Bang theory emerges with, interestingly, a Catholic priest and scientist called Georges Lemaître, who in 1931 published his *Hypothesis Of The Primeval Atom*. Here Lemaître proposed a model of the universe beginning with a cataclysmic explosion that is still expanding - and at an accelerated rate. Despite rival theories from Edwin Hubble and Alexander Friedmann also emerging around the same time, it was Lemaître who described it most accurately, with Albert Einstein moving to endorse the theory after its publication. Lemaître's prediction of the accelerating expansion of the universe would go on to be confirmed in the Nineties by observations made by, ironically, the Hubble Space Telescope.

Lemaître's theory was later ratified by the Hubble telescope in 1991

FLEMING'S GREAT MISTAKE

1928

The development of penicillin was an amazing story of accidental discovery. Working hard in his laboratory for months on end, Scottish scientist Alexander Fleming decided to take a month-long holiday in August 1928 to see his family. Quickly throwing some of his things together he promptly left London, leaving his workplace in a bit of a mess; this mess included a number of Petri dishes filled with the bacteria staphylococci. Little did Fleming realise that these Petri dishes would help him revolutionise the world of medicine.

On returning to London and entering his laboratory Fleming immediately noticed that on one of the Petri dishes a distinctive mould had grown and in doing so killed any of the nearby staphylococci bacteria.

After tidying up, Fleming attempted to regrow the mould himself in a pure culture. He succeeded shortly after and, after trialling the culture on various bacteria, saw that it destroyed several that caused disease. Realising what he had discovered, Fleming published his findings and so was born the precursor to the modern-day antibiotic.

"The very concept of a genetic code was a monumental breakthrough"

THE GENETIC CODE CRACKED 1968

Genetic codes are essentially sets of rules that determine how information which is stored within genetic material like DNA is translated into proteins by living cells. Simply put, it determines how everything about an organism is made and how that organism's cells will be reproduced.

As such, simply discovering the very concept of a genetic code was a monumental breakthrough in the grand scheme of human biology.

Following the discovery of DNA's structure by James Watson and Francis Crick in 1953, numerous scientists embarked on a mission to attempt to determine what bases (or codons) were responsible for encoding the 20 standard amino acids used by living cells to build proteins.

This was eventually achieved in detail by biochemists Har Gobind Khorana, Robert Holley and Marshall Nirenberg, with the trio scooping the Nobel Prize in Physiology or Medicine in 1968 for 'their interpretation of the genetic code'.

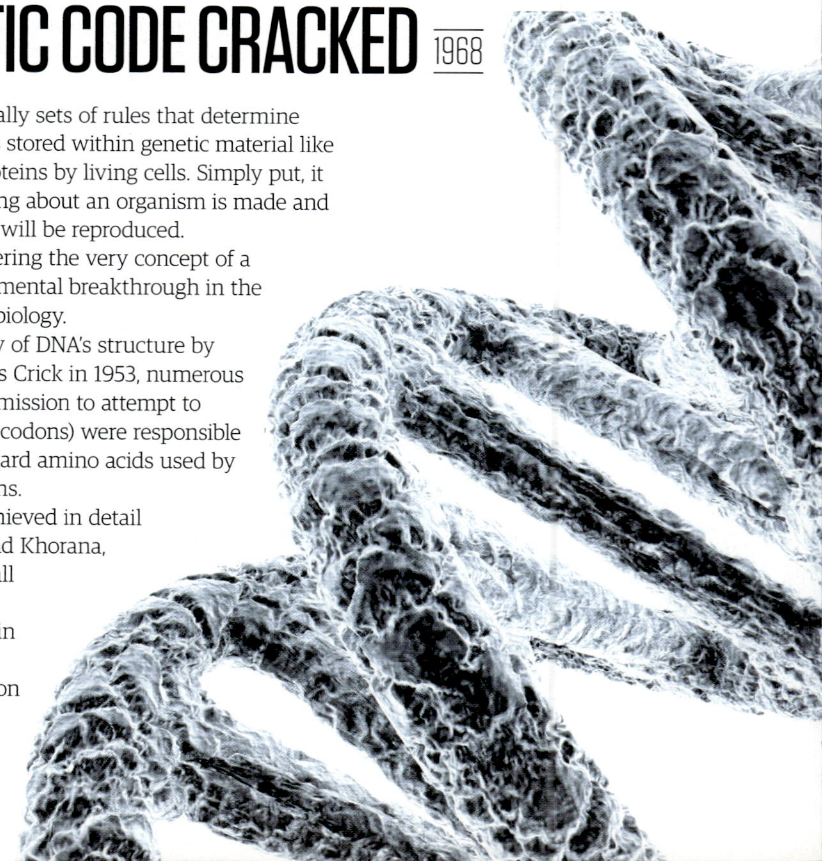

THE SUN IS THE CENTRE OF THE SOLAR SYSTEM 1543

Prior to Nicolaus Copernicus, it was an accepted fact that Earth was at the centre of the galaxy, as laid down in the Ptolemaic model of the heavens (devised by Claudius Ptolemy in the second century CE).

Earth was the focal point of the galaxy (which was considered to be the entire universe in the 16th century) and to dispute this geocentric model of the Solar System was considered heretical by the Catholic Church. Indeed, support for Copernicus's system landed Galileo Galilei under house arrest by the Catholic Inquisition almost a century later and he was considered 'vehemently suspect of heresy'. However, when Copernicus published his treatise *On The Revolution Of The Heavenly Spheres* in 1543, he proposed that this model was a fallacy and that all his research indicated that the galaxy was, in fact, heliocentric (ie centred around the Sun). This heliocentric model of the Solar System, was, as you might expect, strenuously resisted during Copernicus's lifetime and incredibly it would be another 200 years before it was accepted, aided by Isaac Newton's evidence put forward in *Principia Mathematica* in 1687.

QUANTUM THEORY 1920

For centuries the Standard Model of physics - set by Newton and his contemporaries - was considered the definitive set of laws that governed the physical world. But by the start of the 20th century multiple disciplines - such as atomic theory - were hinting there could be a whole other level to physics that was yet unaccounted for.

By 1920 these disciplines loosely intertwined to create quantum theory (or quantum mechanics) - a new branch of physics that focused on physical phenomena on truly microscopic scales, entering the realm of atomic and even subatomic particles. From Albert Einstein's work on electromagnetic radiation, through to Werner Heisenberg's matrix mechanics and Erwin Schrödinger's wave mechanics (the mind behind the famous 'Schrödinger's cat' paradox), increasingly complex models for how physics works have been at the least theorised or in some cases partly demonstrated. Since then quantum theory has become increasingly important to almost all scientific disciplines, with branches such as quantum chemistry, quantum optics and quantum information science expanding our understanding - or, to be more accurate, our current lack of understanding - about how the universe works on the most fundamental of levels.

Einstein's theory of relativity 1905

Containing both Einstein's theories of special and general relativity, this has single-handedly revolutionised modern physics. Since its conception the theory has transformed theoretical physics and astronomy entirely, largely superseding Newton's take on classical mechanics. It enabled the nuclear age to prosper - both for better and worse - as well as furthering our grasp of neutron stars and black holes.

THE SECRETS OF RADIATION 1903

Marie Curie's theory of radioactivity helped us understand how particles move as well as the health risks of radiation

While the discovery of radiation could be attributed to numerous people, ranging from German physicist Johann Wilhelm Ritter who found ultraviolet in 1801, through to the discovery of neutron radiation in the 1930s, one figure arguably stands out. Polish physicist and chemist Marie Curie - along with her husband, Pierre - studied radiation extensively during their lives, with the pair uncovering two new elements in the late-19th century.

Due to her continued work in the field, which included coining the phrase 'radioactivity' and probing into the nature of radioactive half-lives, she was awarded the Nobel Prize in Physics jointly with her husband and fellow French physicist Henri Becquerel for their 'researches on the radiation phenomena' in 1903. Several years later in 1911 - after Pierre had tragically been killed in a road accident - she would receive the Nobel Prize in Chemistry for the discovery of radium and polonium.

Today, Curie's work into radiation - including the huge danger it poses to humans (Marie Curie famously died of radiation poisoning in 1934) - has proven invaluable to modern science, with everything from energy generation, medicine and astronomy benefiting massively from her findings.

The development and refinement of gunpowder was a gradual process that took place over many centuries

WARFARE REDEFINED

CIRCA NINTH CENTURY

Rumoured to have been invented by ancient Chinese alchemists by accident while searching for an elixir of everlasting life, gunpowder has gone on to redefine warfare. Evolving in use from simple firecracker-style explosives, through to fireworks and on to the motive force behind cannons, muskets, rifles and bombs among many other explosive weapons, gunpowder's discovery has resulted in the deaths of countless millions.

According to science historian Joseph Needham's *Science And Civilisation In China*, the development of gunpowder as we know it today was a gradual process and involved many accidents. One of the most notable of these is recorded to have occurred in 1280, where a large gunpowder arsenal at Wei-yang accidentally caught fire. The resultant explosion, which had been completely underestimated by the alchemists at the time, was so powerful that it killed over 100 men instantly and threw the numerous wooden beams and pillars of the arsenal over a distance of five kilometres (three miles) from the site.

"Gunpowder's discovery has resulted in the deaths of countless millions"

PYTHAGORAS LAYS DOWN HIS THEOREM

SIXTH CENTURY BCE

One of the most beautifully simple yet drastically important discoveries in the history of mathematics, the Pythagorean theorem $a^2+b^2=c^2$ - discovered by Ancient Greek Pythagoras in the sixth century BCE - led to great advances in not just academia but also navigation and construction. Despite its abstract appearance, the theorem simply states that in any right-angled triangle, the square of the hypotenuse (the longest side) is equal in length to the sum of the squares of the other two shorter sides.

Pythagoras was one of Ancient Greece's greatest minds

DARWIN AND EVOLUTION 1859

When Charles Darwin set off on his round-the-world voyage on 27 December 1831, little did he realise that history was about to be made. As Darwin moved from port to port of far-flung lands, studying geology, natural history and wildlife, a previously conceived theory of his was being fleshed out before his eyes. Evolution - the change in inherited characteristics of biological populations over generations - was becoming irrefutable.

Of course, it would not be until Darwin published *On The Origin Of Species* in 1859 that he would deliver evolution with compelling evidence - and, at the time, religious institutions and many learned scholars decried it. But arguably it was that five-year trip on the HMS Beagle, studying species like the Galápagos tortoise up close, that was the real point of discovery.

New employees at the Cornhusker Ordnance Plant in Nebraska having their photos and fingerprints taken in 1942

CATALOGUING CRIME 1896

A unique method of identifying criminals gets the thumbs-up

While the use of fingerprints as we know it today - to identify people and as a means of catching criminals - is a relatively modern discovery there is evidence that finger and thumb prints were used in ancient times. For example, the Babylonians in 2000-1000 BCE pressed the tips of their fingers into clay to record business transactions, while thumbprints were also used in ancient China as a means of 'signing' documents.

It wasn't until the 19th century that fingerprints were used to reduce crime. Sir William Herschel, a chief magistrate in India, had residents record their fingerprints when signing business deals to fight fraud in 1858. From this point the path to a more universal adoption of fingerprint records was relatively swift; Scottish doctor Henry Faulds published an article discussing using prints as a means of personal identification in 1880 and 12 years later Argentine police officer Juan Vucetich was the first to use prints to catch criminals.

By 1896 Sir Edward Richard Henry developed a classification system that enabled prints to be classified and sorted - Scotland Yard adopted this system in 1901. This led to the capture of criminals due to their genetic makeup and would indelibly change the way that the police solved crime.

THE EARTH IS NOT FLAT

1522

The idea that Earth was anything other than a flat disc was once inconceivable. Indeed, it was not until the sixth century BCE that just the concept of a spherical Earth was even speculated. Even then it was not until around the third century BCE that Greek astronomy demonstrated Earth was spherical, with this model for the planets of the heavens slowly dispersed via the old trade routes. In reality the notion of a flat Earth lingered until much later. Believe it or not, it wasn't until the early-16th century that conclusive proof of the Earth's shape was attained, with Portuguese explorer Ferdinand Magellan leading the first expedition around the planet. While Magellan died on the three-year journey - killed during battle in the Philippines - a handful of sailors continued the voyage and arrived in Spain on 6 September 1522. Of course, as soon as we ventured into space in the mid-20th century there could no longer be any doubt.

The theory of absolutely everything 1970s

The Standard Model of particle physics addresses the strong, electromagnetic and weak nuclear interactions that control the dynamics of subatomic particles. This robust theory is essential for explaining how the physical world works.

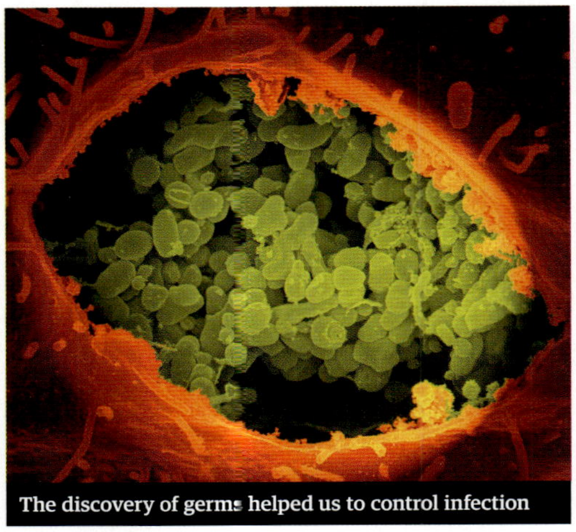

The discovery of germs helped us to control infection

HOW GERMS CAUSE DISEASE 1905

Prior to the discovery of bacteria in 1676 by Dutch scientist Antonie van Leeuwenhoek and the later discovery of the connected germ theory of disease, which states illness can be caused by micro-organisms, a number of wacky and superstitious explanations were commonplace.

Chief among these was the belief in the miasma theory, which stated that deadly diseases such as cholera, chlamydia and the Black Death (plague) were caused by the spreading of a noxious form of air. Indeed, this was the prevailing theory of explaining disease right up until the 19th century. After almost 100 years of research by many scientists, the German Robert Koch conclusively proved with his work on tuberculosis that germ theory was real - a feat that earned him a Nobel prize in 1905. On the back of his success Koch devised a set of rules to test if an organism - such as bacteria - causes disease and these criteria are still used in modern medicine.

Today, thanks to the discovery that certain bacteria and viruses can cause infectious diseases and that they can be spread via environmental mechanisms, like water, air or physical contact, doctors have a far more accurate understanding of how to both prevent and treat many illnesses.

VICTORIA'S EMPIRE

How a tiny island in the Atlantic Ocean came to own an empire so large that the sun never set on it

The date was 22 January 1901 and the British Empire was the largest of any in human history, but the monarch who reigned over it would not live another day. As Queen Victoria lay dying in Osborne House on the Isle of Wight she looked back on a reign that spanned over 63 years. She had seen her empire grow from a collection of scattered isles, separated by vast plains of lands and insurmountable oceans, to the greatest the world had known. It had reached over India, plucked its riches and mounted it as the glimmering jewel in her crown. It had butchered its way mercilessly across Africa at the cost of thousands of British corpses and countless natives who had tried in vain to stand in its way. It was powered forward both by Christian values and colonial greed, so as Victoria drew her last breath, she left a world forever transformed by the empire she had built.

When a young Princess Victoria ascended the steps of Westminster Abbey on her coronation day, few would have foreseen the mighty empire she would eventually rule over. The British public were increasingly disenchanted with the monarchy and her grandfather, the mad king George III, had failed to protect British interest in the Americas, and her uncle George IV's terrible relations with his wife and reckless spending had tarnished the monarchy's prestige. At a mere 18 years and barely 150 centimetres (five feet) tall, Victoria hardly seemed a fitting patron for the vast ambitions of British expansion from the 17th century. But this blue-eyed, silvery-voiced lady possessed a stubborn will of iron and her reign would become the longest in British history. Her ascension marked not the death of the British Empire, but the new dawn of a kingdom so massive that none could ever hope to challenge it.

The world was changing as Victoria took her place on the throne. The tiny, scattered rural villages of England were being abandoned en masse and the cities were transforming into sprawling metropolises. Great towering concrete chimneys rose from the ground and the whirr of machines sounded across the country – the age of steam had arrived. The Industrial Revolution

"The British Empire had the might, ingenuity and limitless ambition to conquer the world"

QUEEN VICTORIA

British, 1819-1901

Brief Bio

Victoria served as monarch of the United Kingdom from 20 June 1837 until her death on 22 January 1901. At 63 years her reign is currently the longest in British history, and is associated with the Industrial Revolution, economic progress and most notably, the expansion of the British Empire to the largest domain of all time.

THE WORLD'S GREATEST EMPIRE

How much of the world Britannia ruled by 1901

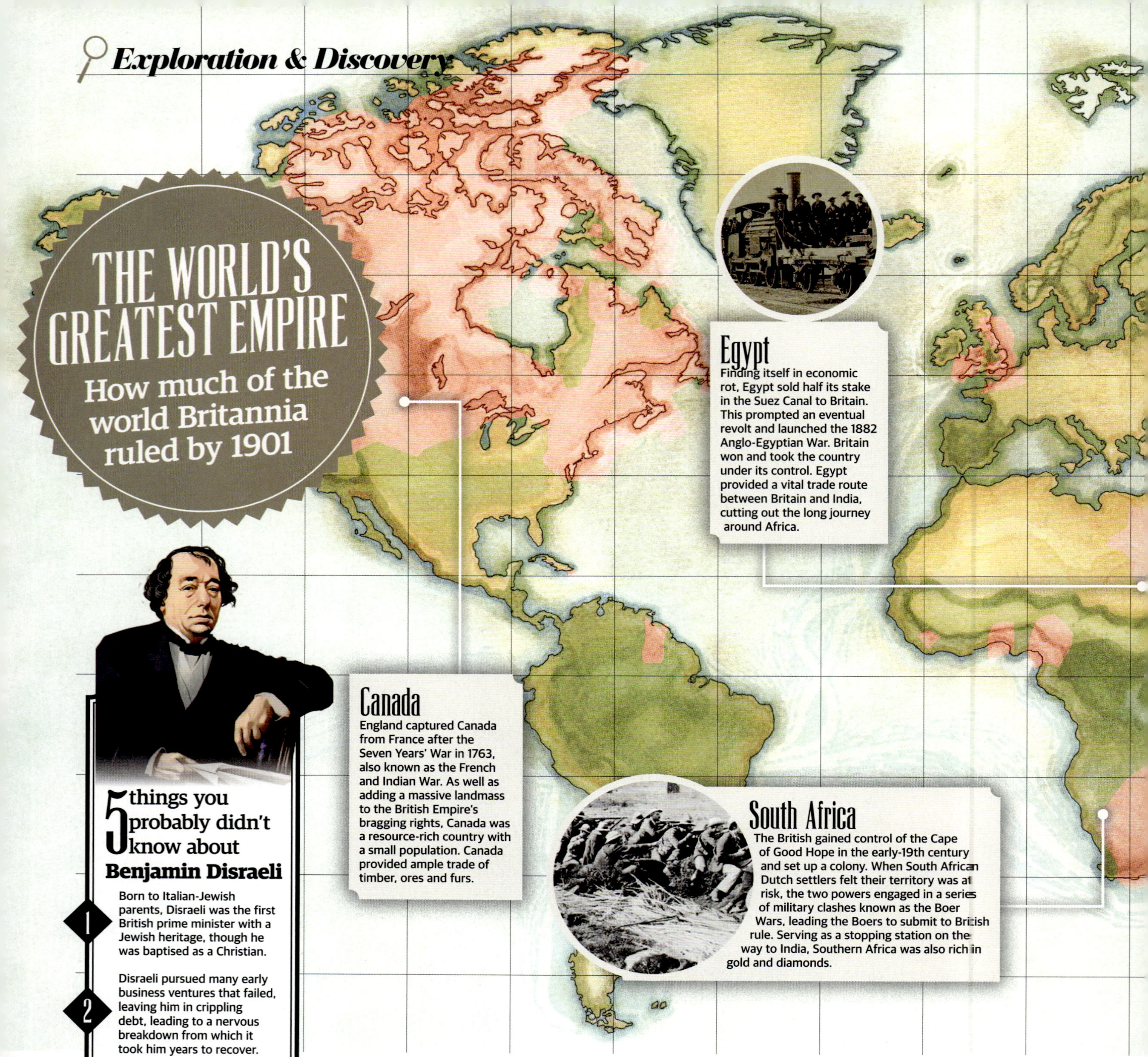

Egypt

Finding itself in economic rot, Egypt sold half its stake in the Suez Canal to Britain. This prompted an eventual revolt and launched the 1882 Anglo-Egyptian War. Britain won and took the country under its control. Egypt provided a vital trade route between Britain and India, cutting out the long journey around Africa.

Canada

England captured Canada from France after the Seven Years' War in 1763, also known as the French and Indian War. As well as adding a massive landmass to the British Empire's bragging rights, Canada was a resource-rich country with a small population. Canada provided ample trade of timber, ores and furs.

South Africa

The British gained control of the Cape of Good Hope in the early-19th century and set up a colony. When South African Dutch settlers felt their territory was at risk, the two powers engaged in a series of military clashes known as the Boer Wars, leading the Boers to submit to British rule. Serving as a stopping station on the way to India, Southern Africa was also rich in gold and diamonds.

5 things you probably didn't know about Benjamin Disraeli

1. Born to Italian-Jewish parents, Disraeli was the first British prime minister with a Jewish heritage, though he was baptised as a Christian.
2. Disraeli pursued many early business ventures that failed, leaving him in crippling debt, leading to a nervous breakdown from which it took him years to recover.
3. He was mocked in Parliament when he made his maiden speech. Later he proclaimed that "the time will come when you will hear me."
4. Disraeli was a notorious flatterer and when asked by a colleague how to deal with Queen Victoria, he replied: "First of all, remember she is a woman."
5. He introduced much legislation that benefited the poor, such as the 1877 Artisans Dwelling Act that provided housing, as well as the Public Health Act the same year.

> "The loss of the love of her life changed not only herself as a person, but the fate of her empire"

changed Britain from a quaint maritime nation into a manufacturing colossus. Railways and steamships brought the British overseas territory closer to the mother country, opening up opportunities for trade and commerce that were previously unfathomable.

It was Albert, Victoria's beloved husband, who opened her and Britain's eyes to the ideas that went on to shape her empire. Fascinated by mechanisms and inventions, Albert organised The Great Exhibition at the Crystal Palace - a temple to the ingenuity of the rapidly developing modern world. Inventions from around the world were displayed, but this was Britain's show, first and foremost. The symbols of British might, which occupied half of the entire display space, served as clear examples of what the British Empire was capable of and fostered the ideas of national supremacy in the eyes of Victoria, the government and the majority of the British population. The Great Exhibition proved that far from the crumbling remains of a once-powerful nation, the British Empire had the might, ingenuity and limitless ambition to conquer the world.

The opportunity to pave the road for this empire arose in 1857 with the Indian Mutiny. India had

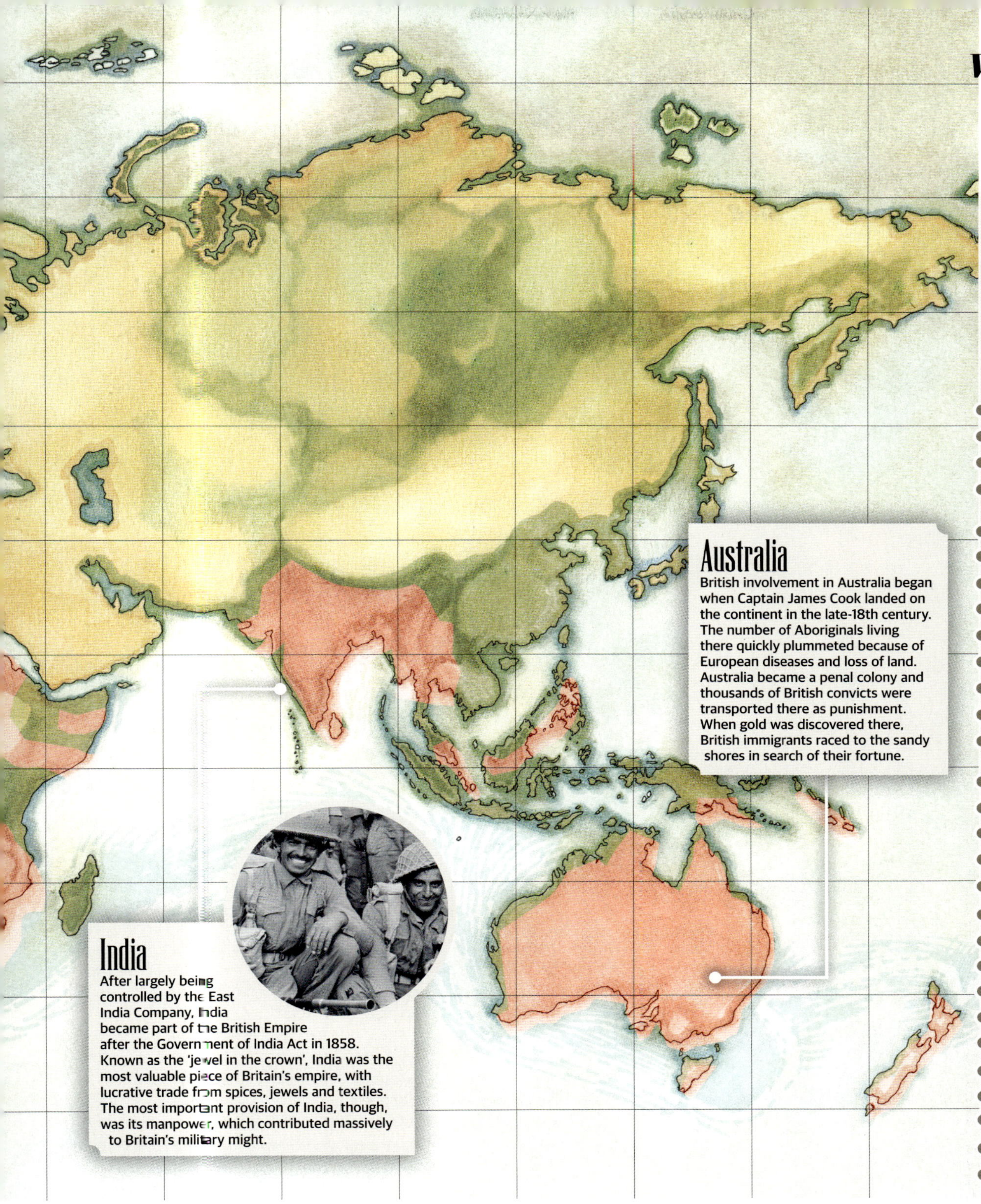

Australia

British involvement in Australia began when Captain James Cook landed on the continent in the late-18th century. The number of Aboriginals living there quickly plummeted because of European diseases and loss of land. Australia became a penal colony and thousands of British convicts were transported there as punishment. When gold was discovered there, British immigrants raced to the sandy shores in search of their fortune.

India

After largely being controlled by the East India Company, India became part of the British Empire after the Government of India Act in 1858. Known as the 'jewel in the crown', India was the most valuable piece of Britain's empire, with lucrative trade from spices, jewels and textiles. The most important provision of India, though, was its manpower, which contributed massively to Britain's military might.

TIMELINE OF CONQUEST

How Victoria's British Empire became the world's biggest

- 1838 PICAIRN ISLANDS
- 1842 HONG KONG
- 1848 INDIA
- 1853 TRUCIAL OMAN (TRINIDAD & TOBAGO)
- 1857 ADEN (YEMEN)
- 1862 BRITISH HONDURAS (BELIZE)
- 1868 BECHUANANLAND (BOTSWANA)
- 1874 FIJI
- 1878 CYPRUS
- 1878 SOUTH WEST AFRICA (NAMIBIA)
- 1881 NORTH BORNEO (SABAH)
- 1884 BASUTOLAND (LESOTHO)
- 1884 BRITISH SOMALILAND (SOMALILAND)
- 1884 PAPUA NEW GUINEA
- 1885 NIGERIA
- 1885 KENYA
- 1887 MALDIVE ISLANDS
- 1888 BRITISH EAST AFRICA (KENYA)
- 1888 BRUNEI
- 1888 COOK ISLANDS (NZ ASSOC)
- 1888 GAMBIA
- 1888 SARAWAK (MALAYSIA)
- 1889 RHODESIA (ZIMBABWE)
- 1889 TRINIDAD (TRINIDAD & TOBAGO)
- 1890 TANGANYIKA (TANZANIA)
- 1891 MALAWI
- 1894 UGANDA
- 1898 SUDAN
- 1899 KUWAIT

been ruled by a private entity - the East India Company - from 1757. The rebellion manifested the discontent felt by the Indian people for the blatant disrespect of their beliefs and customs. The company showed disregard for the Indian caste system and issued new cartridges greased with cow and pig fat that had to be opened with the mouth, highly offensive to Muslim and Hindu soldiers. These actions opened the eyes of the Indian people to the daily injustice they were being subjected to, and unrest snowballed into mass riots and an uprising. Although the mutiny was eventually quelled, the rebellion led to the dissolution of the company, the passing of power to the British state and the creation of what Victoria would call the jewel in her crown - the British Indian Empire.

Queen Victoria welcomed the country to her empire in a lavish ceremony, promising that Indian native customs and religions would be respected and that she would "draw a veil over the sad and bloody past." She presented herself as a maternal figure and a crusader for peace, justice and honest government - ideals largely inspired by her husband. Albert had instilled in her mind the vision of King Arthur's Camelot, an empire ruled not by tyranny but by justice, where the strong serve the weak, where good triumphs over evil, bringing not oppression and bloodshed, but trade, education and welfare. His influence on Victoria was immense and when on 14 December 1861 he died of suspected typhoid fever, the empire veered into an entirely new direction.

When Albert drew his last breath in the blue room at Windsor Castle the queen was inconsolable; the loss of the love of her life changed not only herself as a person, but the fate of her empire. As she donned the mourning clothes she would wear until her own death, she drew a veil over Albert's vision and pursued a different path for her kingdom - one of world domination.

An emerging figure in Parliament would come to foster her views - Benjamin Disraeli. The ambitious and rebellious leader of the Conservatives was led by a passion for imperial power and glory. Inspired by tales of imperial adventures, Disraeli believed Britain should pursue an empire of power and prestige. His most direct political opponent represented everything Albert dreamed the empire

WHAT WAS THE EAST INDIA COMPANY?

Emerging from humble beginnings, the East India Company began as a simple enterprise of London businessmen who wanted to make money from importing spices. The company was granted a royal charter by Queen Elizabeth I in 1600, and in 1601 James Lancaster led its first voyage. The company set up trade outposts in Indian settlements that slowly developed into commercial towns. Steadily increasing its territory, the company claimed vital trading ports from Aden to Penang. As its control extended, the company became the most powerful private company in history, with its own army established by Robert Clive, the first British governor of Bengal. With its great military power behind it, the company controlled India with a combination of direct rule and alliances with Indian princes. The East India Company eventually accounted for half the world's trade and specialised in cotton, silk, tea and opium.

Lancaster was an Elizabethan trader and privateer

A satirical cartoon from 1876 poking fun at the relationship between Queen Victoria and Benjamin Disraeli

The Argyle and Sutherland Highlanders before the 1899 Battle of Modder River during the Second Boer War

could be. William Gladstone, the leader of the Liberals, thought the empire should serve a high moral purpose, to follow not a path of conquest but one of commerce, sharing their moral vision with the rest of the world.

These two fiery and driven men fought over these opposing visions in Parliament as Victoria continued to mourn. Without Albert she felt incompetent and unable to face the immense duty that her role dictated. With her strong conservative views she found Gladstone and his liberal reforms dangerous and unpredictable. Disraeli, suave, coy and dripping with forthright confidence, enchanted the lonely queen. With his constant flattery and sharp wit, Disraeli reignited her interest in politics and captivated her, as Albert had done so previously, with his vision of just how mighty the empire could be. However, Gladstone's liberal vision and Albert's quest for Camelot had not completely faded. The British people, led by strong Protestant beliefs Victoria herself had instilled in them, felt it was Britain's role - their duty even - to civilise people around the world. They believed the British cause was to export not only trade, but also gospel values of morality and justice.

It was in pursuit of this lofty goal that many missionaries

A British marketing poster promoting the Suez Canal - the waterway was an important factor in the growth of the empire

FIVE REASONS THE BRITISH EMPIRE CAME TO RULE THE WORD

DOMINANCE OF THE SEAS

Britain employed a 'two-power standard' in 1889 which called for the Royal Navy to maintain a force at least equal to the combined strength of the next two largest navies in the world. This policy ensured British dominance of the seas with a string of naval bases encompassing the whole world. The pure size and strength of the navy served its purpose - deterring any would be competitors and confirming its position as ruler of the waves.

THE INDUSTRIAL REVOLUTION

Britain was the first nation to harness the power of steam and the first to undergo an industrial revolution. This resulted in mass production of low-cost goods to trade around the world. It also gave Britain's military an array of resources like rifles, steamships and trains, equipping it to defeat any possible enemies. Medical advances also allowed British explorers to penetrate remote areas without fear of tropical diseases.

THE QUEST TO SPREAD DEMOCRACY

Land grabbing aside, the British Empire was led by a strong Protestant desire to improve the world. Britain saw itself as an agent of civilisation - one they wanted to spread worldwide, bringing peace, order and stability. This belief that they were doing genuine good led men like David Livingstone to travel to Africa to spread the word of God, and with it, the British Empire.

TAKING ADVANTAGE OF THE COMPETITION

As major powers of the world such as Spain, France, the Netherlands and the Ottomans were losing power, the British began to peak in strength. Britain was able to take advantage of the European wars that had weakened other nations as it enjoyed a period of relative peace, allowing uninterrupted expansion of its empire. Any threats that did emerge, such as Russia, just gave Britain new zeal to cement its powerful hold on the world.

STRONG LEADERSHIP

Britain was ruled by a single monarch throughout most of the 19th century - Queen Victoria. The record-breaking length of her reign brought a sense of stability and contributed to the unconquerable notion of the British Empire. Although Victoria did involve herself in government, her role was symbolic rather than one of direct power, which ensured stability of British politics. While other nations were dealing with socialist movements, Britain enjoyed a long period of relative domestic peace.

> "The Industrial Revolution changed Britain from a quaint maritime nation into a manufacturing giant"

turned their attention to Africa. Little was known of the 'Dark Continent', but the common perception was that it was a place of pagan worship ravaged by tribal wars. One missionary in particular would capture the attention of the British nation. Tall, handsome and heroic, David Livingstone embodied everything the British believed their nation to represent. A medical missionary, Livingstone's daring adventures around the continent were followed by a captivated British public. Fighting vicious beasts, battling through dense jungles and suffering a multitude of illnesses, Livingstone was the heroic face of the empire's Christian ideals.

Livingstone's horrific confrontation with African chain gangs was to drive the British cause of expansion. The slavery rife in Africa was abhorrent to Livingstone and the British public, as the practice had been abolished across the empire in 1833. The queen and government united behind Livingstone's quest to find a suitable trade route, hoping that by doing so, the African people would find ways to make a living that wasn't built on the backs of slaves. Livingstone's journey was a failure and he returned to scathing criticism - something the imperialist Disraeli leapt on with glee. His flattery of Victoria had completely won her over and the monarchy and government became united in pursuit of one goal - the expansion of the empire.

The perfect opportunity to begin this new empire emerged as another nation struggled to survive. The Egyptian ruler, Isma'il Pasha, was confronted with crippling debts after reckless spending on lavish ceremonies and a costly war with Ethiopia. In an act of desperation he made an offer to sell to the British Egypt's shares in the Suez Canal. The canal was more than a mere trading port; it opened up a short route to India across Egypt and down the Red Sea, cutting out the lengthy journey around Africa. The Egyptian ruler's offer would give the British controlling influence over the jugular of the empire, so Disraeli urged Victoria to accept. She immediately did and the Suez Canal fell into British hands.

With control of India, Britain was already the most powerful nation on Earth and three-quarters of the world's trade was transported in British ships, but this control was being threatened. The Russian Empire had been steadily expanding east

How Britannia ruled the waves

The anatomy of the HMS Prince George

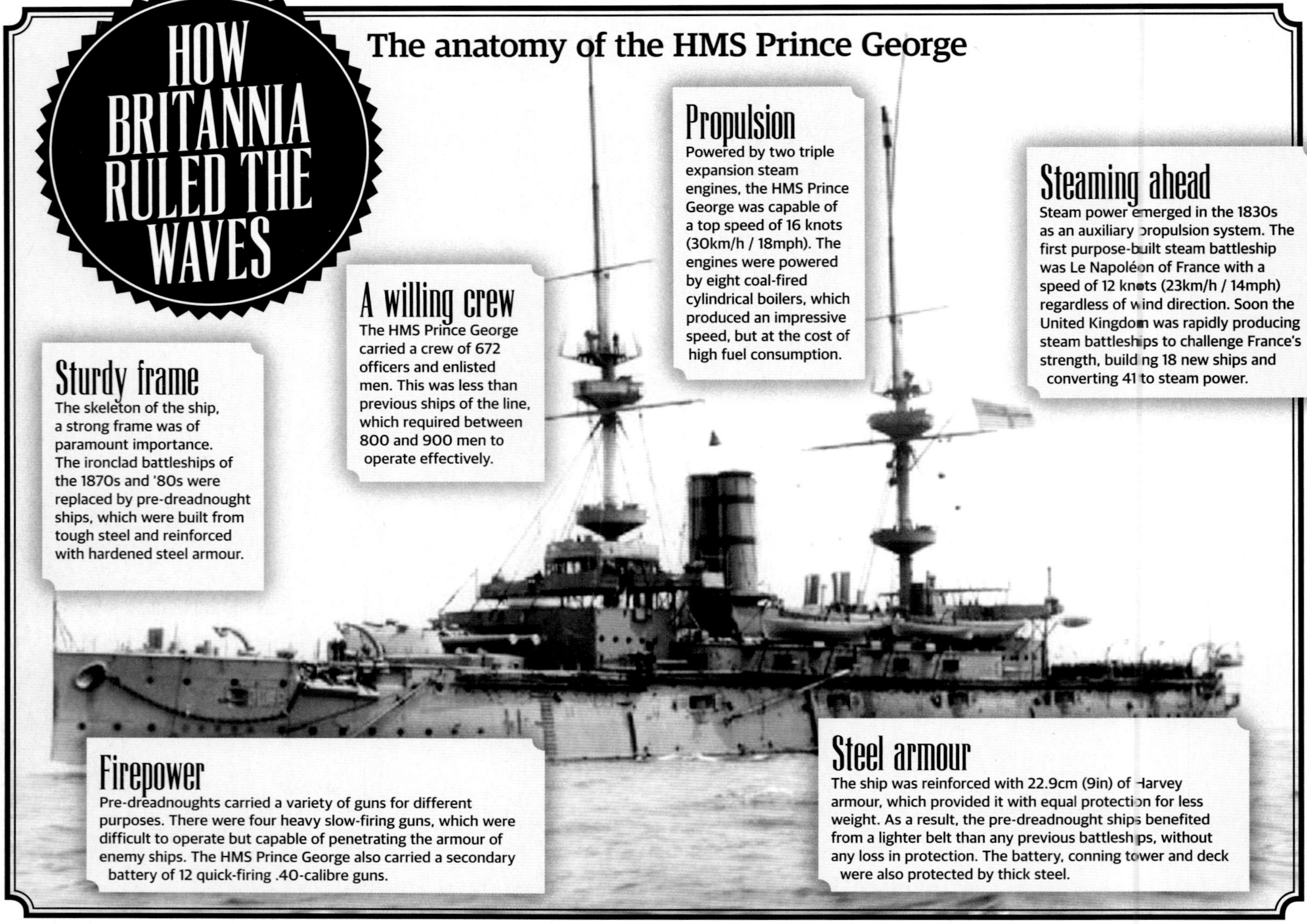

Propulsion
Powered by two triple expansion steam engines, the HMS Prince George was capable of a top speed of 16 knots (30km/h / 18mph). The engines were powered by eight coal-fired cylindrical boilers, which produced an impressive speed, but at the cost of high fuel consumption.

Steaming ahead
Steam power emerged in the 1830s as an auxiliary propulsion system. The first purpose-built steam battleship was Le Napoléon of France with a speed of 12 knots (23km/h / 14mph) regardless of wind direction. Soon the United Kingdom was rapidly producing steam battleships to challenge France's strength, building 18 new ships and converting 41 to steam power.

A willing crew
The HMS Prince George carried a crew of 672 officers and enlisted men. This was less than previous ships of the line, which required between 800 and 900 men to operate effectively.

Sturdy frame
The skeleton of the ship, a strong frame was of paramount importance. The ironclad battleships of the 1870s and '80s were replaced by pre-dreadnought ships, which were built from tough steel and reinforced with hardened steel armour.

Firepower
Pre-dreadnoughts carried a variety of guns for different purposes. There were four heavy slow-firing guns, which were difficult to operate but capable of penetrating the armour of enemy ships. The HMS Prince George also carried a secondary battery of 12 quick-firing .40-calibre guns.

Steel armour
The ship was reinforced with 22.9cm (9in) of Harvey armour, which provided it with equal protection for less weight. As a result, the pre-dreadnought ships benefited from a lighter belt than any previous battleships, without any loss in protection. The battery, conning tower and deck were also protected by thick steel.

and south and was getting uncomfortably close to Victoria's prized jewel - India. The Middle East was largely controlled by the Turks, but they were busy dealing with violent rebellions. The Turkish treatment of their Christian subjects was shocking and atrocious, but as Russia backed the rebels the British had no option but to support the Turks. The British public, to whom Russia stood for everything Britain opposed - ignorance, slavery and subjugation - largely supported this choice. Facing the prospect of imminent war with the strongest nation on the planet, Russia agreed to peace talks and thanks in part to the charisma and negotiation skills of Disraeli, agreed to stop their advance on the Middle East.

Imperial spirit rushed through the public as the might of British muscle flexed and proved itself again. As the empire continued its steady expansion across the continent it came face to face with the most powerful African nation - the Zulus. The British, with a bloated ego, underestimated the strength of their spear-wielding enemies and suffered a crushing initial defeat. In the end it took 16,000 British reinforcements to prise the Zulus' independence from their grip. Expecting to return to a wave of praise for their daring exploits, the victorious army were surprised to discover that British opinions were changing once again.

Gladstone, the "half-mad firebrand", as Victoria dubbed him, preached his outraged opinions about the mass slaughter of Zulus and rampant destruction of their homes. Victoria was outraged but the public sided with Gladstone and, much to the queen's dismay, the power of the government switched hands once more. Liberal leader or not, all of Europe's attention was firmly fixed on Africa as nations began a scramble to establish colonies there. In amongst this mad rush to establish new territory by European powers, it was arguably one man's actions that would determine the ultimate fate of Victoria's empire.

Led by Muhammad Ahmed, revolution was tearing through the Sudan as tribes rose against their corrupt rulers. As this holy war drew uncomfortably close to the Suez Canal, Victoria urged Gladstone to utilise the British troops stationed there to defend it. The liberal leader refused. In order to buy time he sent one man, General Charles Gordon, to secure the evacuation of loyal civilians and soldiers.

Like Livingstone, Gordon was a national hero. He was brave, dashing, popular and his decorated military career had painted him in the British public's eyes as a gleaming knight of old. Despite these qualities Gordon was also wild and unpredictable. When he reached the Sudan he was horrified by the slavery rife in the region and decided to face the Mahdi in battle. With limited forces, Gordon soon found himself besieged in the city of Khartoum. His appeals for aid, to the adoring public's outrage, fell on deaf ears in the government. It took more than eight months of public fury to finally force Gladstone's hand, but it was too late - Gordon, the nation's hero of Christianity, was dead.

In an instance the liberal vision was shattered, Gladstone was voted out and his moral influence departed with him. The renewed crusading spirit of British imperialism found its poster boy in a

Right 1892 caricature of Cecil Rhodes, after he announced plans for a telegraph line and railroad from Cape Town to Cairo

"They believed the British cause was to export not only trade, but also gospel values of morality and justice"

man who would lead the empire down a dark and dangerous path. Moving from England to Africa to work on a cotton farm, Cecil John Rhodes had become outrageously wealthy from the diamond rush, but he wanted more - the whole of Africa. Driven by greed and lust for power, Rhodes wished to create a British colony across Africa, not for the betterment of its people or to spread Christian values, but for profit and business.

Using the tenacity and cunning that had elevated him to success, Rhodes tricked and butchered his way across the continent with the British government backing him every bloody step of the way. Rhodes made it his purpose to make the world English and famously said: "If there be a God, I think that what he would like me to do is paint as much of the map of Africa British Red as possible." His path of colonial greed led Britain head-first into a conflict now known as the Boer Wars.

Gold had been found in Transvaal in northern South Africa and Rhodes worried that this would prompt an alliance with the Germans, thus cutting off his route to the north of the continent. Rhodes planned an uprising to overthrow the Boer leaders, but it did not go as planned - far from the naked, spear-wielding foes he had previously conquered, the Boers had guns, and they fought back hard with skill and courage.

Outrage tore across Europe against what was seen as an unprovoked attack on an independent state, but not in Britain. Fully convinced of their noble mission, the British people believed the Boers to be vicious and uncompromising. More soldiers poured into the region into a war they believed would be short and glorious, but as more British bodies piled up - Victoria's own grandson among them - British confidence in their own unconquerable might began to wane.

As British reinforcements continued to flood into the territory the tide slowly began to turn. Rhodes had managed to squeeze a win from the jaws of defeat and the Boer territories became British colonies. The empire had grown, but at a cost. Rhodes' controversial actions during the war - including forming what would come to be known as the first concentration camps - had been a step too far for the British public. What had begun as a noble quest of Christianity had transformed into a greedy and brutal scramble for power. When Rhodes died his merciless version of imperialism was buried with him in the dry African dirt.

When Victoria passed away she was finally rid of the black mourning clothes she had worn for 40 years and was dressed entirely in white. Spring flowers were scattered around her body and her wedding veil was placed on her head as she prepared to reunite with the dearest love of her life. She was, however, leaving another behind; the Empire she had mothered now stretched across the globe with large parts of maps of the word coloured in the pink that showed British rule. As the sun set on the quiet room in which she lay in Osborne House, it was rising on the bustling spice markets of India, and soon the vast plains of British land in Africa would be bathed in warm golden light. Victoria had died, but the legacy she left behind expanded over the face of the entire planet. The cogs of the British Empire whirred steadily on.

"The monarchy and government became united in pursuit of one goal - the expansion of the empire"

STEPHENSON'S ROCKET

INNOVATIVE STEAM LOCOMOTIVE, BRITAIN 1829

"Stephenson had incorporated new ideas to make better use of its steam-powered pistons"

01 The crew Although the Rocket was not complicated to operate, it needed two people. One to 'drive' the engine and look out for obstructions on the track and another to feed coke (derivative of coal which burned more cleanly) into the firebox and keep an eye on the amount of heat being produced by the boiler.

02 Cylinder The cylinder compressed the steam, which then pushed down on the piston rod, creating a downward motion. As the steam was released through the exhaust pipe, steam entered from the other side of the piston rod by the eccentric rod D-valve, which forced the piston rod back up.

03 Multiple firetube boiler One of the key innovations of the Rocket was the multiple firetubes through which the hot gas from the firebox traveled. Previous models relied on one tube surface for the gas to travel through to produce steam but The Rocket had multiple tubes, increasing the heated surface area within the boiler, which produced more steam.

10 Wheels The Rocket's wheels were designed to take two and a half tons of weight on its front set while the back wheels were considerably lighter. This reduced the weight of the second axle behind it, making it faster.

How do we know this?

Stephenson's famous Rocket experiment was examined and documented not only by the judges present at the day of the Rainhill trials but also by spectators gathered at the unveiling of the Liverpool and Manchester railway line the day after, where British prime minister Arthur Wellesley, Duke of Wellington saw the latest breakthrough in steam locomotion for himself. Stephenson, like all the great engineers of the time, wrote technical specifications on all of his inventions and the Rocket's design was used as a template for all future steam engine production. It has gone down in history as a triumph of British engineering and as such has been studied and written about extensively. The Rocket is currently housed and displayed at the Science Museum in London.

Stephenson's famous Rocket on display

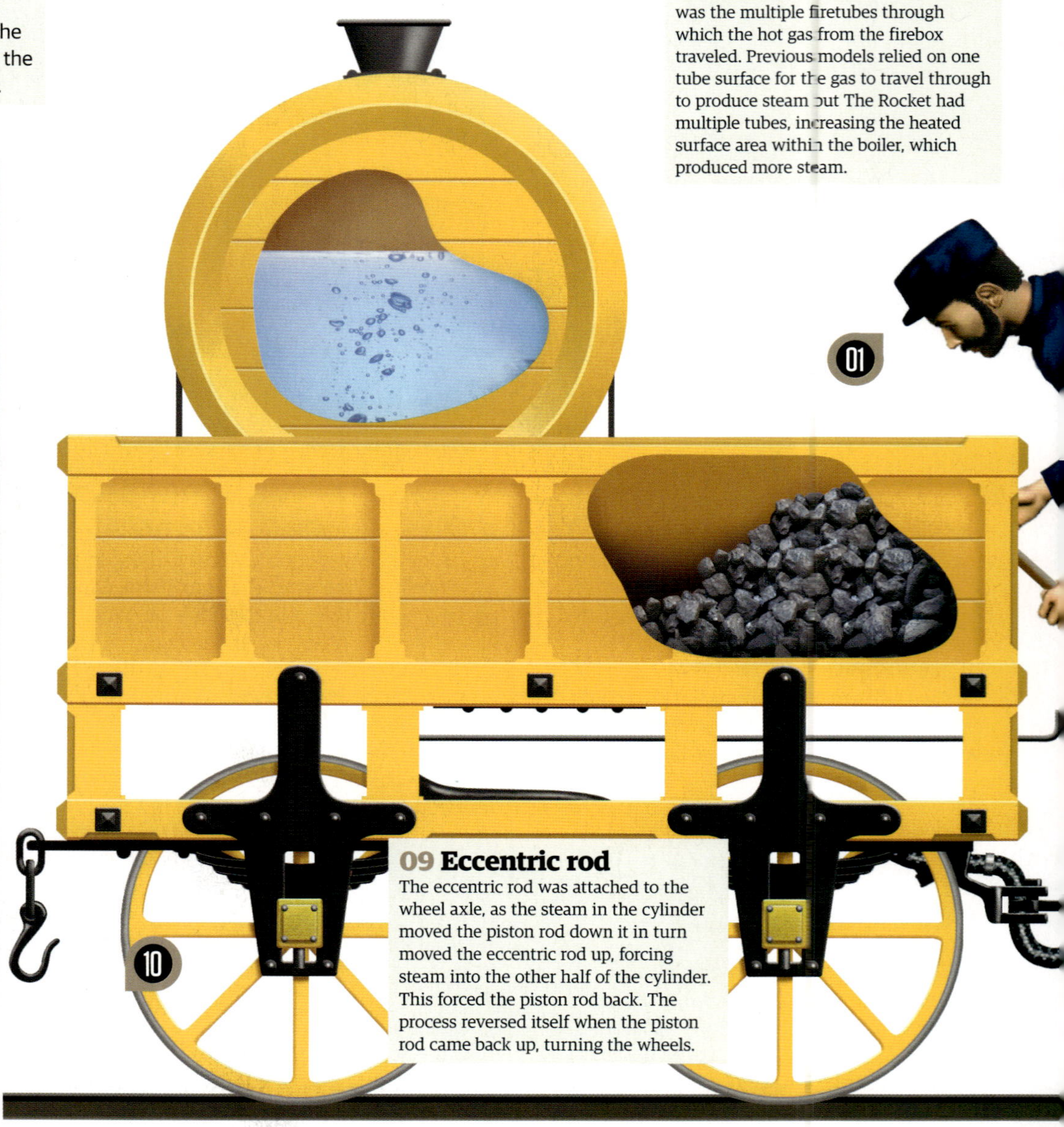

09 Eccentric rod The eccentric rod was attached to the wheel axle, as the steam in the cylinder moved the piston rod down it in turn moved the eccentric rod up, forcing steam into the other half of the cylinder. This forced the piston rod back. The process reversed itself when the piston rod came back up, turning the wheels.

Very few inventions in history have changed the fabric of British society quite as much as Robert Stephenson's steam locomotive prototype – popularly known as Stephenson's Rocket. With its successful test at the Rainhill trials in Liverpool in October 1829, a new dawn of steam locomotion was born which brought every community in Britain together through speedy and reliable rail travel.

Stephenson had a lot riding on the success of the Rocket, as the engineering company he co-owned with his father had created its engine with many costly new refinements. Adding to this pressure was the fact that Stephenson's rivals had produced bigger machines with seemingly more powerful engines. The Rocket did have one advantage over its competitors though – it was not reliant on redundant technology. Stephenson had incorporated new ideas to make better use of its steam-powered pistons.

The design combined established principles of locomotion with some new enhancements. These included a multiple firetube boiler, which enabled the Rocket to punch above its weight when hauling freight and passengers. The Rocket also had a blast pipe, which increased the intensity of the fire that produced the steam, making the boiler more effective.

The result of these refinements was remarkable. The Rainhill grandstand spectators were astonished to see Stephenson's small yellow engine pull carriages three times its own weight on the train tracks, reach a maximum speed of 30 mph (48kmh) – unheard of at the time – and even climb up a shallow incline while hauling material. The other locomotives had either broken down or could not reach the required minimum average speed. Stephenson was awarded the £500 prize money for creating the first reliable steam-powered train locomotive which could be used for passenger and material transport. He was also given two different contracts to produce locomotives.

The design set the standard for steam locomotives and all trains produced by workshops from that moment were based on this invention.

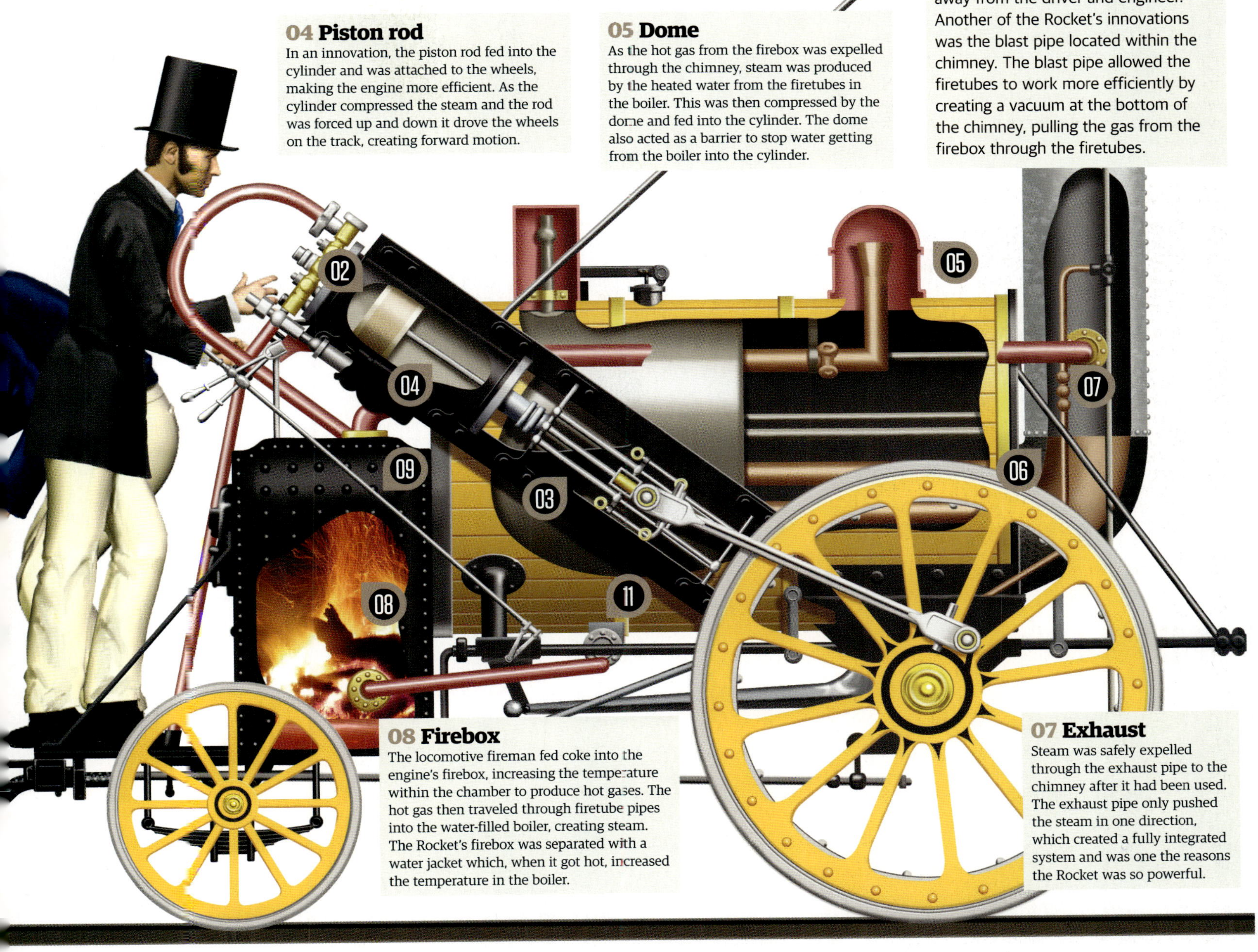

06 Chimney

The chimney expelled the hot gas through a vertical pipe safely away from the driver and engineer. Another of the Rocket's innovations was the blast pipe located within the chimney. The blast pipe allowed the firetubes to work more efficiently by creating a vacuum at the bottom of the chimney, pulling the gas from the firebox through the firetubes.

04 Piston rod

In an innovation, the piston rod fed into the cylinder and was attached to the wheels, making the engine more efficient. As the cylinder compressed the steam and the rod was forced up and down it drove the wheels on the track, creating forward motion.

05 Dome

As the hot gas from the firebox was expelled through the chimney, steam was produced by the heated water from the firetubes in the boiler. This was then compressed by the dome and fed into the cylinder. The dome also acted as a barrier to stop water getting from the boiler into the cylinder.

08 Firebox

The locomotive fireman fed coke into the engine's firebox, increasing the temperature within the chamber to produce hot gases. The hot gas then traveled through firetube pipes into the water-filled boiler, creating steam. The Rocket's firebox was separated with a water jacket which, when it got hot, increased the temperature in the boiler.

07 Exhaust

Steam was safely expelled through the exhaust pipe to the chimney after it had been used. The exhaust pipe only pushed the steam in one direction, which created a fully integrated system and was one the reasons the Rocket was so powerful.

10 INSPIRING INVENTORS

Meet those who see the world a little differently and whose inventions and imagination have changed the world

Maria Telkes

HUNGARIAN 1900-1995

Fascinated by the power of the sun from a young age, Maria Telkes studied physical chemistry at the University of Budapest before travelling to the United States to work and study solar energy. Sculptor Amelia Peabody asked her to work with her, and together they invented the world's first solar-powered house. Telkes noted in 1948: "I envisage the day when solar heat-collecting shelters like power stations will be built apart from the house to develop enough heat from the sun for pumping into an entire community.'

Telkes envisaged the age of solar power over half a century ago

ISAAC NEWTON

ENGLISH 1642-1727

Isaac Newton was the inventor of the world's first reflecting telescope. Newton had studied and lectured on the optical theories behind the reflecting telescope for a number of years before finally inventing one, and used his creation to prove that white light was made up of a spectrum of colours. The main advantage of the Newtonian telescope was that it gave a clearer picture since it did not suffer from the chromatic aberration problem of the refracting designs available at the time.

GALILEO GALILEI

ITALIAN 1564-1642

Few inventors have earned the titles 'father of' in more than one field, but Galilei has that honour for astronomy and modern science. Galileo's stamp on these diverse disciplines emphasises the extraordinary mind he possessed. He has been credited as the inventor of a number of devices, including a basic thermometer and a compass used for working out the trajectory of cannonballs. His work did have its critics though, and he was condemned by the Catholic Church on charges of 'vehement suspicion of heresy' because of his scientific beliefs.

Leonardo da Vinci

ITALIAN 1452-1519

Da Vinci was a master painter, sculptor and inventor in Renaissance Italy. His talent and curiosity allowed him to rub shoulders with the upper echelons of Italian society. His inventions included a grinding machine, hydraulic engines and contraptions used for draining water from harbours. Many of the inventions he designed never saw use, as they were too outlandish to be constructed, such as a flying machine and an armoured tank.

Many of da Vinci's inventions were discovered through his sketches

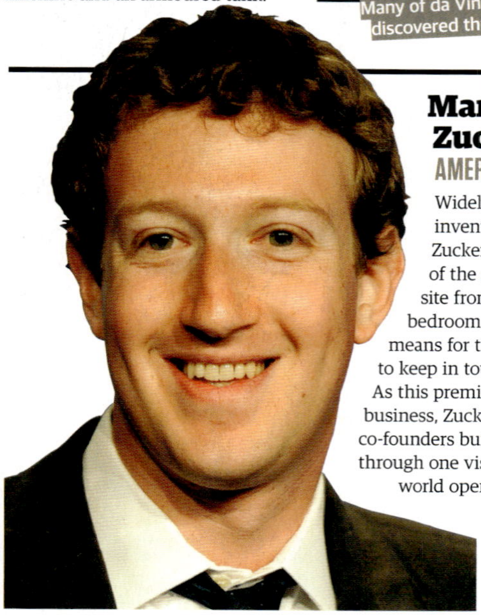

Mark Zuckerberg

AMERICAN 1984-

Widely credited as the inventor of Facebook, Zuckerberg created the idea of the social networking site from his college bedroom at Harvard as a means for the college fraternity to keep in touch with each other. As this premise developed into a business, Zuckerberg and his four co-founders built their company through one vision - to make the world open. Facebook has over one billion active users throughout the world.

Archimedes
ITALIAN 287-212 BCE

Regarded as the most prominent mind of the ancient world, his advances in mathematics and designs for mechanical equations are still used as the basis for mathematics and physics. He is perhaps best known for the Archimedes screw, which is reputed to have been invented in the Hellenistic period. The screw revolutionised irrigation techniques in Ancient Greece and Egypt by allowing farmers to transfer water from a low to a high position.

Many of Archimedes' inventions are still in use today

JAMES DYSON
ENGLISH 1947-

One of the late-20th-century's most iconic inventors, James Dyson's first invention was the Ballbarrow, a modified version of a wheelbarrow using a ball instead of a wheel. Other inventions also using a ball followed – including a trolley that launched boats – before he became frustrated at the poor performance of his vacuum cleaner and decided he could do better. After five years of different prototypes, his invention was completed, but no UK manufacturer would take the product so he launched it in Japan through catalogue sales. Dyson vacuum cleaners are now one of that industry's premier brands and Dyson continues to invent, with his latest product a fan without external blades. He is worth an estimated £3 billion ($4.85 billion).

James Dyson is one of the most iconic inventors of the modern age

Thomas Edison
AMERICAN 1847-1931

Edison revolutionised communication in 1877 when he invented the carbon microphone, which allowed one person to hear another through a telephone. The invention was essential in radio broadcasting and saw widespread application in telephones until the 1980s. He also delivered power to thousands of American homes using his direct current distribution system transferring electricity from power generators to homes, although this was superseded by Tesla's alternating current system.

Tim Berners-Lee
ENGLISH 1955-

The creation of the World Wide Web was a combination of inspiration and abstract thinking by Tim Berners-Lee while he was working for CERN, the European organisation for nuclear research. Originally designed for researchers to instantly share information with each other through computers, Berners-Lee combined pre-existing systems to create a network where people could access information.

> "We should be glad of an opportunity to serve others by any invention of ours"
> *Benjamin Franklin*

Benjamin Franklin
AMERICAN 1706-1790

Inventor, revolutionary and one of the founding fathers of the United States, Benjamin Franklin is credited as the inventor of a number of contraptions, such as the lightning rod, harnessing electricity from storms, and the Franklin stove. He also proposed a number of theories to harness the power of nature, including a thesis on kites being used to pull ships across waterways. He never patented his inventions, as he believed everybody should be able to enjoy them.

HISTORY OF AVIATION

From the ambitious dreams of the Wright brothers, to the glory of supersonic flight – discover the story of man's conquest of the skies

Pioneering age

Adventure and glory awaited the brave pioneers during the early years of aviation

The Wright Flyer was first demonstrated in total secrecy

1903

Wright Flyer

The Wright Flyer was as much a moral triumph as it was a triumph of aerial engineering. There had been countless failures, crashes and accidents resulting in near death before Orville Wright's successful flight on December 17 1903. The first flight ended in failure, as a problem with one of the Flyers' elevators sent it crashing into the sand around the takeoff zone. The brothers persevered though and finally the rudimentary pusher engine, the huge wingspan and the pulley system the flyer sat on – which was designed to overcome the power-to-weight problem – all worked perfectly. The result was the first powered flight and landing of an aircraft.

1928

Ford 5-AT Tri-Motor

The first true airliner, big enough inside for rudimentary luxuries, was fast and reasonably safe. Crucially, it could also be mass-produced.

1928

Page H.P.42

Based on the designs of World War I bombers, the Page was big, ugly and slow because of the drag it produced. It did offer its passengers a reasonably safe ride though.

1925

Curtiss flying boat

While the design for the first flying boat looked ungainly, Glenn H Curtiss' pusher proved to be a success, enabling the pilot to take off and land from the ocean.

Brief Bio

LOUIS BLERIOT

French, 1872-1936

Louis Bleriot made his fortune in the automobile industry but nearly lost all his money after his initial ill-fated first steps into the aviation industry. His designs did not achieve the recognition his enormous skill deserved until he made a great breakthrough with his Bleriot XI flyer that channel-hopped from England to France in 1909, winning the *Daily Mail* English Channel challenge. After his daredevil flight he stopped flying altogether and founded the SPAD aviation company because of his wife's concerns over his safety.

1909

Bleriot XI

The Wright Flyer may have proved it was possible for an aircraft that was 'heavier than air' to fly, but it was the Bleriot Flyer that showed that air travel was a viable form of transportation. The Bleriot XI was the first plane to fly across the English Channel in 1909. As the *Daily Express* newspaper commented: 'Britain is no longer an island.'

When the Wright brothers made their first successful 'heavier than air' flight in 1903 in their Wright Flyer, they were keenly aware that they had invented a machine that would change the face of the earth forever. The brothers flew their craft in absolute secrecy barring a few select witnesses who could testify that they'd done it. Orville Wright said afterwards: "It was only a flight of 12 seconds, it was uncertain, wavy, creeping, but it was a real flight at last and not a glide." They knew the great potential of their new contraption. The problem was, no one else did. To the public at large flight was in the purview of socially awkward inventors and university professors, not on the horizon of wider society. The great breakthroughs made during this tenuous pioneering period were ground-breaking: man could now fly in the Wright brother's Flyer, he could fly over the English Channel on a mono-wing with the Bleriot IX and he could even sail and fly at the same time with Glenn H. Curtiss' new water craft. But these contraptions were little more than unreliable, flimsy experiments; good for the inventors who professed that it could be done, but good for little more than this. Until 1914 there simply wasn't the pioneering spirit outside of the brave experiments of Wright and Bleriot for serious attention to be given to flight.

"As the memories of World War I slowly ebbed away into the new hope of the roaring Twenties, pilots started to break records"

The horrors of World War I changed this niche status. War gave inventors the opportunity they needed to bring their designs to the attention of powerful men. With the resources of industrialised nations preparing for war, the gentlemen flyers were given the time and money they needed to truly get off the ground. Terrible weapons were invented and the war brought the concept of the aerial bomber capable of levelling cities and ever-faster single-seat fighters that filled the skies with deadly dogfights. As the war drew to its catastrophic conclusion, the aircraft of the early 1900s bore little resemblance to the reliable, skinned war birds of 1918. Man could now fly into the heavens and have a reasonable expectation that he would make it back to earth in one piece. Budding entrepreneurs saw these developments and were impressed. During the war, planes were used to transport goods and people around the battlefields of Europe, why couldn't they be used

Golden age

Record-breakers, pilot tycoons and truly luxurious aerial travel exemplified the golden era

1927

Pan Am

Pan Am, or Pan-American Airlines, offered non-stop luxurious flying boat services to the exotic Pacific and Far East during the Twenties and Thirties. The airline started out in the freight industry, offering a mail service from America to the Caribbean. The company then branched out to offer passenger routes to the Caribbean, Cuba and the paradise locations of Hawaii and the Philippines. The airline was renowned for the destinations it would fly to, even offering a service to Hong Kong, opening the wonders of the Far East.

1927

Spirit of St Louis

The Spirit of St Louis was the first plane to cross the Atlantic nonstop. Taking off in New York it arrived in Paris 33 hours and 30 minutes later flown by aviation pioneer Charles Lindbergh.

Flying boat

Imperial Airways, later to be known as British Airways, offered comfort and style. Initially offering its services as a carrier for colonial officials in the ugly but reliable Page H.P.42, the airline quickly grew to accommodate civil passengers flying to exotic destinations. Part of the appeal of flying 'imperial' was its safety record – the planes were reliable and dependable in the air.

1924

Brief Bio

HOWARD HUGHES

American, 1905-1976

The eccentric millionaire Howard Hughes was a maverick designer and test pilot of the air industry during the golden age of flight. He was a man who strived for bigger and better aircraft, designing his Hughes H-1 racer to be the fastest aircraft on earth and then his H-4 Hercules to be the largest. He broke a number of aviation records including a round-the-world trip, which he completed in 91 hours – he returned to New York city ahead of the photographers covering the event in 1938.

Hughes H-1 Racer

Howard Hughes, the eccentric legend whose millionaire status meant that he could afford to design and build aircraft, designed the Hughes racer. His H-1 Racer epitomised this wealth and pioneering spirit and it was designed to do just one thing: be the fastest man-made aircraft on the planet.

It was Hughes himself who was at the controls of the racer when he broke the speed record in 1935. In the attempt he even flew the plane until it ran out of petrol, resulting in him having to make an emergency landing. There was little apparent damage to the aircraft and he was reported to say as he emerged from the scene: "We can fix her, she'll go faster!"

1935

The H-1 Racer was designed to be the fastest in the world

> "The answer to convince people to use air travel was found in its appeal – the dream of flight"

in the same way during the new peace? What's more the designs currently in circulation could easily be modified to create passenger planes. However, the ungainly results were for practical uses only. Converted military bomber designs such as the Page H.P.42 offered few luxuries apart from the bonus that it no longer took colonial officials weeks to get anywhere in their vast empires. Ferrying around the masters of Europe kept fledgling aviation businesses like Imperial Airways (later British Airways) afloat, but it didn't make them the super corporations we know them to be today.

As the memories of World War I slowly ebbed away into the new hope of the roaring twenties, pilots started to break records once again. There were air speed records broken by Jimmy Doolittle in the Curtiss R3C-2 racer and by the millionaire Howard Hughes in his H-1 Racer at 245mph and 352 mph respectively. Charles Lindbergh broke distance records across the Atlantic ocean in the elegant Spirit of St Louis in 1927. In 1933 the eccentric one-eyed pilot Wiley Post flew his Vega 5C the 'Winnie Mae' around the world in seven days. The courageous and pioneering Amelia Earhart became the first female pilot to cross the Atlantic and the first female pilot to fly solo from Hawaii to California, also in a Vega 5C. Planes became more and more powerful with new designs to their wings and bodies to make them slick and streamlined. Reginald Mitchell's designs for Supermarine created the Supermarine K5054 later to be known as the Spitfire. On its maiden test flight, standing in his tweed jacket and smoking his pipe at Eastleigh Airfield Hampshire, Mitchell muttered: "Spitfire was just the sort of bloody silly name they would choose." This was truly a pioneering age of flight. Yet flight was still only in the sights of a select few. It was still not commercially viable for everyone despite the immense interest and press that was lavished on the heroes of the industry.

The first problem facing the fledgling airline companies was people. It wouldn't be enough to fund such a risky business into a mass market on the expectation that people would simply want to travel in planes as an extremely expensive alternative to sea travel. Travelling from A to B was the only expected outcome and nothing more. The answer to convince people to use air travel was found in its appeal - the dream of flight. The aspirational luxury of travelling in a wonderful flying machine to an exotic destination. It was easy to capitalise on the press received by Hughes

World War II

Powerful, sleek war birds faced off against one another in a battle for rule of the skies

1936

Supermarine Spitfire

This outstanding plane represented a unique blend of power and agility. Tricky to handle for the inexperienced pilot, due to it's sensitive characteristics, but an absolute dream if there was enough experience behind the control stick, the Spitfire could out-climb and outrun the German Me 109 in the deadly months of 1940 when Britain and Germany fought for dominance of British skies. In the words of fighter ace Adolf Malan: "The spitfire had style and was obviously a killer."

Brief Bio

CHUCK YEAGER

American, 1923-

One of the greatest test pilots in the world, Chuck Yeager saw the advent of a new age of air travel from the propeller to the jet. Starting from humble beginnings in Virginia, Yeager left school and immediately joined the Army Air Corps as a mechanic. After proving his ability as a pilot he was awarded a field commission and went on to become one of the top fighter aces of World War II. His adventures in flight did not stop there and in 1947 he became the first man to break the sound barrier in the Bell X-1.

1944

Messerschmitt Me 262

The first jet fighter ever to enter service, the Me 262 was faster than anything else flying in 1944. Billed as one of Hitler's 'war-winning' weapons, the Me 262 was deadly to slow allied bombers and could out-run any rival fighter aircraft. Ace American fighter pilot Chuck Yeager was reportedly one of the only men to ever shoot down an Me-262.

1940

F4U-4 Corsair

The odd shape of the Corsair's wings enabled it to maintain outstanding power and speed while at the same time survive the enormous stresses of landing on an aircraft carrier.

1938

The turbo prop

The secret to the success of the large aircraft designed in the Forties was the dedicated engine of the turbo prop. The turbo prop allowed the propeller to be driven by compressed air making it faster and more fuel-efficient. Today, most propeller-driven aircraft feature turbo props.

and Lindbergh. People wanted to travel and they fell in love with the romanticism of the great pilot-explorers of the age.

The next problem was designing an aircraft that matched the dream's expectations. The romanticism of air travel would die a quick death if passengers were forced into cramped, dirty, cold, converted bomb bays of a dressed-up warplane. There was also the question of cost. How could airlines make operating routes financially practical? The answer lay in a standardised, cheap-to-construct plane that could offer comfort and style for customers and keep the operator in business. So, in 1926, the airliner was invented and adopted by American Airlines. Henry Ford, who had been interested in developing a production line base model for the airline industry, created the first of these new 'air trains' in the form of the Ford 5 AT Tri-Motor. The cabins were still cramped but uncle Ford's planes offered leather interiors, in-flight meals, room for luggage and a host of air stewardesses on-hand to offer stiff drinks and hearty reassurance. The noise of the engine and the juddery ride didn't make for a restful flight, however.

As the appeal of air travel grew, so did the planes. Designs were proposed for safer craft that offered all the luxury of a sea voyage, the air industry's biggest competitor. The new flying boats of Boeing encapsulated this drive for luxury travel. The designs were wild, opulent and captured the essence of glamour inside and out of the aircraft. The Boeing 314 Yankee Clipper, which flew the transatlantic service, was equipped with a full saloon bar, its cabin resembled a society lounge with wicker basket chairs and full sliver service. The opulence and adventure was also captured by the Pacific routes made by the Martin Model 130 that opened up the mystery and promise of the Far East to travellers. Domestic airlines started to set the standard for modern airline services. Routes within the United States and beyond started to be serviced by the new DC-4s and Boeing 307s, with the great rival companies of Douglas and Boeing going head-to-head to offer more luxury, comfort and safety with smoother rides and faster flights. It also awarded airline companies with the great Holy Grail of the skies: air travel that paid for itself through customer tickets.

World War II changed the aircraft industry yet again - this time by unprecedented propositions. The advent of the jet engine created bigger, faster and more numerous aircraft. The industry had developed from the domain of the super rich to a service attainable by the new middle classes of the free world. But with a new era came new challenges. Aerial regulation, tighter business control and the ever-increasing need to make air travel cost-effective meant that much of the golden age extravagance was lost. There were to be no more flying boats - they were simply too expensive to operate. No longer could the airlines offer three-course gourmet dinners in a saloon-style bar in-flight, as it was too dangerous

Cold War

Competition between East and West created a drive for faster and bigger flying machines

1969

Boeing 747

The 747 gave the air industry what it needed: a passenger plane with huge capacity. It could accommodate 409 passengers in three separate classes.

Mrs Nixon visits the cockpit of the first commercial Boeing 747

1946

Bell X-1

A rocket with a cockpit, the Bell X-1 was the first plane to travel faster than the speed of sound. Its shape was modelled on a bullet, with its oval nose and thin wings making it as aero-dynamic as possible. The X-1 was equipped with four rocket chambers that, if fired all at once, created an, "impact [that] nearly knocks you back into next week", in the words of test pilot Chuck Yeager.

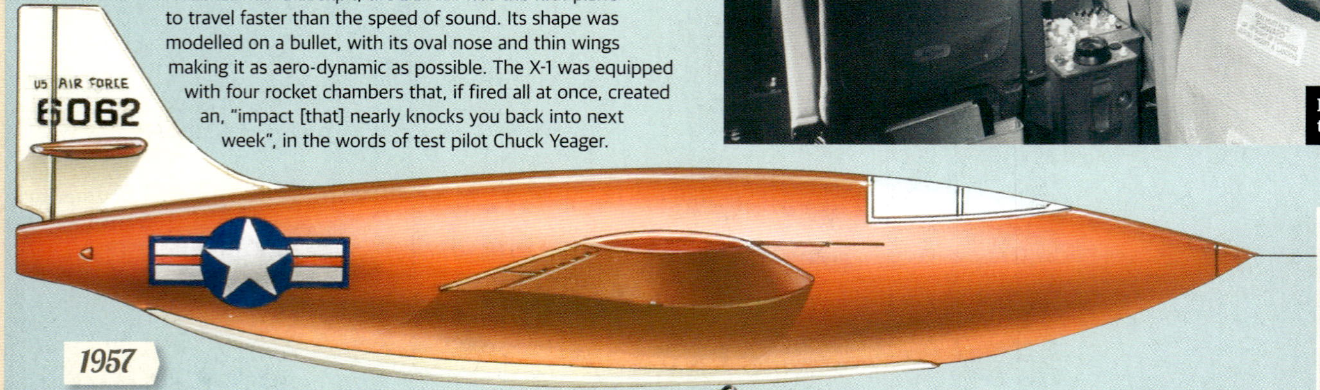

1957

Boeing 707

The first truly successful airliner, the Boeing 707 was fast, sleek and benefitted from four fan jet engines that were more fuel-efficient than other models.

1958

Ejection seats

Travelling faster than the speed of sound in a military aircraft presented a unique challenge for pilots bailing out. The aircraft would be travelling too fast for pilots to simply open the canopy and jump. Instead, a seat combining vertical rockets and seat restraints was designed. In order to get the pilot clear of the tail fin, the seat had to accelerate the occupant vertically to 100mph in 0.4 seconds.

Brief Bio

JACQUELINE AURIOL

French, 1917-2000

Jacqueline Auriol was one of the only female test pilots during the Cold War. As daughter-in-law to the French President during the Forties she was already a minor celebrity. In 1953 she broke the sound barrier in a Sassult Mystere II. She than set a world speed record in 1963 with the Dassault Mirage flying at 1,274mph.

to have half-drunk passengers wandering around the cabin if the plane experienced an emergency. This meant that as standard shapes and sizes in plane design emerged, such as the Boeing model 377, the elaborate styles of the Twenties and Thirties were lost forever. Big corporations now decided what flew and what didn't based on profit margins. No one could put this principle better than the American test pilots in the Mojave Desert – the men who had broken the sound barrier in the Bell X-1. Their funding was being cut to make way for space rockets, the next great adventure into the heavens. In the quiet on-base bars the pilots would mutter one thing over their drinks: 'No bucks, no Buck Rogers.'

In-keeping with this tight eye on business, standard safety features and the need for ever-greater passenger capacity per aircraft was the new Holy Grail airlines were forced to pursue. With the new long-range airliners by 1957 more people were crossing the Atlantic by plane than they were by boat. The jet engine was gratefully acquired and adapted from the military and soon the propeller-driven airliner was a thing of the past. There were high-profile problems though. The first-ever jet-powered passenger plane, the De Havilland Comet, had an horrendous safety record but finally, in 1957, Boeing unveiled the plane that gave airlines their first huge commercial success: The Boeing 707. The 707 served as the blueprint for all future airline designs to follow, with external engine nacelles, roomy cabins, in-flight movies and cabin service. The power of the media was harnessed; the sex appeal of air travel with beautiful women and the huge jet planes they could be found in was used to attract the rich and powerful. As the money started to finally roll in, the market began to shrink to the big players. Imperial Airways became British Airways, independent American airline companies became united under United Airlines and Pan Am, unable to sustain its fleet of flying boats or its routes adequately without incurring huge losses, finally folded. The 707 gave way to the double-decker 747 that was in turn overtaken by the giant Airbus 380 as the goliath of the sky. It was now possible to travel from London to Sydney in less than 24 hours non-stop in the global village that the airlines had created.

Planes were no longer designed to offer extravagance but rather a safe and comfortable ride. There was no need for airlines to see themselves in competition with sea voyages, the by-gone years of sea travel in luxury was an expense few modern people could afford. Business became so successful that airlines could offer ever-cheaper fares, opening up more markets to well and truly stamp their dominance over the travel industry. It soon became a dreary era of bigger planes for bigger capacity based on the same basic designs. In amongst this mediocrity stood one machine that was a piece of breathtaking aero-engineering genius. It blended the envelope of technological advancement with pure style and luxury worthy of the golden age of flight. It also gave a new kind of adventure for its passengers

Modern age

Technology and refined aviation techniques combined to create the new giants of the sky

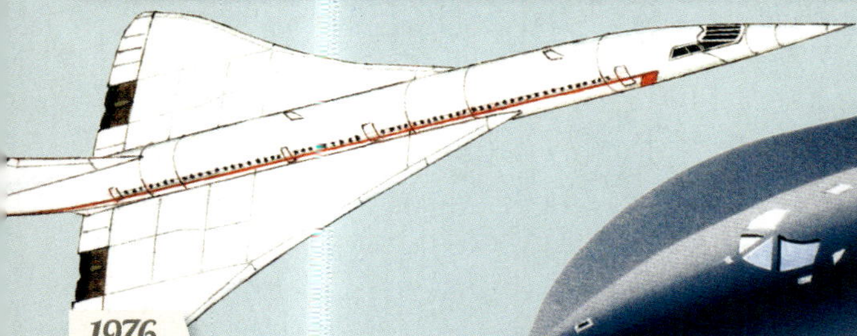

2007

Airbus A380

The Airbus 380 is the single biggest passenger plane currently flown by airlines. Many airports have had to modify their facilities to accommodate their gigantic size.

1976

Concorde

First appearing in 1973 Concorde still represents the cutting edge of civil aviation technology. The technical challenge of getting an airliner to perform like a fighter aircraft was so huge that when British-French aerial engineers started working on the designs more than one critic said it could never be done. Everything about Concorde was built for speed, its delta wings, its four Rolls Royce engines and its airflow control system were designed to give maximum velocity with minimal drag.

1966

Lockheed SR-71 Blackbird

Reaching a velocity of over three times the speed of sound and a height of 100,000 feet (18 miles) the SR-71 Blackbird was the highest and fastest aircraft in the world. Used by the US military for spy missions, its aerodynamics aimed to give maximum power for the least amount of drag, prompting its rather unique appearance. In order for its pilots to survive the extreme conditions of near space flight, they had to don a space suit with its own oxygen and heat supply.

2006

F-35 Lightning II

The most technically advanced fighter aircraft and widely rumoured to be the last manned fighter, the F-35 is a true stealth, fly-by-wire, air-superiority fighter.

Brief Bio

RICHARD BRANSON

British, 1950-

A true pioneer in the modern age of flight, he founded one of the world's most important airlines, Virgin Atlantic, and has since been involved in a number of different air challenges. One of his most famous record attempts was to be the first man to travel around the world in a hot air balloon, which failed in 1998.

"Concorde's retractable nose and delta wing enabled it to pierce the sound barrier"

totally unique to its own characteristics. The plane's name was Concorde and it offered its passengers the chance to travel faster than a speeding bullet. Described by its principle test pilot Brian Trubshaw as nothing short of "a miracle", the Concorde offered the extremely wealthy the chance to fly from London Heathrow at breakfast and arrive in New York in time for their eggs and bacon. Everything about the plane screamed modernity. Concorde's retractable nose and delta wing enabled it to pierce the sound barrier, while its four custom-made Rolls Royce engines were powerful enough to give a cruising speed of mach 2. Inside, style and elegance were once again reborn, offering 128 passengers first-class service as they crossed the Atlantic at supersonic speeds. As one journalist put it: "Moving a mile every 2.7 seconds [my coffee] doesn't even ripple." Yet Concorde was launched into a world that was becoming increasingly hostile to air travel. Flight was no longer viewed as the glamorous adventure it was three decades before. Some of the crucial factors stacked against the plane were fuel and noise pollution, the cost of a ticket - which for Concorde clocked in at £6,000 return - and the extraordinary expense the Concorde planes took to maintain. There were also serious questions being asked about the aircraft's safety, when in 2000 an Air France-run flight crashed shortly after take-off, killing over a hundred people. All this meant that in 2003 the whole fleet was grounded permanently. Peoples' perceptions of flight had changed. Luxury and speed was now seen as optional extras rather than requirements. In this competitive world the Concorde represented a technical marvel but one meant for a different age, an age where air travel was something special rather than a mundane day-to-day activity.

From the tentative first flight of the Wright Flyer lifting a few feet off the ground, to the roaring sound of Concorde's Rolls Royce engines at the cusp of the sound barrier, the air industry has always inspired and been inspired by the dreams of entrepreneurs, pilots and adventurers. Greater and more-powerful machines continue to be designed by the top names in the industry, from the smart fighter jets of the F-22 and F-35, to the first green aircraft of NASA's Helios, ensuring that people continue to take to the air and conquer the heavens above. In the words of Claude Grahame-White in 1914: "This conquest of the air will prove, ultimately, to be man's greatest and most glorious triumph."